MARVEL

BLACK PANTHER

PRELUDE

BLACK PANTHER PRELUDE

WRITER: **WILL CORONA PILGRIM**

ARTIST: **ANNAPAOLA MARTELLO**

COLORIST: **JORDAN BOYD**

LETTERER: **VC'S TRAVIS LANHAM**

EDITORS: **MARK BASSO** with **SARAH BRUNSTAD**

FOR MARVEL STUDIOS

EXECUTIVE, PRODUCTION & DEVELOPMENT: **NATE MOORE**

MANAGER, PRODUCTION & DEVELOPMENT: **ZOIE NAGELHOUT**

PRESIDENT: **KEVIN FEIGE**

BLACK PANTHER CREATED BY STAN LEE & JACK KIRBY

COLLECTION EDITOR: JENNIFER GRÜNWALD

ASSISTANT EDITOR: CAITLIN O'CONNELL

ASSOCIATE MANAGING EDITOR: KATERI WOODY

EDITOR, SPECIAL PROJECTS: MARK D. BEAZLEY

VP PRODUCTION & SPECIAL PROJECTS: JEFF YOUNGQUIST

SVP PRINT, SALES & MARKETING: DAVID GABRIEL

EDITOR IN CHIEF: C.B. CEBULSKI

CHIEF CREATIVE OFFICER: JOE QUESADA

PRESIDENT: DAN BUCKLEY

MARVEL'S BLACK PANTHER PRELUDE. Contains material originally published in magazine form as MARVEL'S BLACK PANTHER PRELUDE #1-2, JUNGLE ACTION #6-7, BLACK PANTHER (1998) #19, BLACK PANTHER (2005) #2 and BLACK PANTHER (2016) #1. Second printing 2018. ISBN# 978-1-302-90942-0. Published by MARVEL WORLDWIDE, INC., a subsidiary of MARVEL ENTERTAINMENT, LLC. OFFICE OF PUBLICATION: 135 West 50th Street, New York, NY 10020. Copyright © 2018 MARVEL No similarity between any of the names, characters, persons, and/or institutions in this magazine with those of any living or dead person or institution is intended, and any such similarity which may exist is purely coincidental. **Printed in Canada.** DAN BUCKLEY, President, Marvel Entertainment; JOHN NEE, Publisher; JOE QUESADA, Chief Creative Officer; TOM BREVOORT, SVP of Publishing; DAVID BOGART, SVP of Business Affairs & Operations, Publishing & Partnership; DAVID GABRIEL, SVP of Sales & Marketing, Publishing; JEFF YOUNGQUIST, VP of Production & Special Projects; DAN CARR, Executive Director of Publishing Technology; ALEX MORALES, Director of Publishing Operations; SUSAN CRESPI, Production Manager; STAN LEE, Chairman Emeritus. For information regarding advertising in Marvel Comics or on Marvel.com, please contact Vit DeBellis, Custom Solutions & Integrated Advertising Manager, at vdebellis@marvel.com. For Marvel subscription inquiries, please call 888-511-5480. **Manufactured between 3/1/2018 and 3/12/2018 by SOLISCO PRINTERS, SCOTT, QC, CANADA.**

1 0 9 8 7 6 5 4 3 2

MARVEL'S BLACK PANTHER
PRELUDE #1

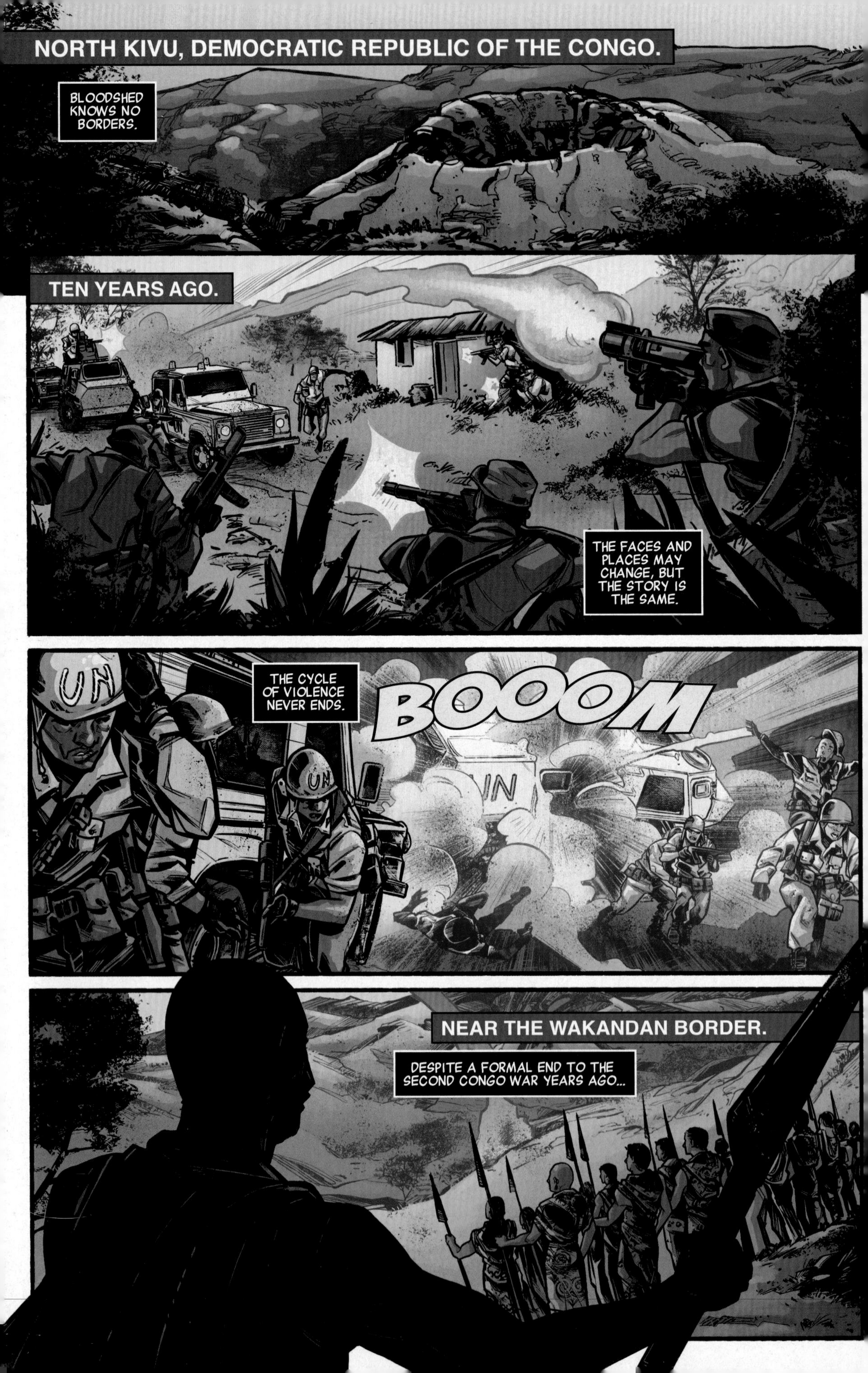
NORTH KIVU, DEMOCRATIC REPUBLIC OF THE CONGO.
BLOODSHED KNOWS NO BORDERS.
TEN YEARS AGO.
UN
THE FACES AND PLACES MAY CHANGE, BUT THE STORY IS THE SAME.
UN
THE CYCLE OF VIOLENCE NEVER ENDS.
BOOOM
UN
UN
NEAR THE WAKANDAN BORDER.
DESPITE A FORMAL END TO THE SECOND CONGO WAR YEARS AGO...

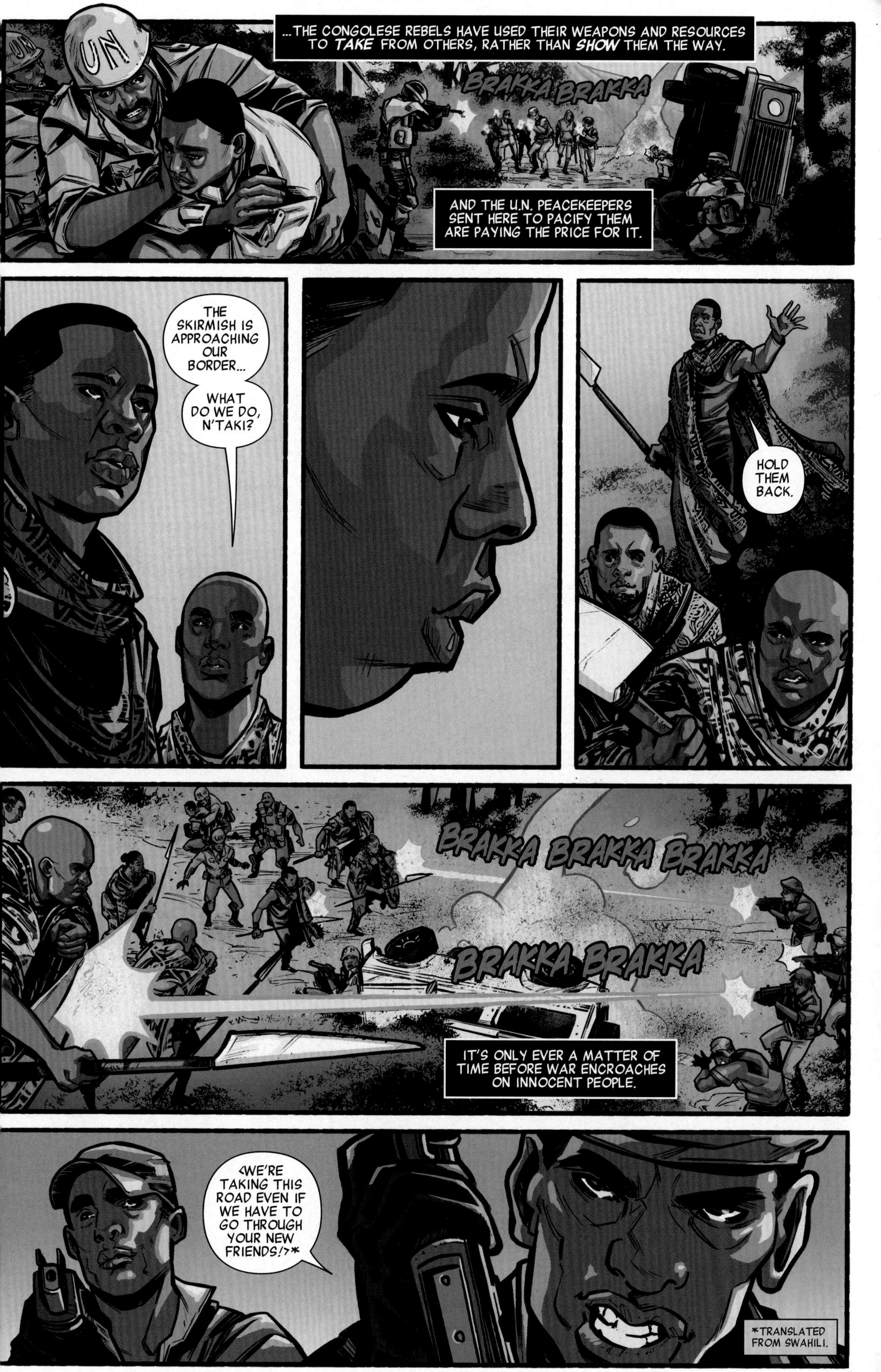

...THE CONGOLESE REBELS HAVE USED THEIR WEAPONS AND RESOURCES TO TAKE FROM OTHERS, RATHER THAN SHOW THEM THE WAY.
UN
BRAKKA BRAKKA
AND THE U.N. PEACEKEEPERS SENT HERE TO PACIFY THEM ARE PAYING THE PRICE FOR IT.
THE SKIRMISH IS APPROACHING OUR BORDER...
WHAT DO WE DO, N'TAKI?
HOLD THEM BACK.
BRAKKA BRAKKA BRAKKA
BRAKKA BRAKKA
IT'S ONLY EVER A MATTER OF TIME BEFORE WAR ENCROACHES ON INNOCENT PEOPLE.
<WE'RE TAKING THIS ROAD EVEN IF WE HAVE TO GO THROUGH YOUR NEW FRIENDS!>*
*TRANSLATED FROM SWAHILI.

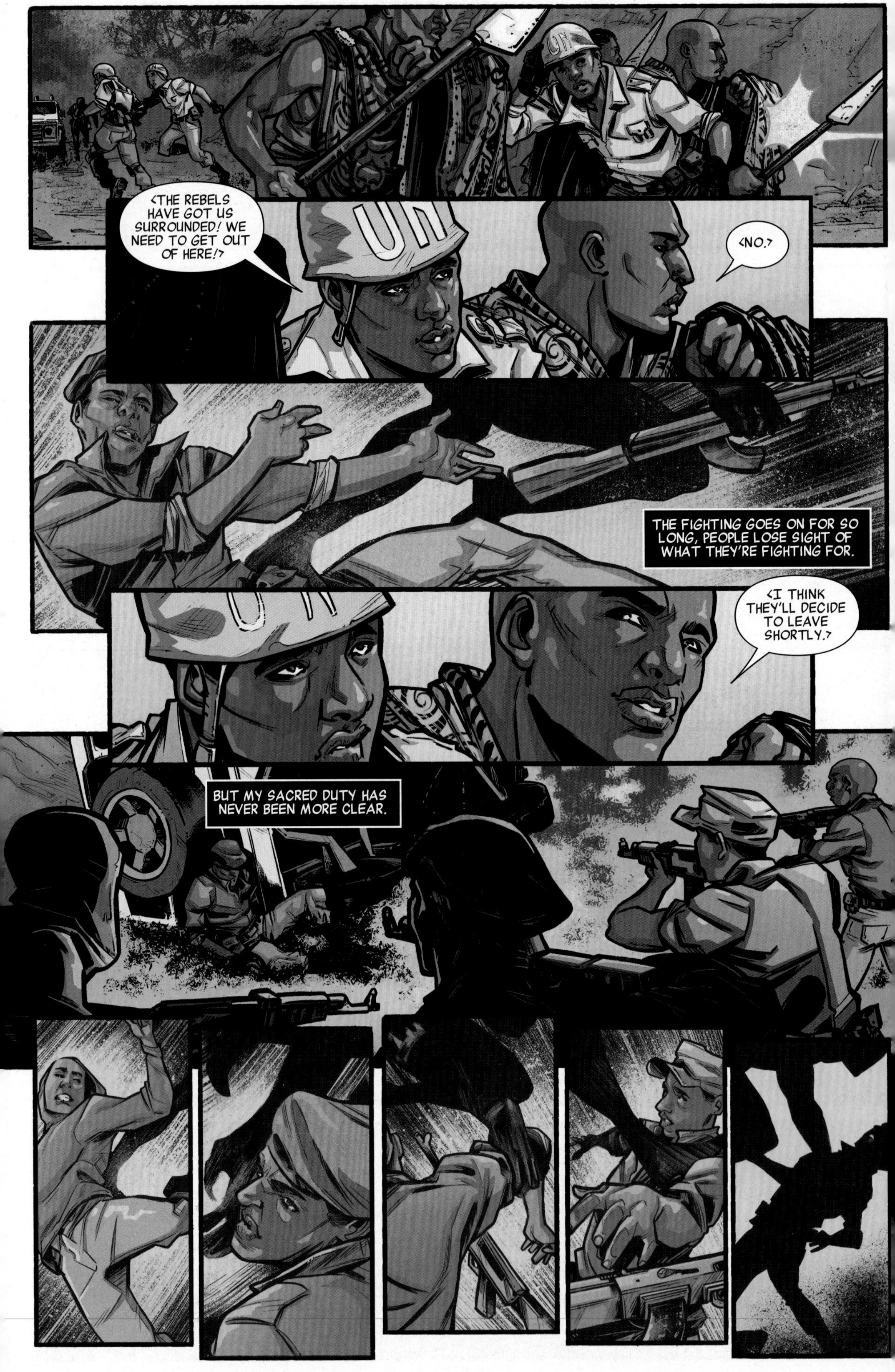
<THE REBELS HAVE GOT US SURROUNDED! WE NEED TO GET OUT OF HERE!>
<NO.>
THE FIGHTING GOES ON FOR SO LONG, PEOPLE LOSE SIGHT OF WHAT THEY'RE FIGHTING FOR.
<I THINK THEY'LL DECIDE TO LEAVE SHORTLY.>
BUT MY SACRED DUTY HAS NEVER BEEN MORE CLEAR.

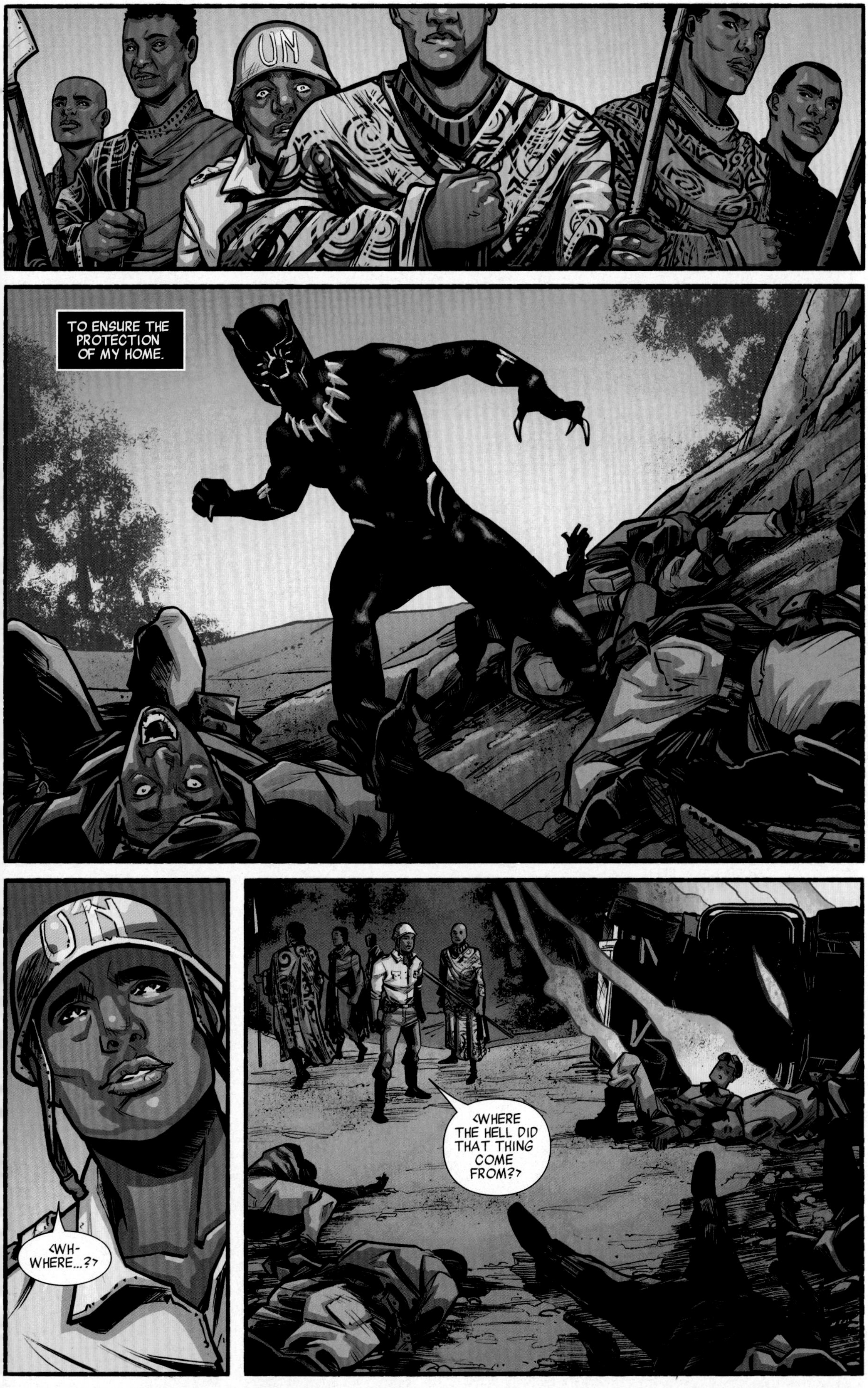
TO ENSURE THE PROTECTION OF MY HOME.
<WH- WHERE...?>
<WHERE THE HELL DID THAT THING COME FROM?>

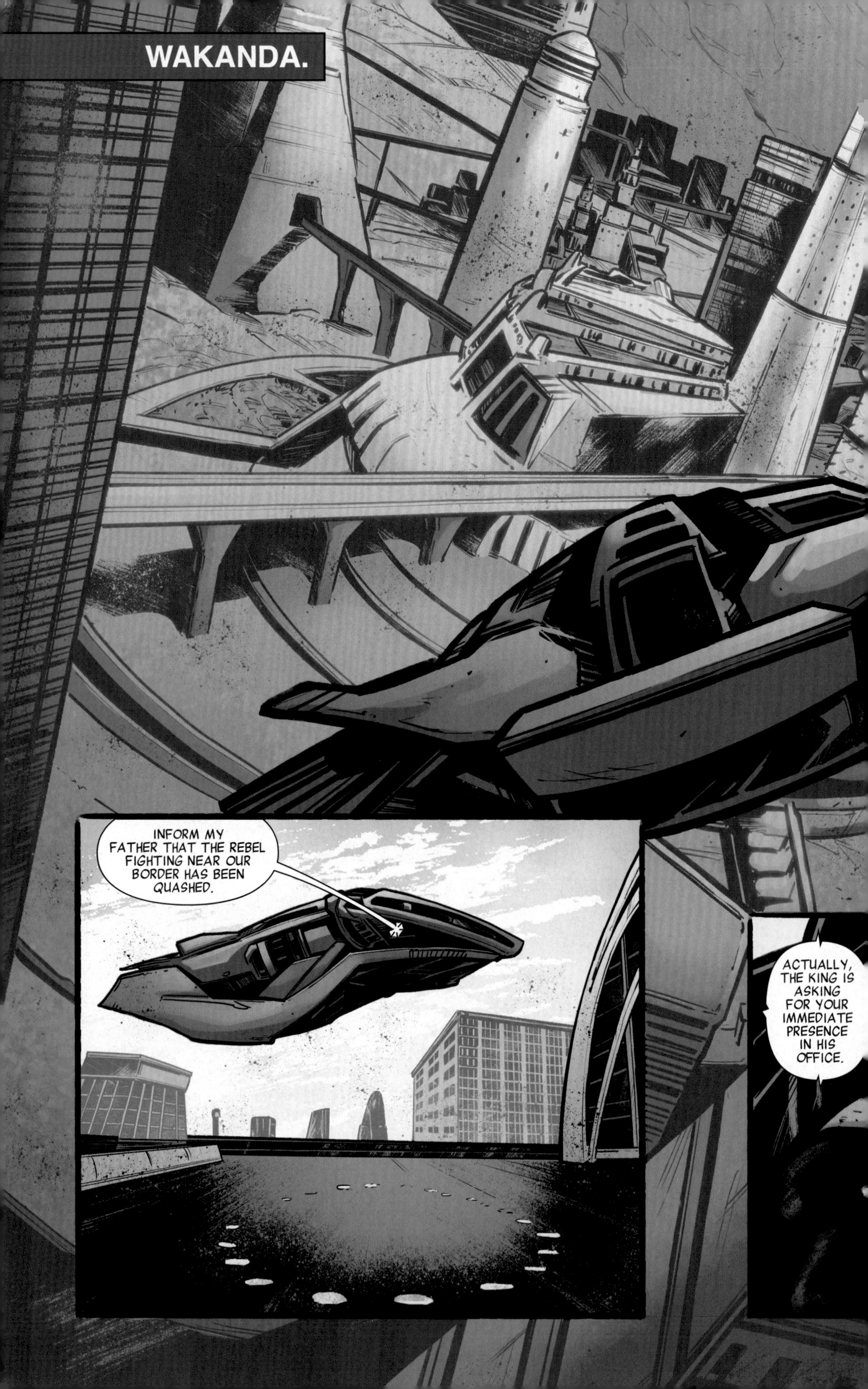
WAKANDA.
INFORM MY FATHER THAT THE REBEL FIGHTING NEAR OUR BORDER HAS BEEN QUASHED.
ACTUALLY, THE KING IS ASKING FOR YOUR IMMEDIATE PRESENCE IN HIS OFFICE.

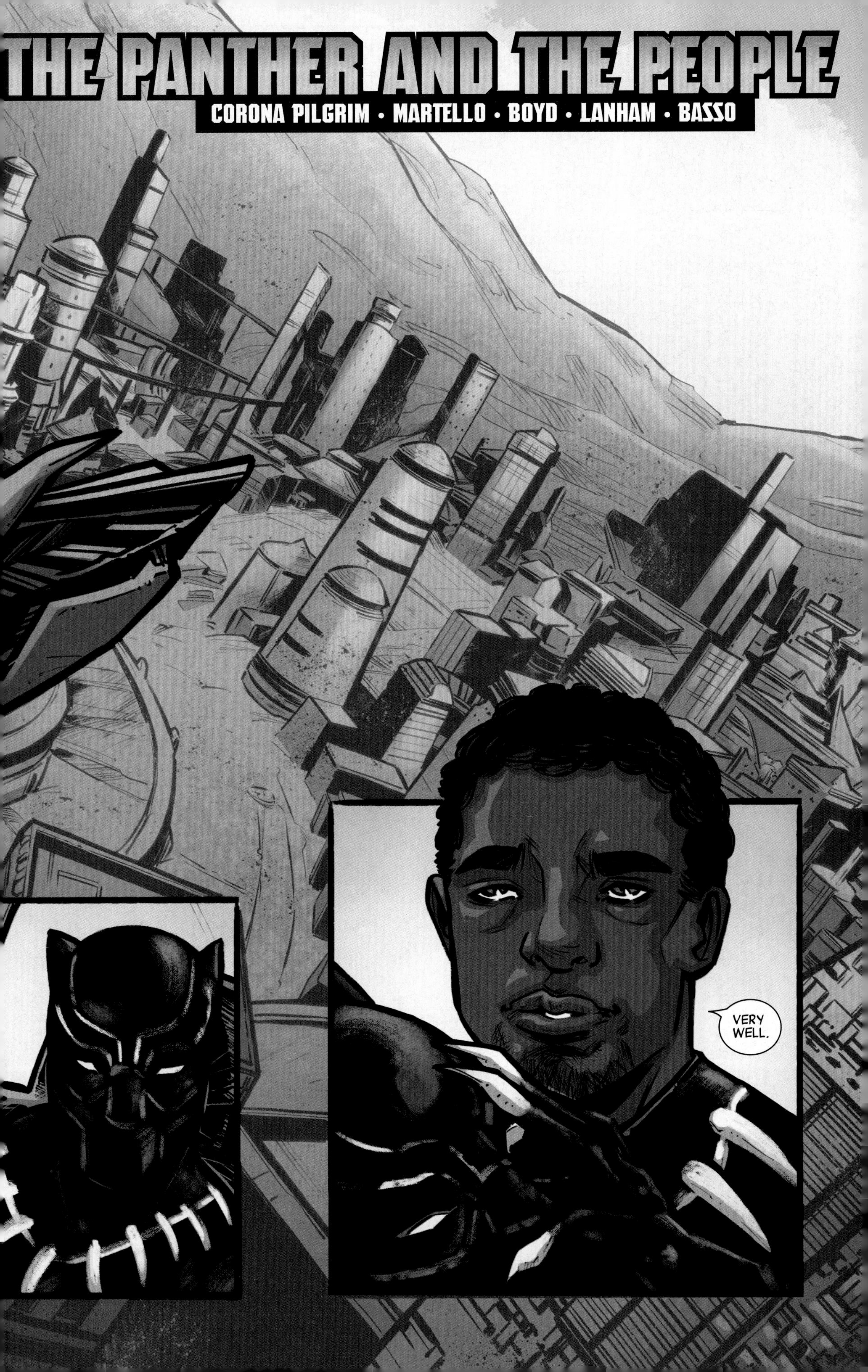
THE PANTHER AND THE PEOPLE
CORONA PILGRIM • MARTELLO • BOYD • LANHAM • BASSO
VERY WELL.

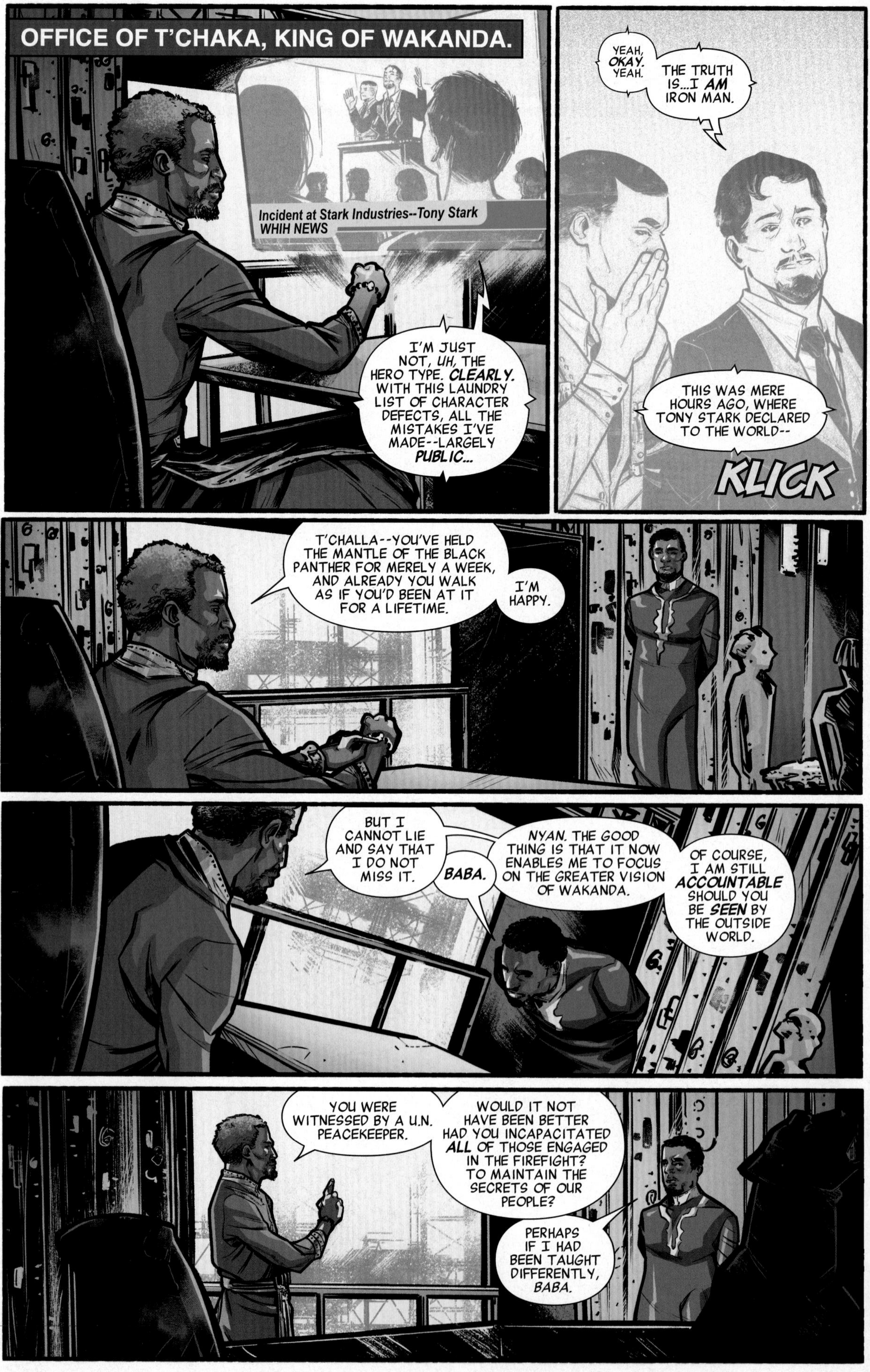
OFFICE OF T'CHAKA, KING OF WAKANDA.
Incident at Stark Industries--Tony Stark
WHIH NEWS
I'M JUST NOT, UH, THE HERO TYPE. CLEARLY. WITH THIS LAUNDRY LIST OF CHARACTER DEFECTS, ALL THE MISTAKES I'VE MADE--LARGELY PUBLIC...
YEAH, OKAY. YEAH.
THE TRUTH IS...I AM IRON MAN.
THIS WAS MERE HOURS AGO, WHERE TONY STARK DECLARED TO THE WORLD--
KLICK
T'CHALLA--YOU'VE HELD THE MANTLE OF THE BLACK PANTHER FOR MERELY A WEEK, AND ALREADY YOU WALK AS IF YOU'D BEEN AT IT FOR A LIFETIME.
I'M HAPPY.
BUT I CANNOT LIE AND SAY THAT I DO NOT MISS IT.
BABA.
NYAN. THE GOOD THING IS THAT IT NOW ENABLES ME TO FOCUS ON THE GREATER VISION OF WAKANDA.
OF COURSE, I AM STILL ACCOUNTABLE SHOULD YOU BE SEEN BY THE OUTSIDE WORLD.
YOU WERE WITNESSED BY A U.N. PEACEKEEPER.
WOULD IT NOT HAVE BEEN BETTER HAD YOU INCAPACITATED ALL OF THOSE ENGAGED IN THE FIREFIGHT? TO MAINTAIN THE SECRETS OF OUR PEOPLE?
PERHAPS IF I HAD BEEN TAUGHT DIFFERENTLY, BABA.

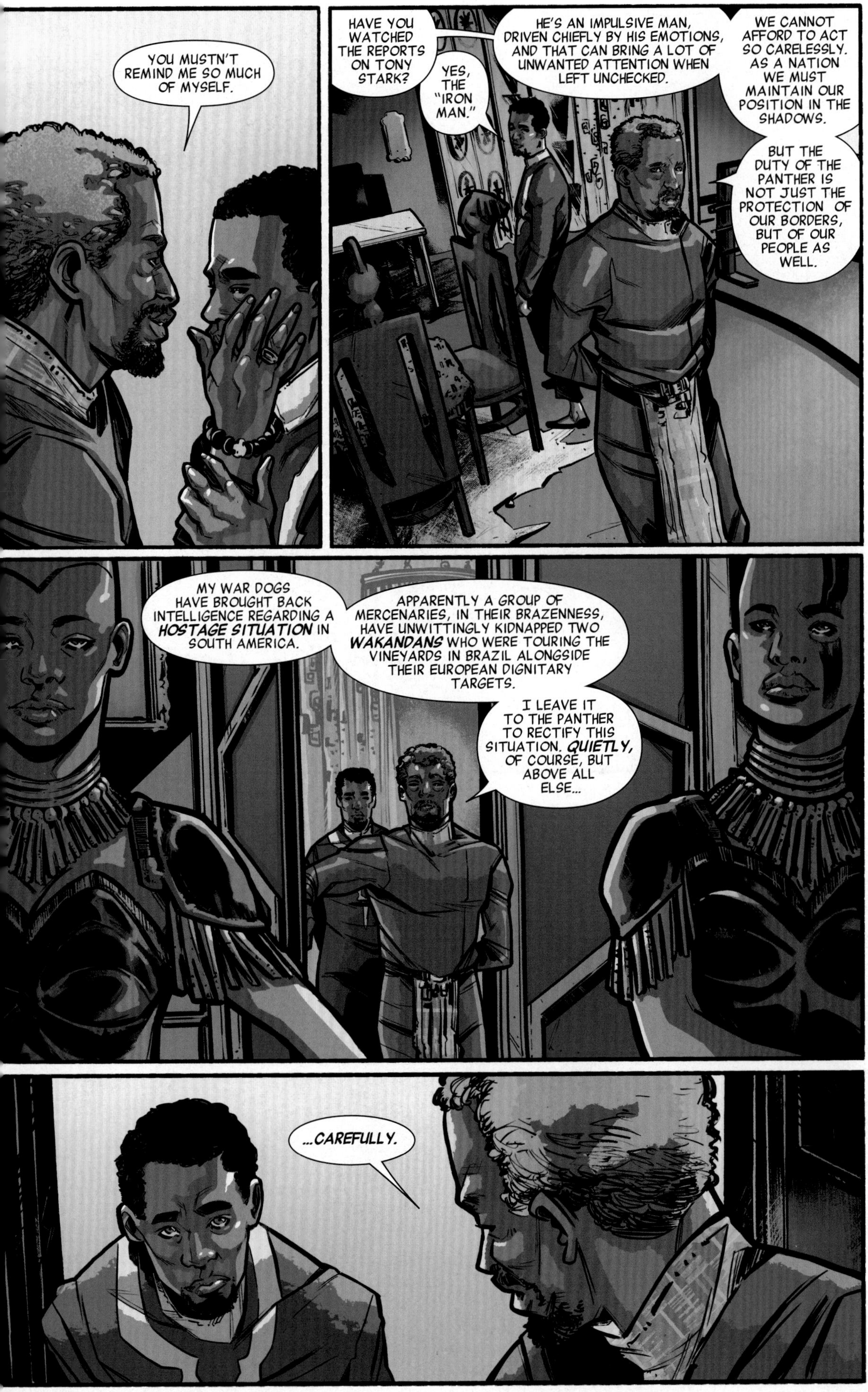
YOU MUSTN'T REMIND ME SO MUCH OF MYSELF.
HAVE YOU WATCHED THE REPORTS ON TONY STARK?
YES, THE "IRON MAN."
HE'S AN IMPULSIVE MAN, DRIVEN CHIEFLY BY HIS EMOTIONS, AND THAT CAN BRING A LOT OF UNWANTED ATTENTION WHEN LEFT UNCHECKED.
WE CANNOT AFFORD TO ACT SO CARELESSLY. AS A NATION WE MUST MAINTAIN OUR POSITION IN THE SHADOWS.
BUT THE DUTY OF THE PANTHER IS NOT JUST THE PROTECTION OF OUR BORDERS, BUT OF OUR PEOPLE AS WELL.
MY WAR DOGS HAVE BROUGHT BACK INTELLIGENCE REGARDING A *HOSTAGE SITUATION* IN SOUTH AMERICA.
APPARENTLY A GROUP OF MERCENARIES, IN THEIR BRAZENNESS, HAVE UNWITTINGLY KIDNAPPED TWO *WAKANDANS* WHO WERE TOURING THE VINEYARDS IN BRAZIL ALONGSIDE THEIR EUROPEAN DIGNITARY TARGETS.
I LEAVE IT TO THE PANTHER TO RECTIFY THIS SITUATION. *QUIETLY,* OF COURSE, BUT ABOVE ALL ELSE...
...CAREFULLY.

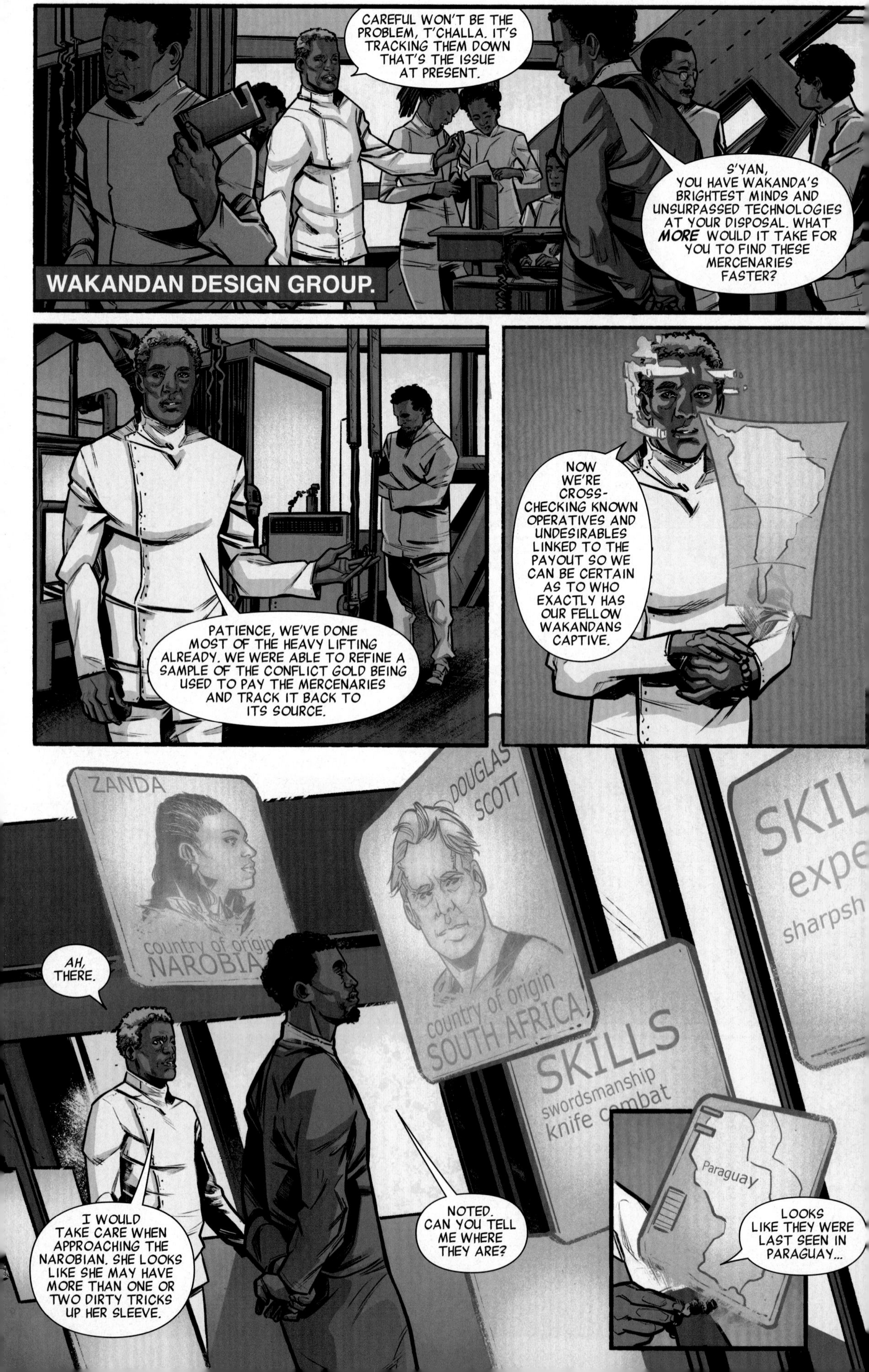
CAREFUL WON'T BE THE PROBLEM, T'CHALLA. IT'S TRACKING THEM DOWN THAT'S THE ISSUE AT PRESENT.
S'YAN, YOU HAVE WAKANDA'S BRIGHTEST MINDS AND UNSURPASSED TECHNOLOGIES AT YOUR DISPOSAL. WHAT MORE WOULD IT TAKE FOR YOU TO FIND THESE MERCENARIES FASTER?
WAKANDAN DESIGN GROUP.
PATIENCE, WE'VE DONE MOST OF THE HEAVY LIFTING ALREADY. WE WERE ABLE TO REFINE A SAMPLE OF THE CONFLICT GOLD BEING USED TO PAY THE MERCENARIES AND TRACK IT BACK TO ITS SOURCE.
NOW WE'RE CROSS-CHECKING KNOWN OPERATIVES AND UNDESIRABLES LINKED TO THE PAYOUT SO WE CAN BE CERTAIN AS TO WHO EXACTLY HAS OUR FELLOW WAKANDANS CAPTIVE.
ZANDA
country of origin NAROBIA
DOUGLAS SCOTT
country of origin SOUTH AFRICA
SKILLS swordsmanship knife combat
SKIL expe sharpsh
AH, THERE.
I WOULD TAKE CARE WHEN APPROACHING THE NAROBIAN. SHE LOOKS LIKE SHE MAY HAVE MORE THAN ONE OR TWO DIRTY TRICKS UP HER SLEEVE.
NOTED. CAN YOU TELL ME WHERE THEY ARE?
Paraguay
LOOKS LIKE THEY WERE LAST SEEN IN PARAGUAY...

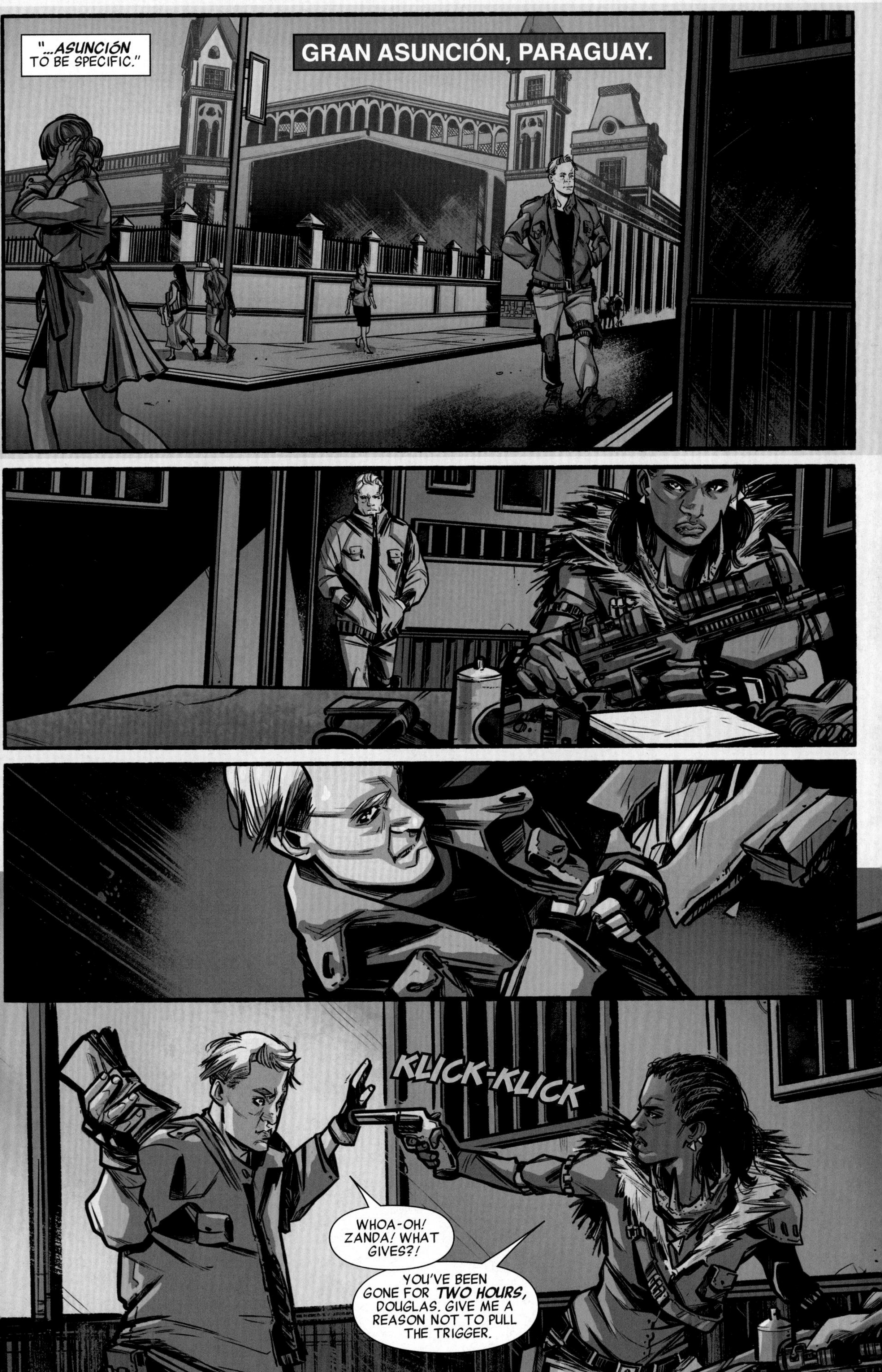
"...ASUNCIÓN TO BE SPECIFIC."
GRAN ASUNCIÓN, PARAGUAY.
KLICK-KLICK
WHOA-OH! ZANDA! WHAT GIVES?!
YOU'VE BEEN GONE FOR TWO HOURS, DOUGLAS. GIVE ME A REASON NOT TO PULL THE TRIGGER.

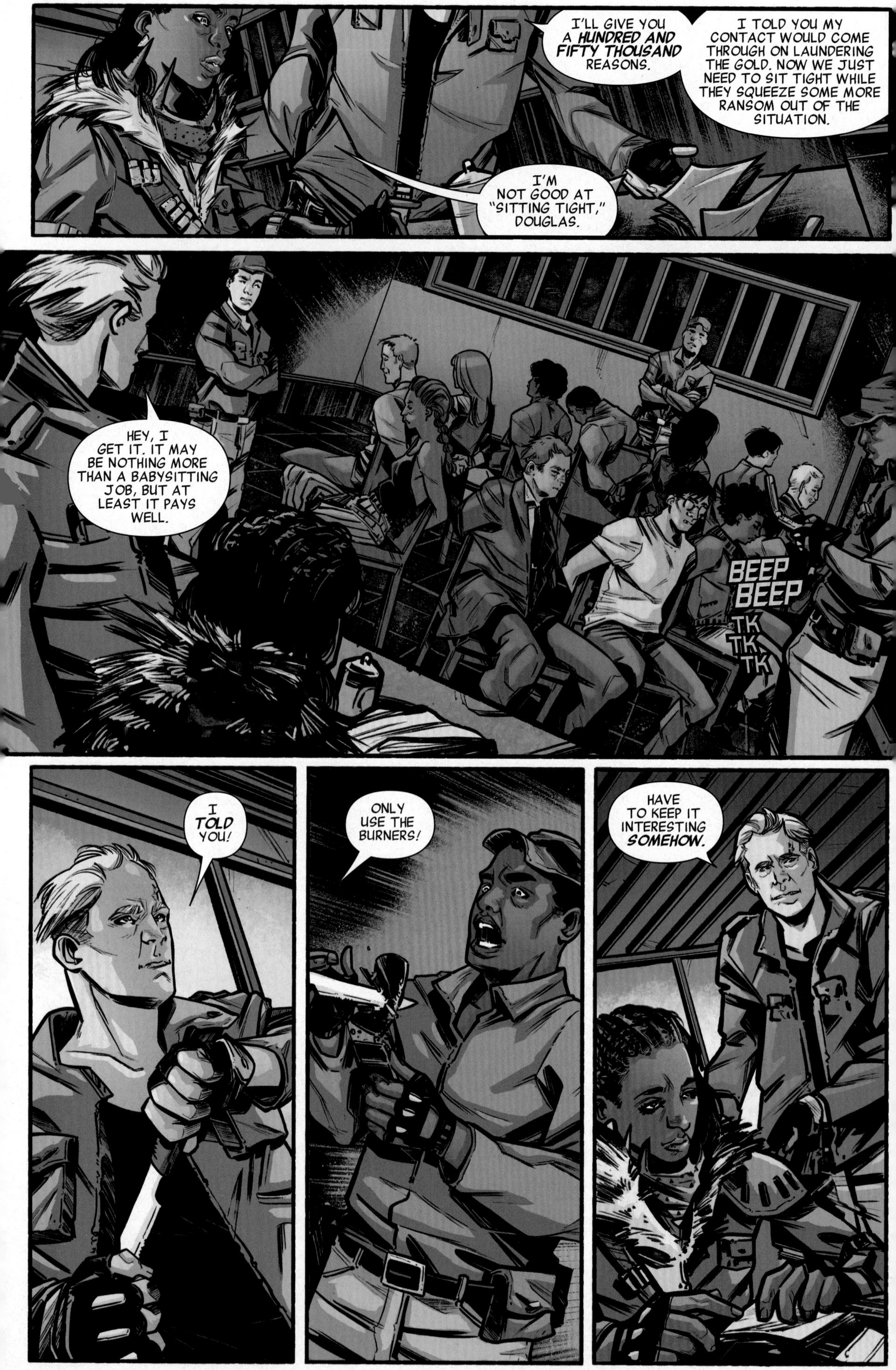

I'LL GIVE YOU A HUNDRED AND FIFTY THOUSAND REASONS.
I TOLD YOU MY CONTACT WOULD COME THROUGH ON LAUNDERING THE GOLD. NOW WE JUST NEED TO SIT TIGHT WHILE THEY SQUEEZE SOME MORE RANSOM OUT OF THE SITUATION.
I'M NOT GOOD AT "SITTING TIGHT," DOUGLAS.
HEY, I GET IT. IT MAY BE NOTHING MORE THAN A BABYSITTING JOB, BUT AT LEAST IT PAYS WELL.
BEEP BEEP
TK TK TK
I TOLD YOU!
ONLY USE THE BURNERS!
HAVE TO KEEP IT INTERESTING SOMEHOW.

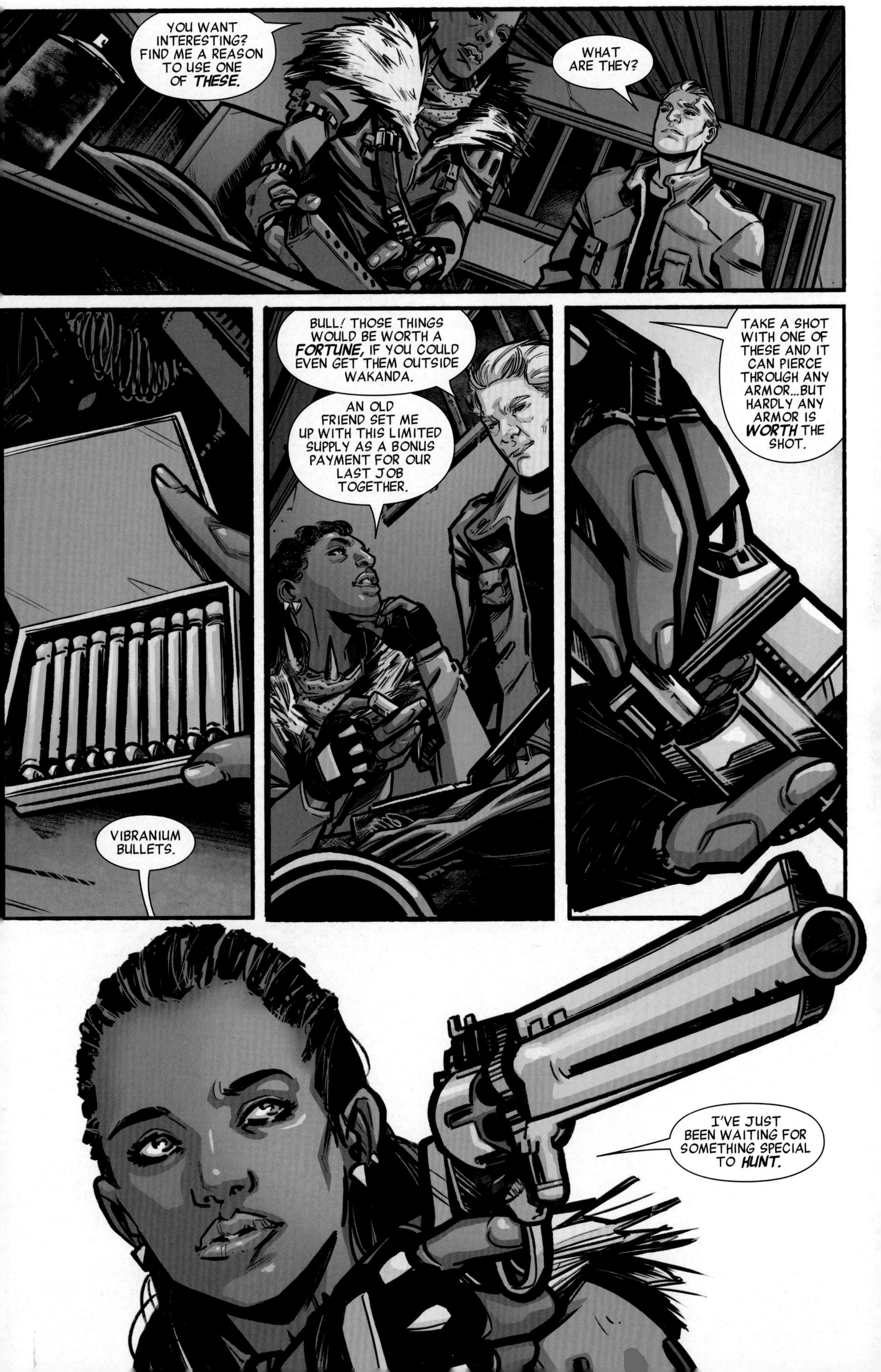
YOU WANT INTERESTING? FIND ME A REASON TO USE ONE OF THESE.
WHAT ARE THEY?
VIBRANIUM BULLETS.
BULL! THOSE THINGS WOULD BE WORTH A FORTUNE, IF YOU COULD EVEN GET THEM OUTSIDE WAKANDA.
AN OLD FRIEND SET ME UP WITH THIS LIMITED SUPPLY AS A BONUS PAYMENT FOR OUR LAST JOB TOGETHER.
TAKE A SHOT WITH ONE OF THESE AND IT CAN PIERCE THROUGH ANY ARMOR...BUT HARDLY ANY ARMOR IS WORTH THE SHOT.
I'VE JUST BEEN WAITING FOR SOMETHING SPECIAL TO HUNT.

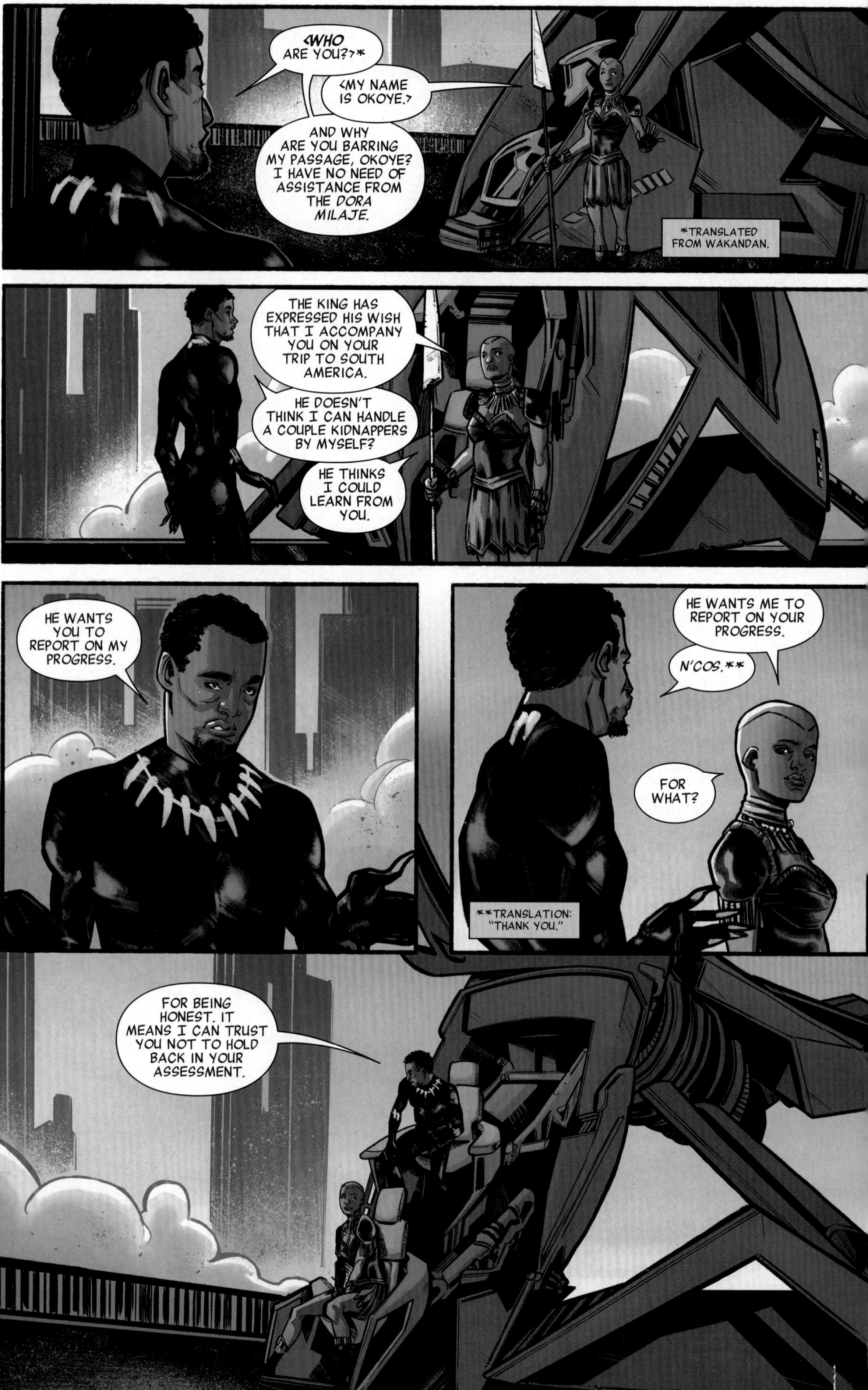

<WHO ARE YOU?>*
<MY NAME IS OKOYE.>
AND WHY ARE YOU BARRING MY PASSAGE, OKOYE? I HAVE NO NEED OF ASSISTANCE FROM THE *DORA MILAJE*.
*TRANSLATED FROM WAKANDAN.
THE KING HAS EXPRESSED HIS WISH THAT I ACCOMPANY YOU ON YOUR TRIP TO SOUTH AMERICA.
HE DOESN'T THINK I CAN HANDLE A COUPLE KIDNAPPERS BY MYSELF?
HE THINKS I COULD LEARN FROM YOU.
HE WANTS YOU TO REPORT ON MY PROGRESS.
HE WANTS ME TO REPORT ON YOUR PROGRESS.
*N'COS.***
FOR WHAT?
**TRANSLATION: "THANK YOU."
FOR BEING HONEST. IT MEANS I CAN TRUST YOU NOT TO HOLD BACK IN YOUR ASSESSMENT.

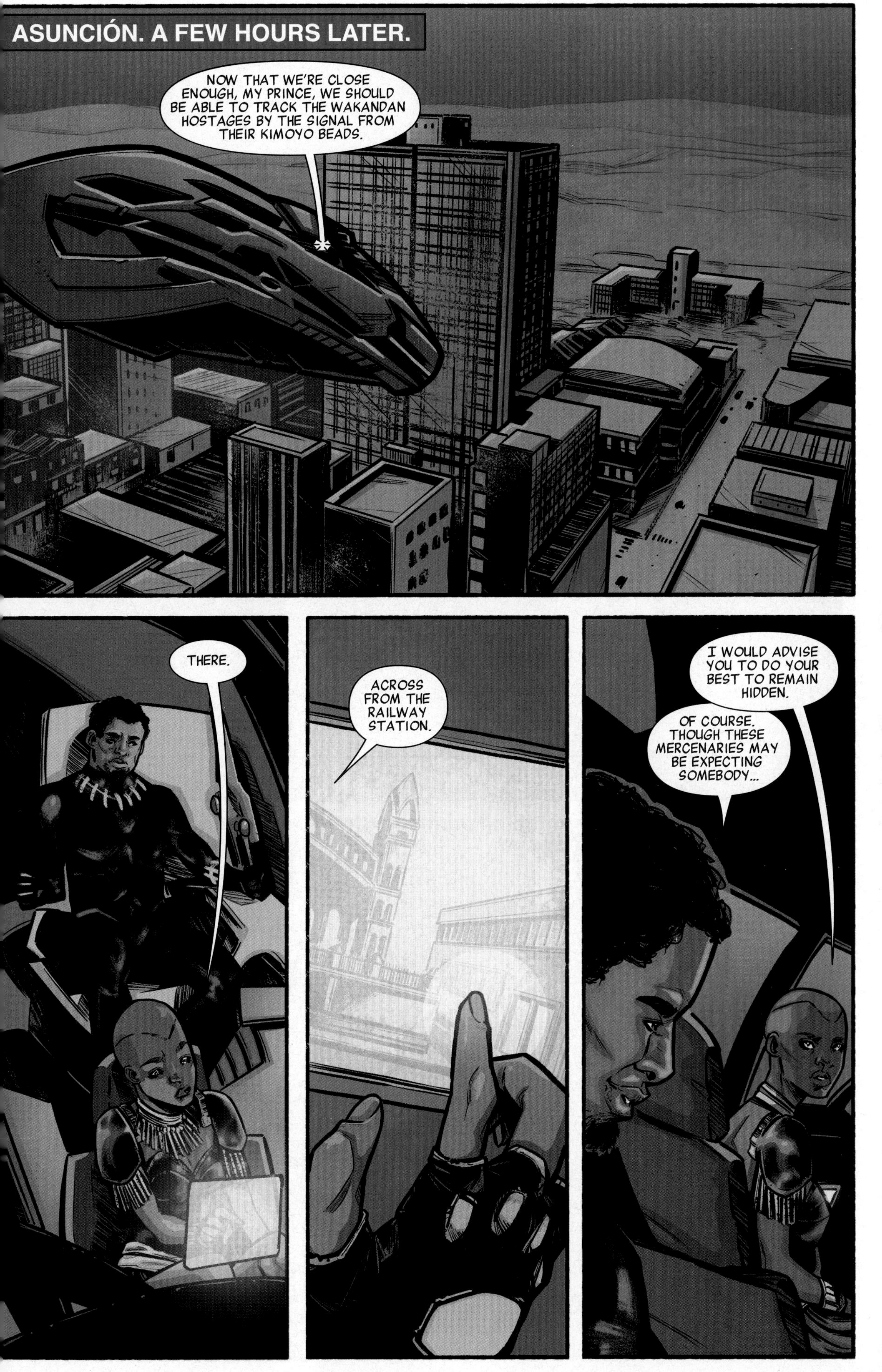
ASUNCIÓN. A FEW HOURS LATER.
NOW THAT WE'RE CLOSE ENOUGH, MY PRINCE, WE SHOULD BE ABLE TO TRACK THE WAKANDAN HOSTAGES BY THE SIGNAL FROM THEIR KIMOYO BEADS.
THERE.
ACROSS FROM THE RAILWAY STATION.
I WOULD ADVISE YOU TO DO YOUR BEST TO REMAIN HIDDEN.
OF COURSE. THOUGH THESE MERCENARIES MAY BE EXPECTING SOMEBODY...

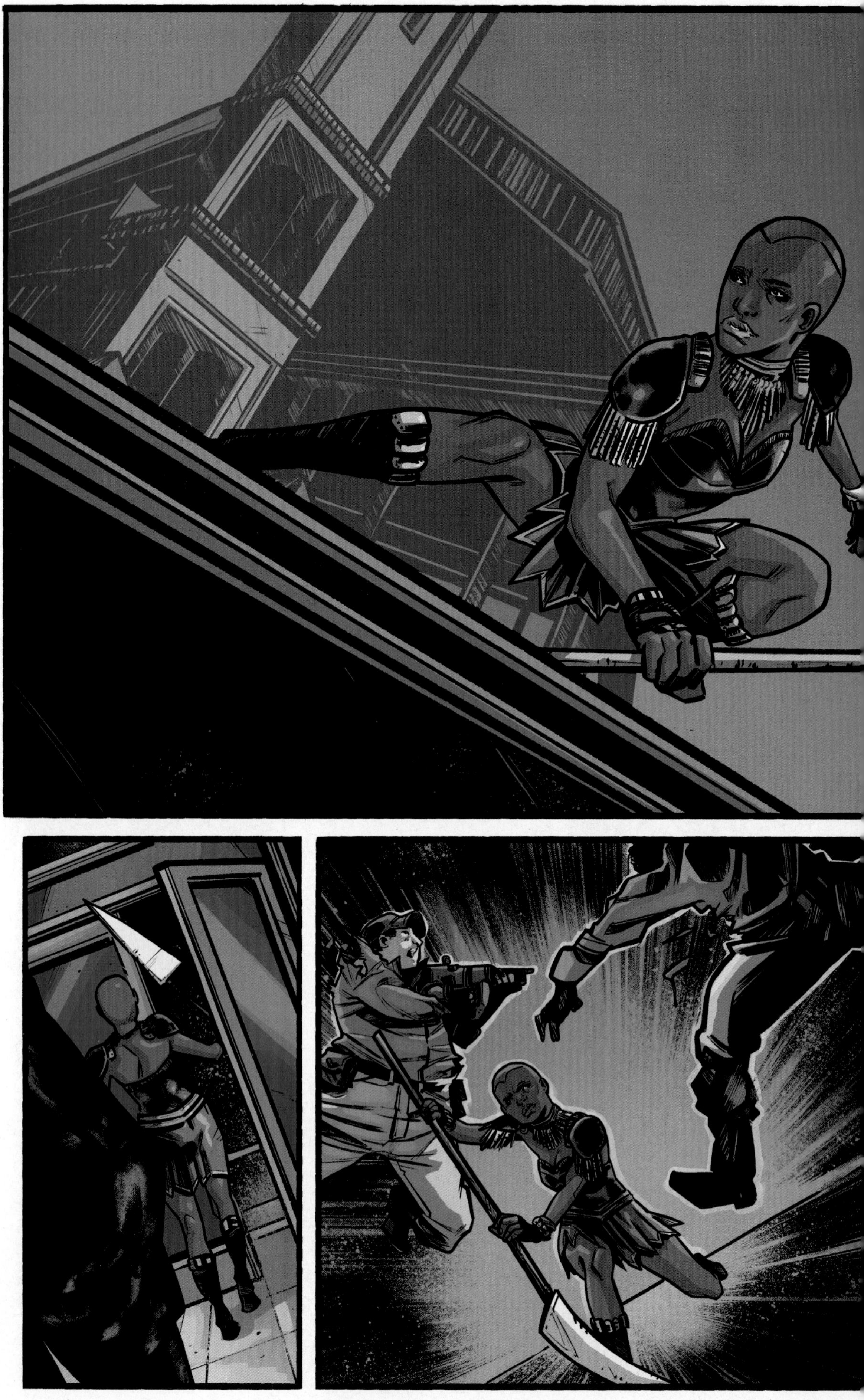

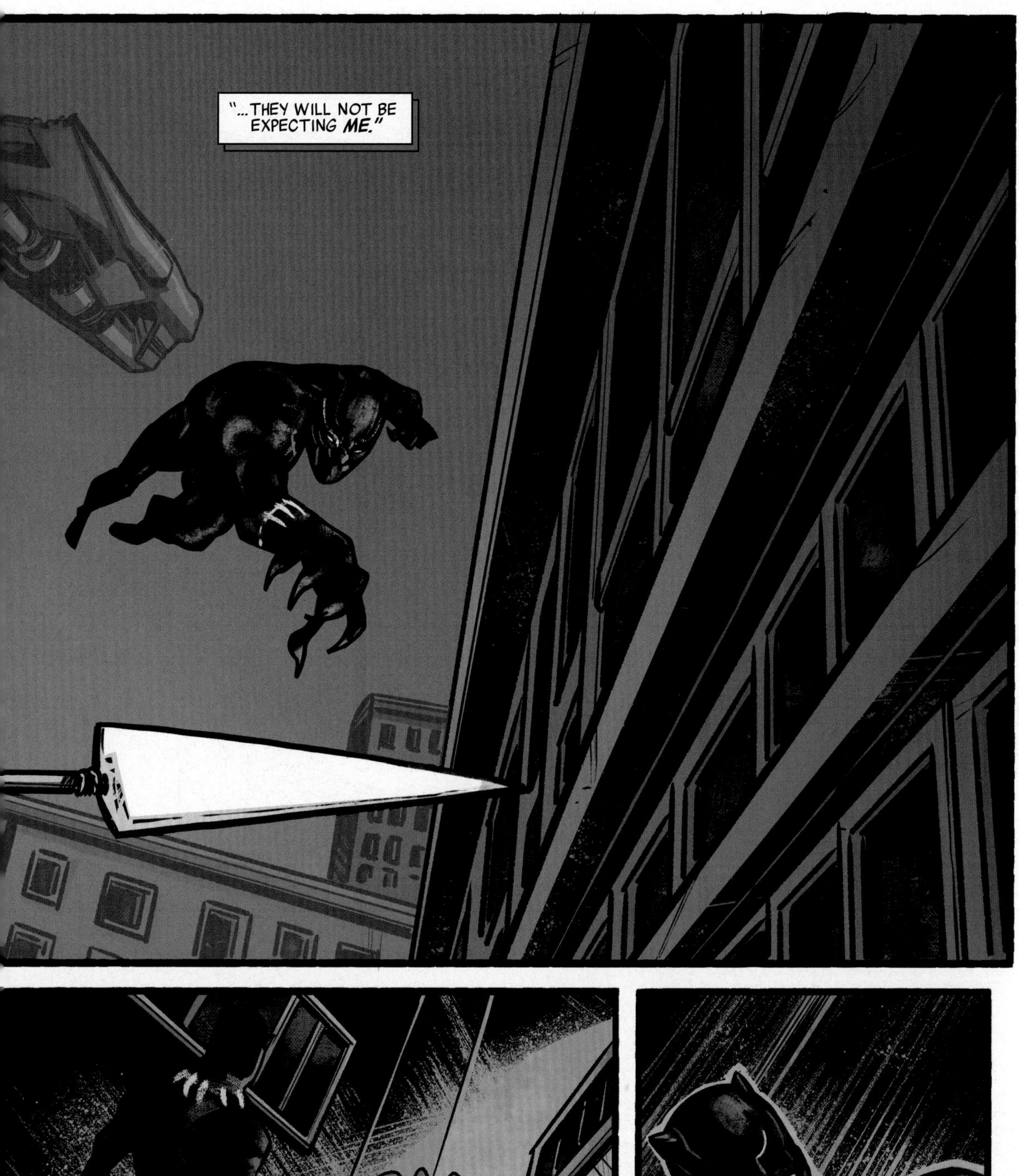
"...THEY WILL NOT BE
EXPECTING ME."

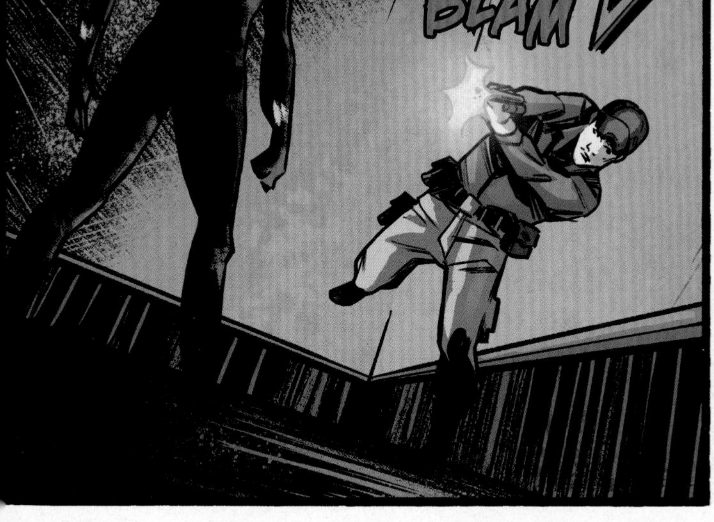
BLAM

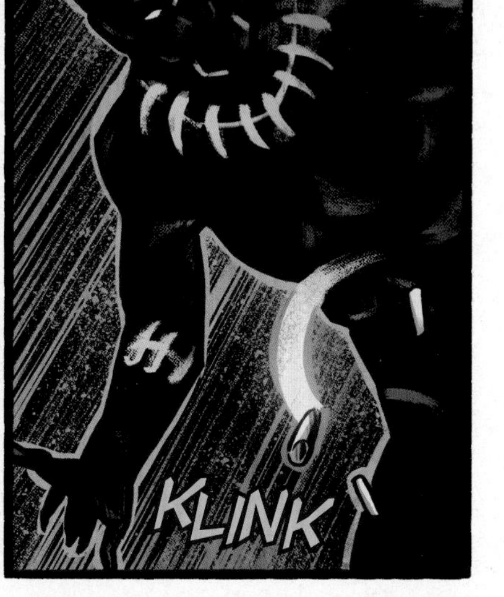
KLINK

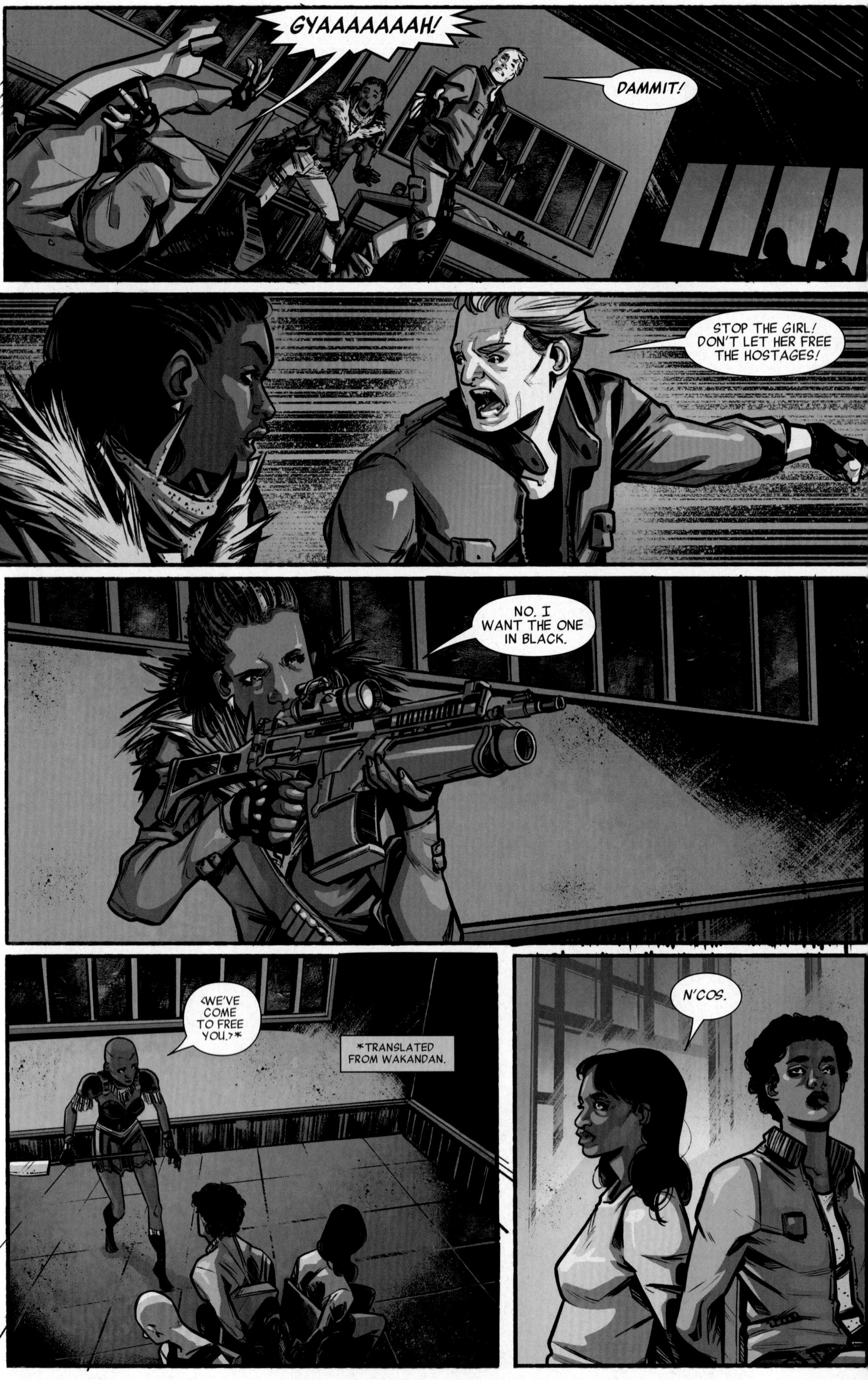
GYAAAAAAAH!
DAMMIT!
STOP THE GIRL! DON'T LET HER FREE THE HOSTAGES!
NO. I WANT THE ONE IN BLACK.
<WE'VE COME TO FREE YOU.>*
*TRANSLATED FROM WAKANDAN.
N'COS.

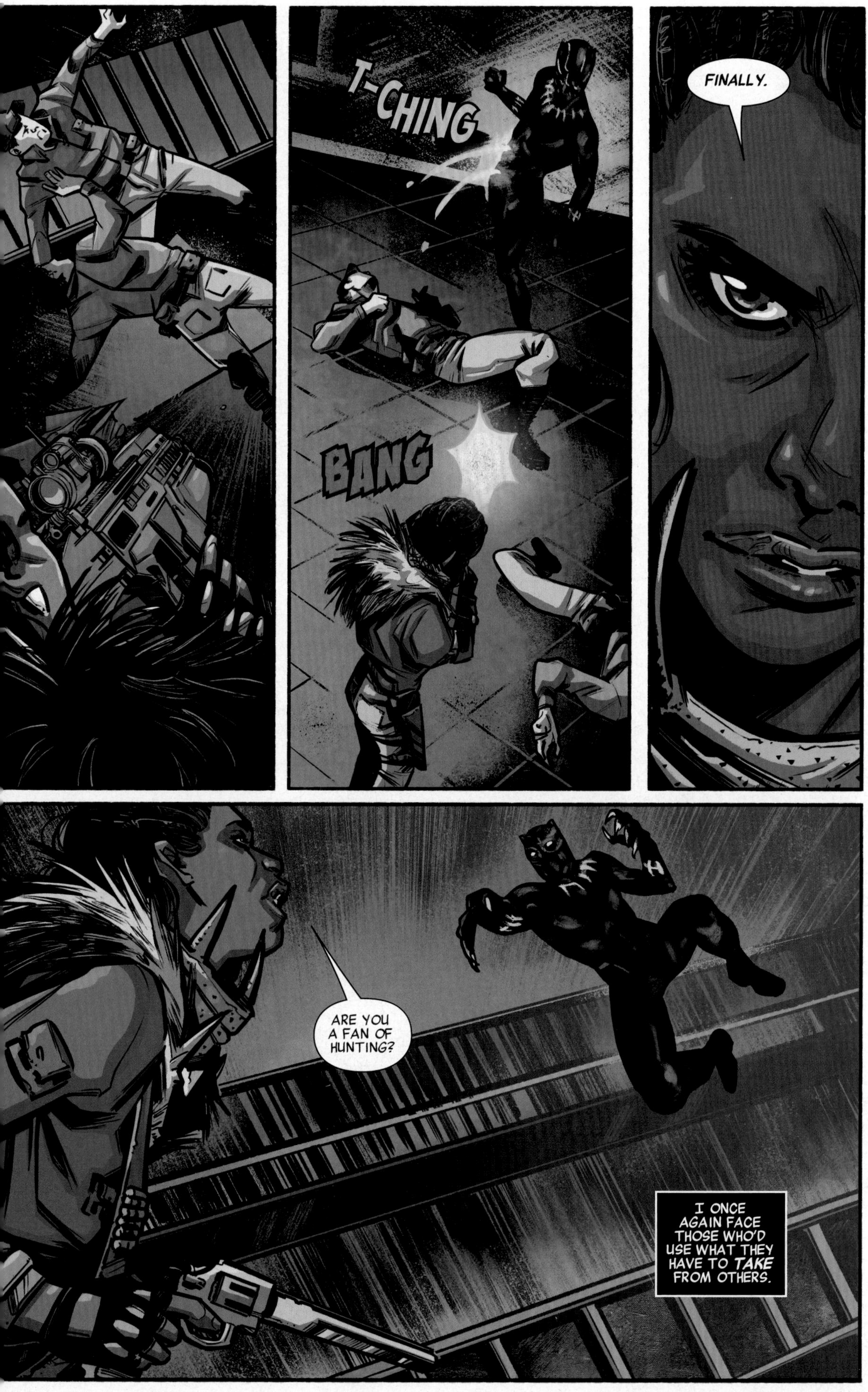
T-CHING
BANG
FINALLY.
ARE YOU A FAN OF HUNTING?
I ONCE AGAIN FACE THOSE WHO'D USE WHAT THEY HAVE TO *TAKE* FROM OTHERS.

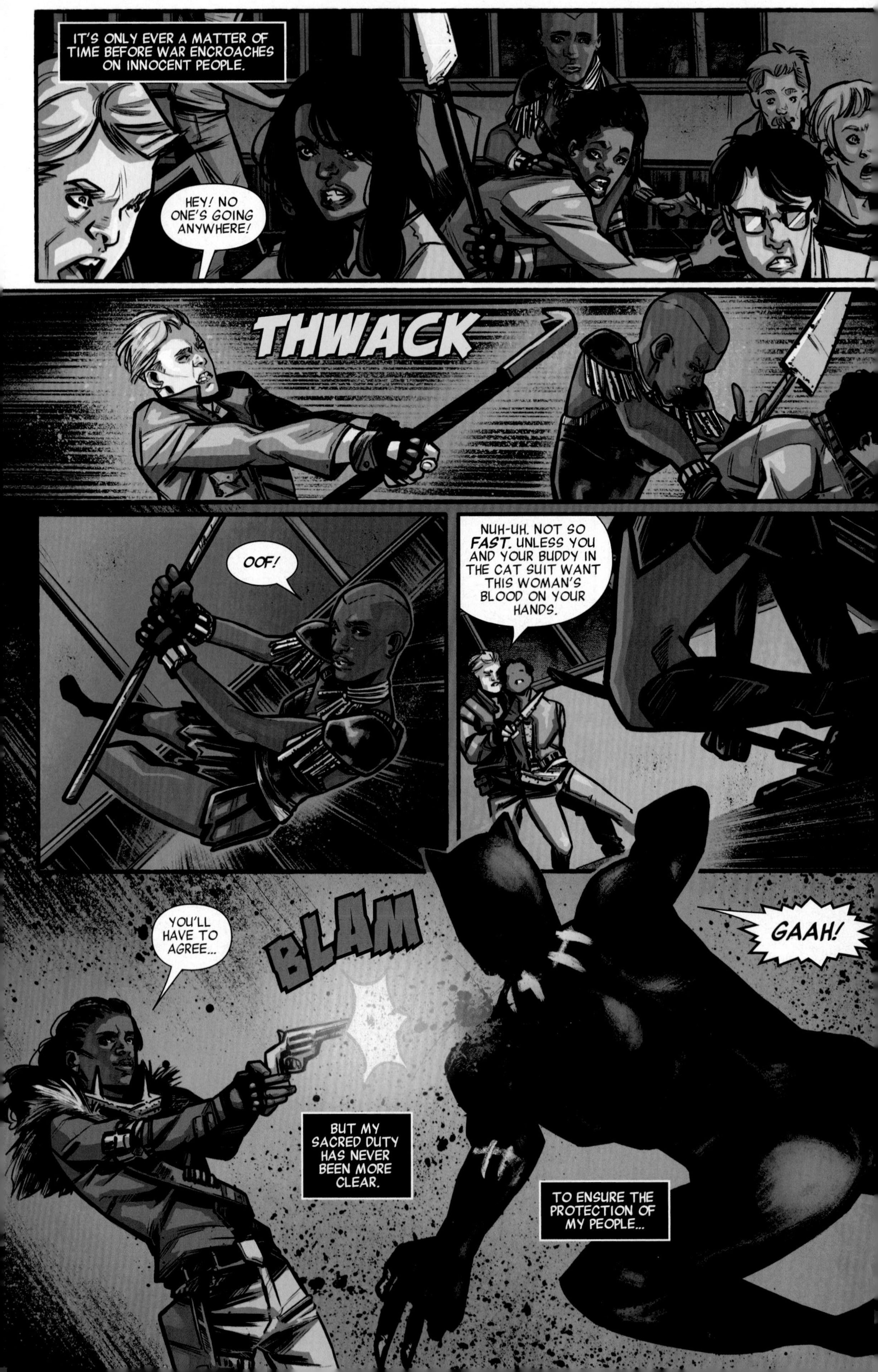
IT'S ONLY EVER A MATTER OF TIME BEFORE WAR ENCROACHES ON INNOCENT PEOPLE.
HEY! NO ONE'S GOING ANYWHERE!
THWACK
OOF!
NUH-UH. NOT SO FAST. UNLESS YOU AND YOUR BUDDY IN THE CAT SUIT WANT THIS WOMAN'S BLOOD ON YOUR HANDS.
YOU'LL HAVE TO AGREE...
BLAM
GAAH!
BUT MY SACRED DUTY HAS NEVER BEEN MORE CLEAR.
TO ENSURE THE PROTECTION OF MY PEOPLE...

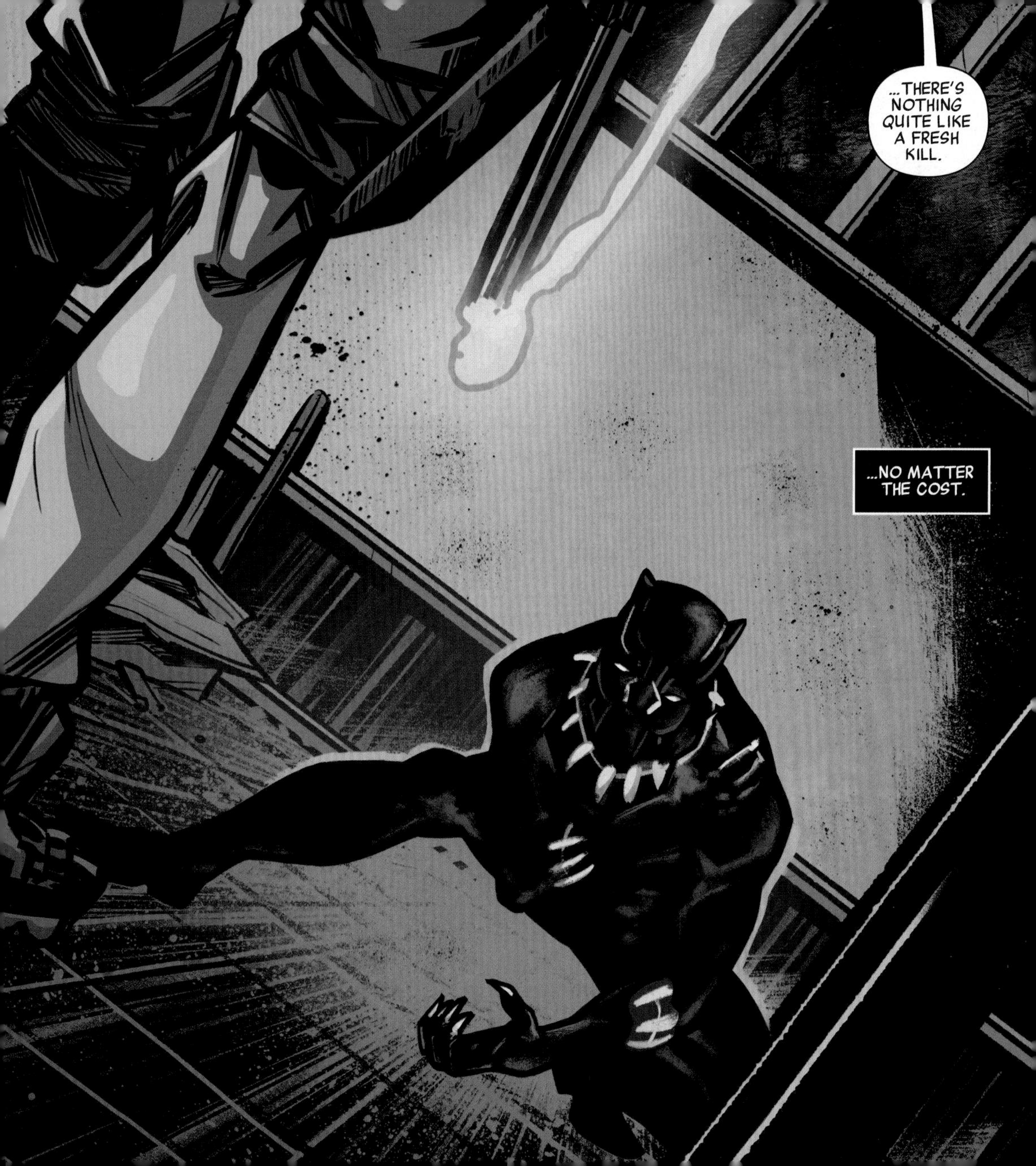
...THERE'S NOTHING QUITE LIKE A FRESH KILL.
...NO MATTER THE COST.

**MARVEL'S BLACK PANTHER
PRELUDE #2**

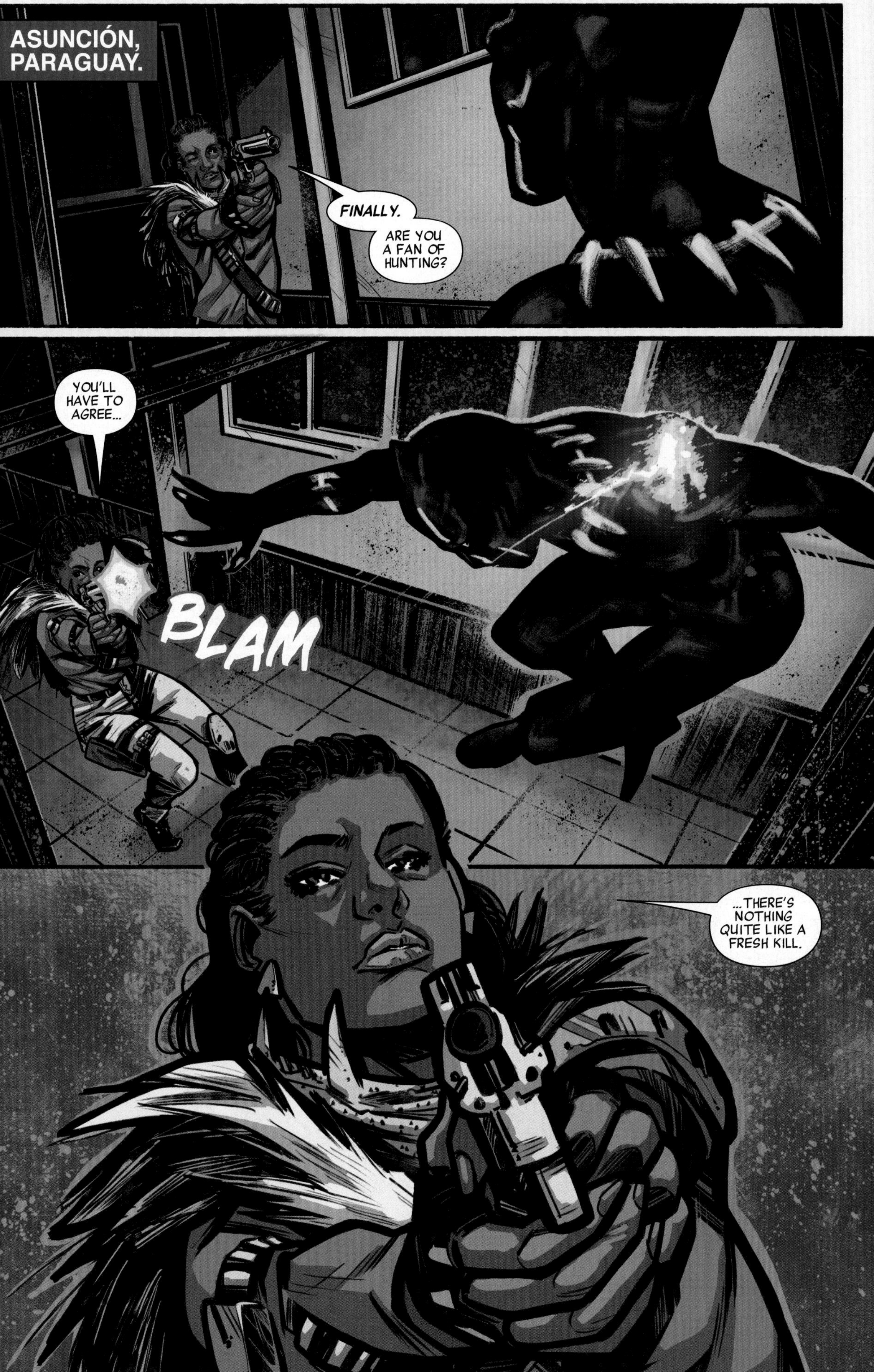
ASUNCIÓN, PARAGUAY.
FINALLY.
ARE YOU A FAN OF HUNTING?
YOU'LL HAVE TO AGREE...
BLAM
...THERE'S NOTHING QUITE LIKE A FRESH KILL.

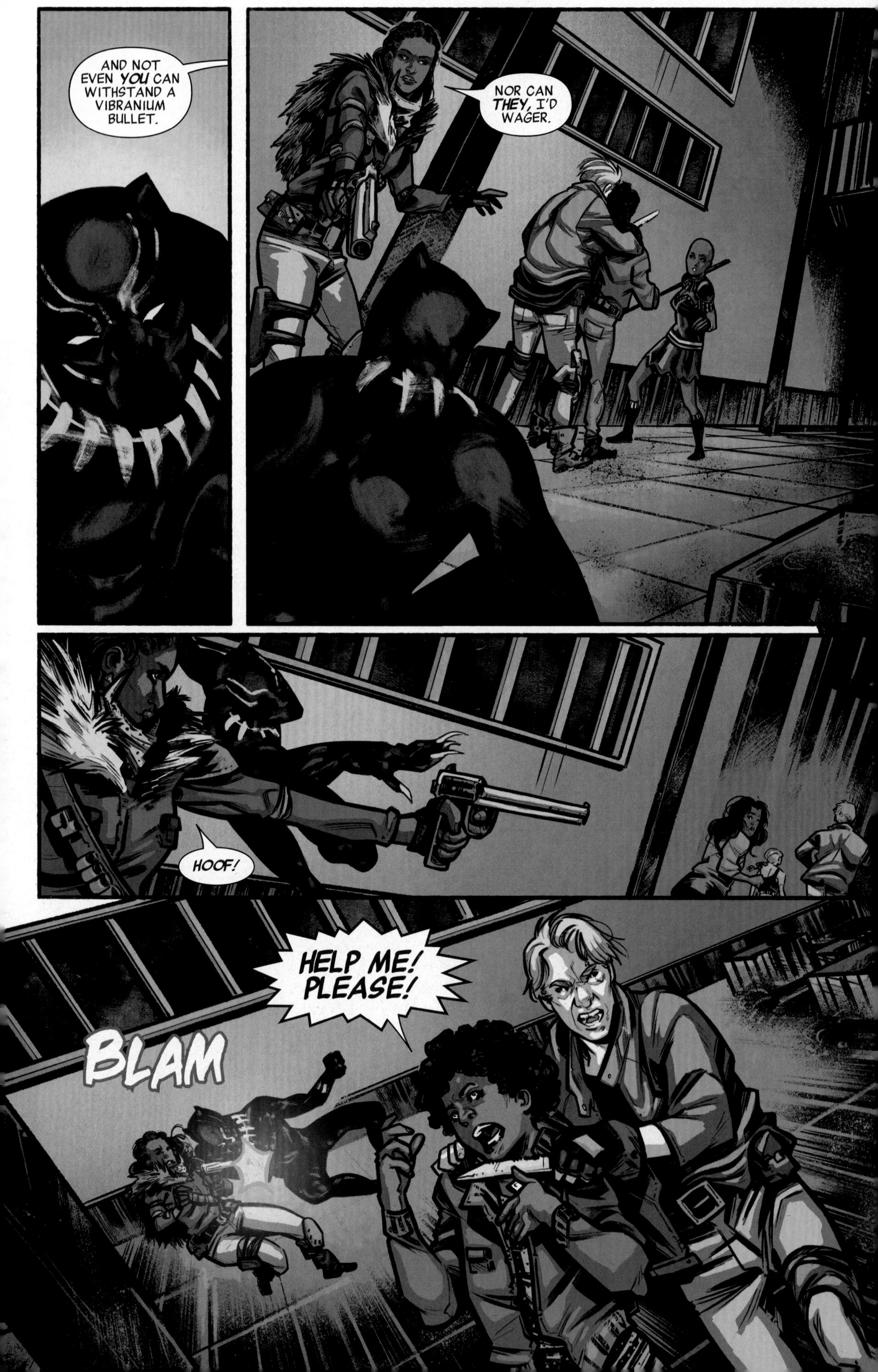
AND NOT EVEN YOU CAN WITHSTAND A VIBRANIUM BULLET.
NOR CAN THEY, I'D WAGER.
HOOF!
HELP ME! PLEASE!
BLAM

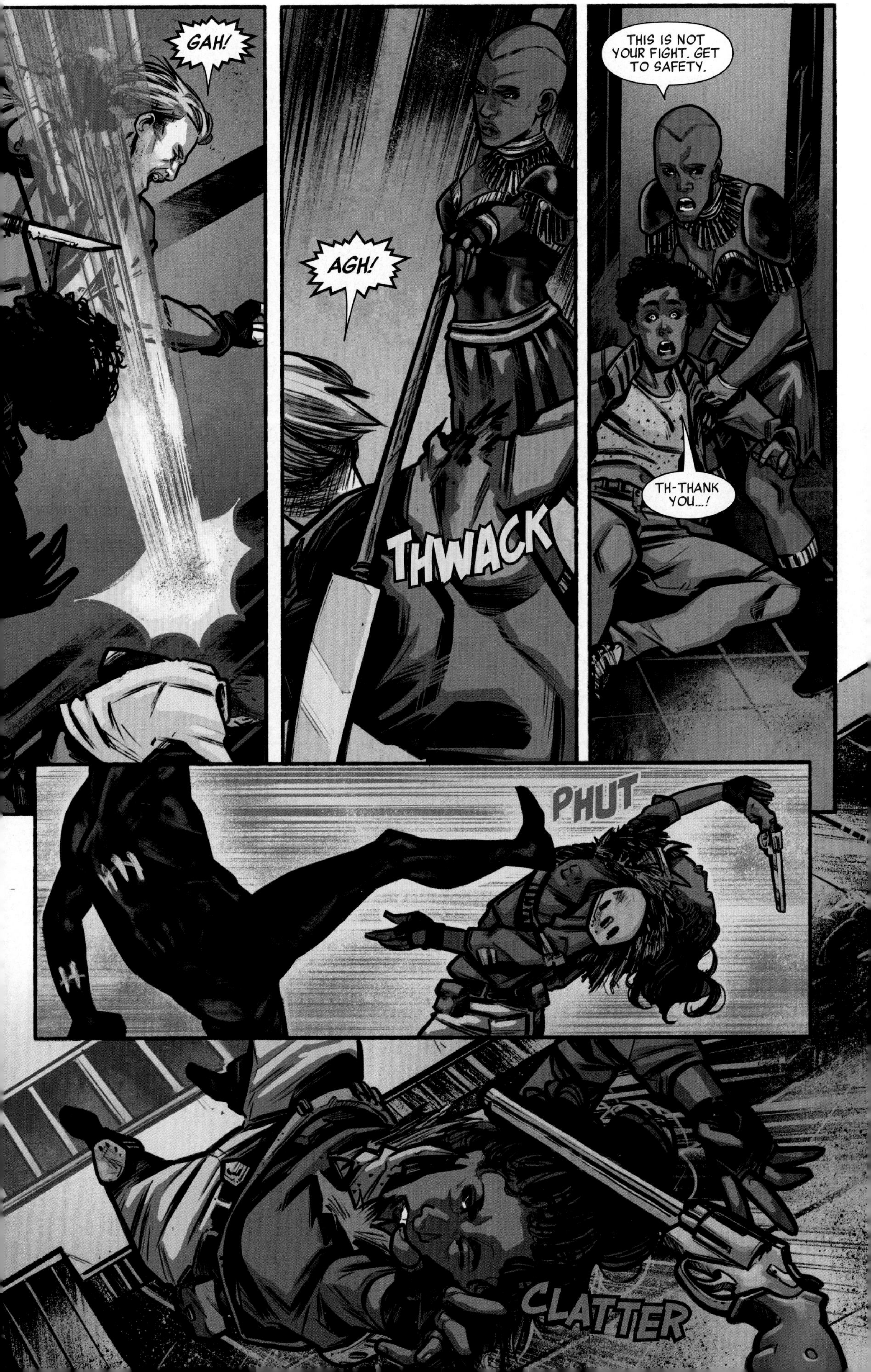
GAH!
AGH!
THWACK
THIS IS NOT YOUR FIGHT. GET TO SAFETY.
TH-THANK YOU...!
PHUT
CLATTER

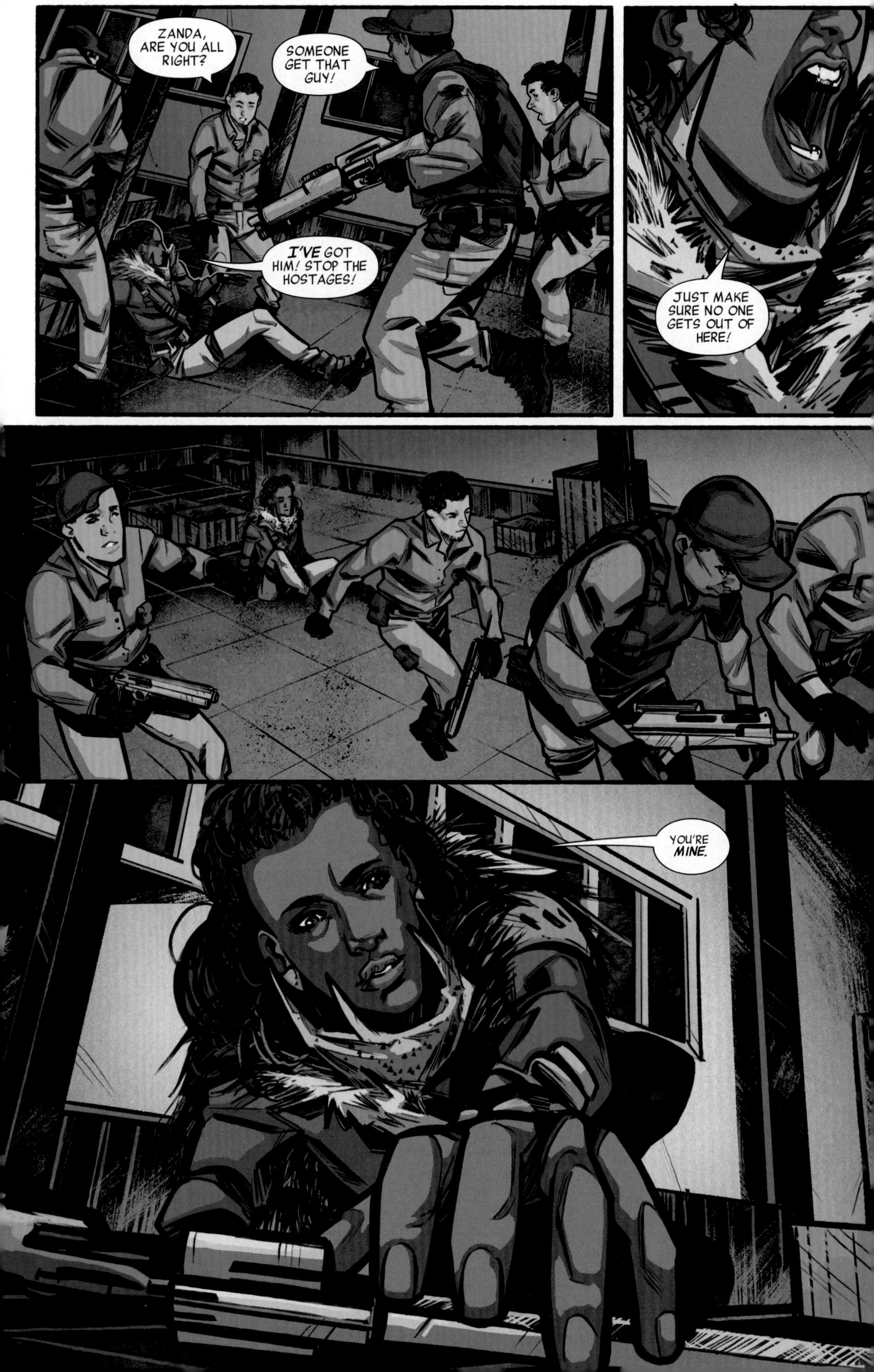
ZANDA, ARE YOU ALL RIGHT?
SOMEONE GET THAT GUY!
I'VE GOT HIM! STOP THE HOSTAGES!
JUST MAKE SURE NO ONE GETS OUT OF HERE!
YOU'RE MINE.

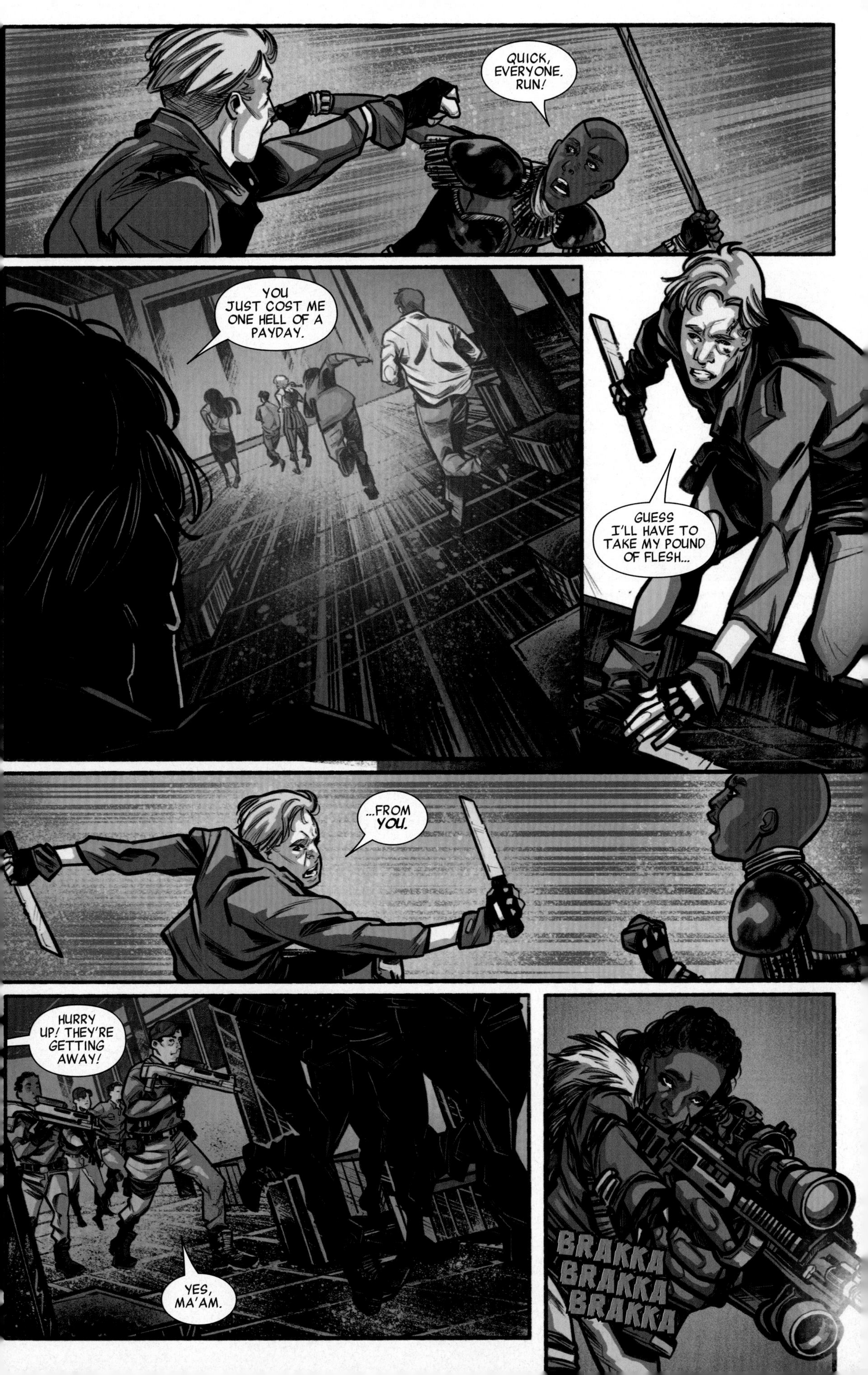
QUICK, EVERYONE. RUN!
YOU JUST COST ME ONE HELL OF A PAYDAY.
GUESS I'LL HAVE TO TAKE MY POUND OF FLESH...
...FROM YOU.
HURRY UP! THEY'RE GETTING AWAY!
YES, MA'AM.
BRAKKA BRAKKA BRAKKA

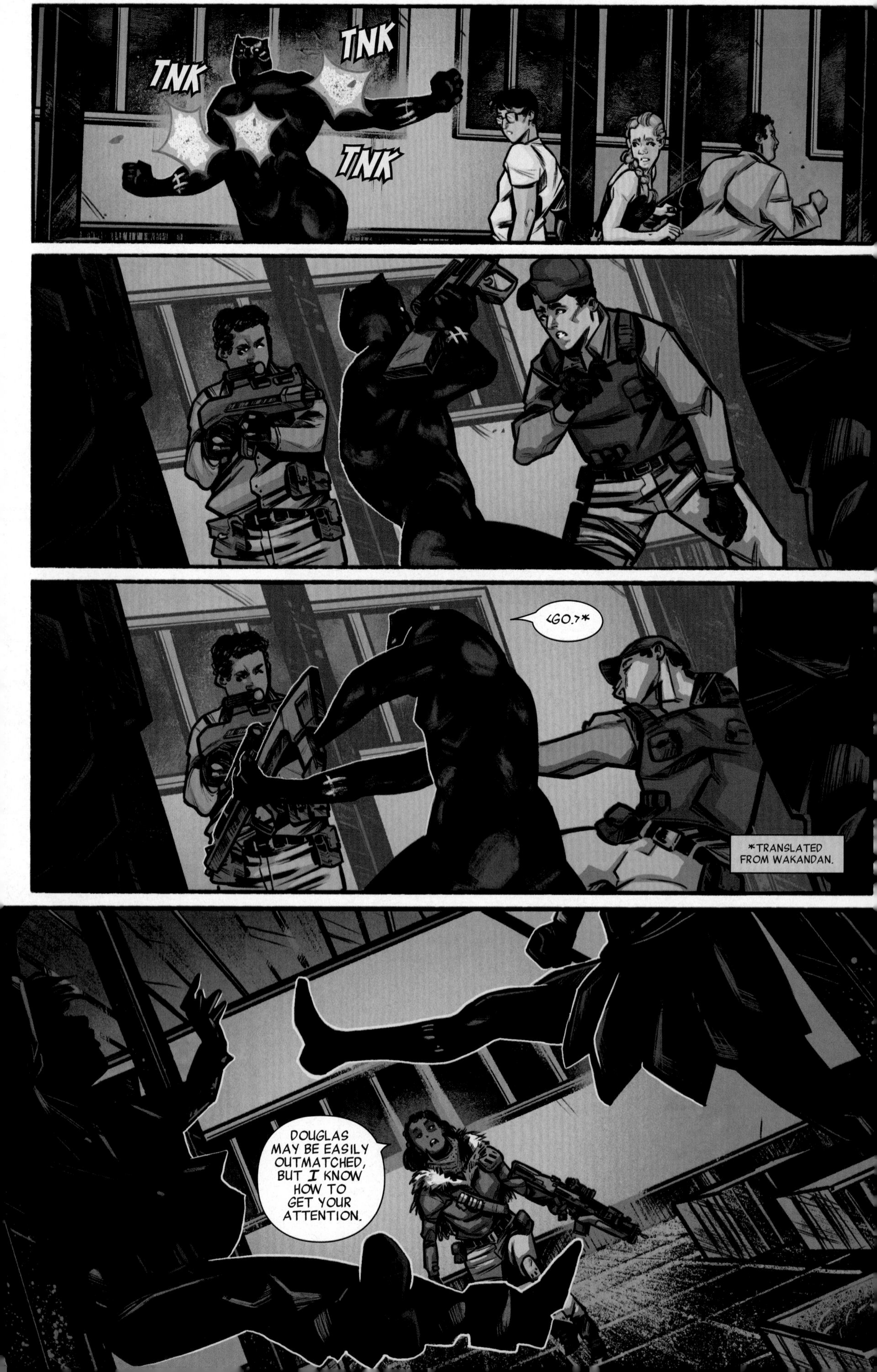
TNK
TNK
TNK
<GO.>*
*TRANSLATED FROM WAKANDAN.
DOUGLAS MAY BE EASILY OUTMATCHED, BUT I KNOW HOW TO GET YOUR ATTENTION.

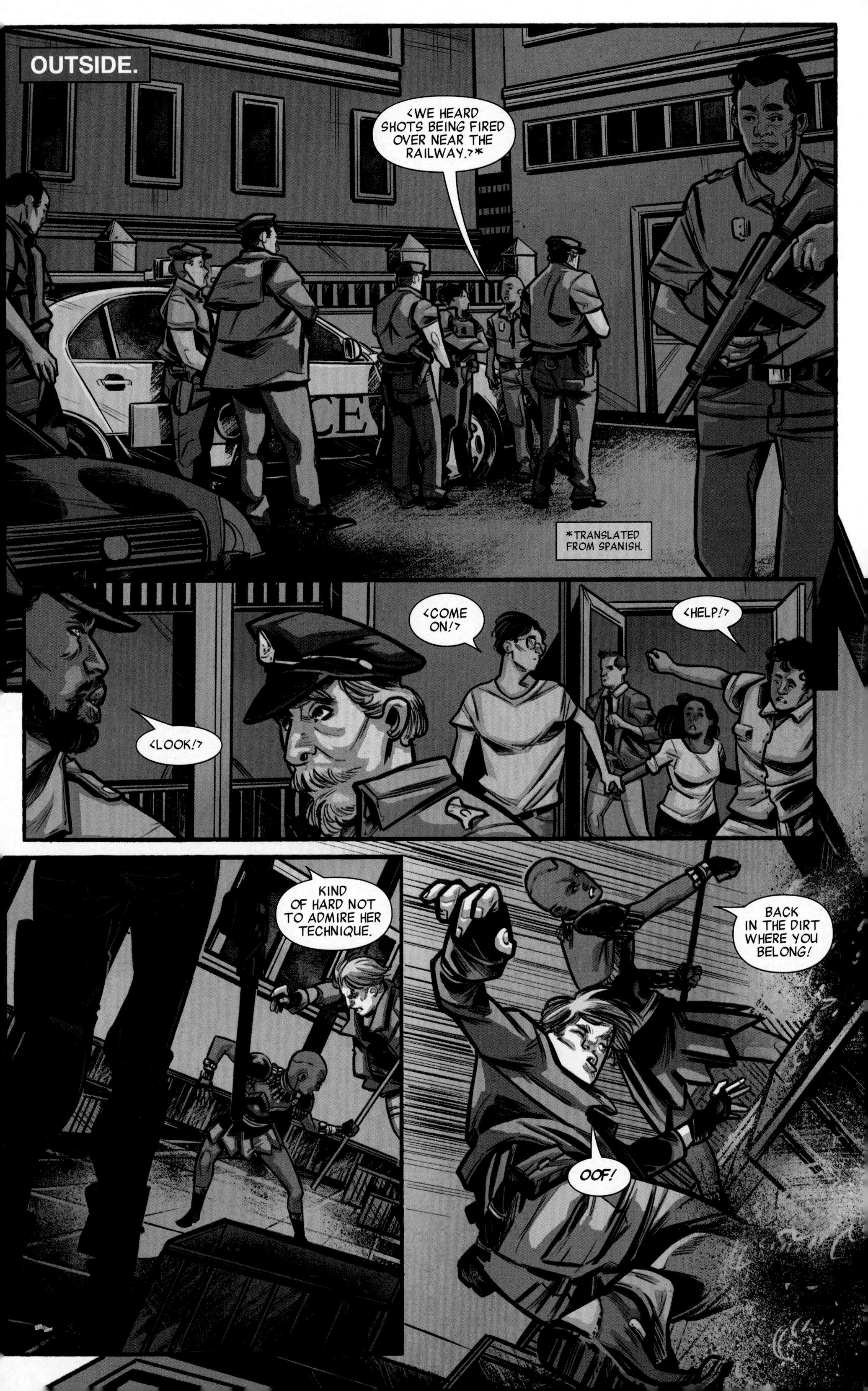
OUTSIDE.
<WE HEARD SHOTS BEING FIRED OVER NEAR THE RAILWAY.>*
*TRANSLATED FROM SPANISH.
<LOOK!>
<COME ON!>
<HELP!>
KIND OF HARD NOT TO ADMIRE HER TECHNIQUE.
BACK IN THE DIRT WHERE YOU BELONG!
OOF!

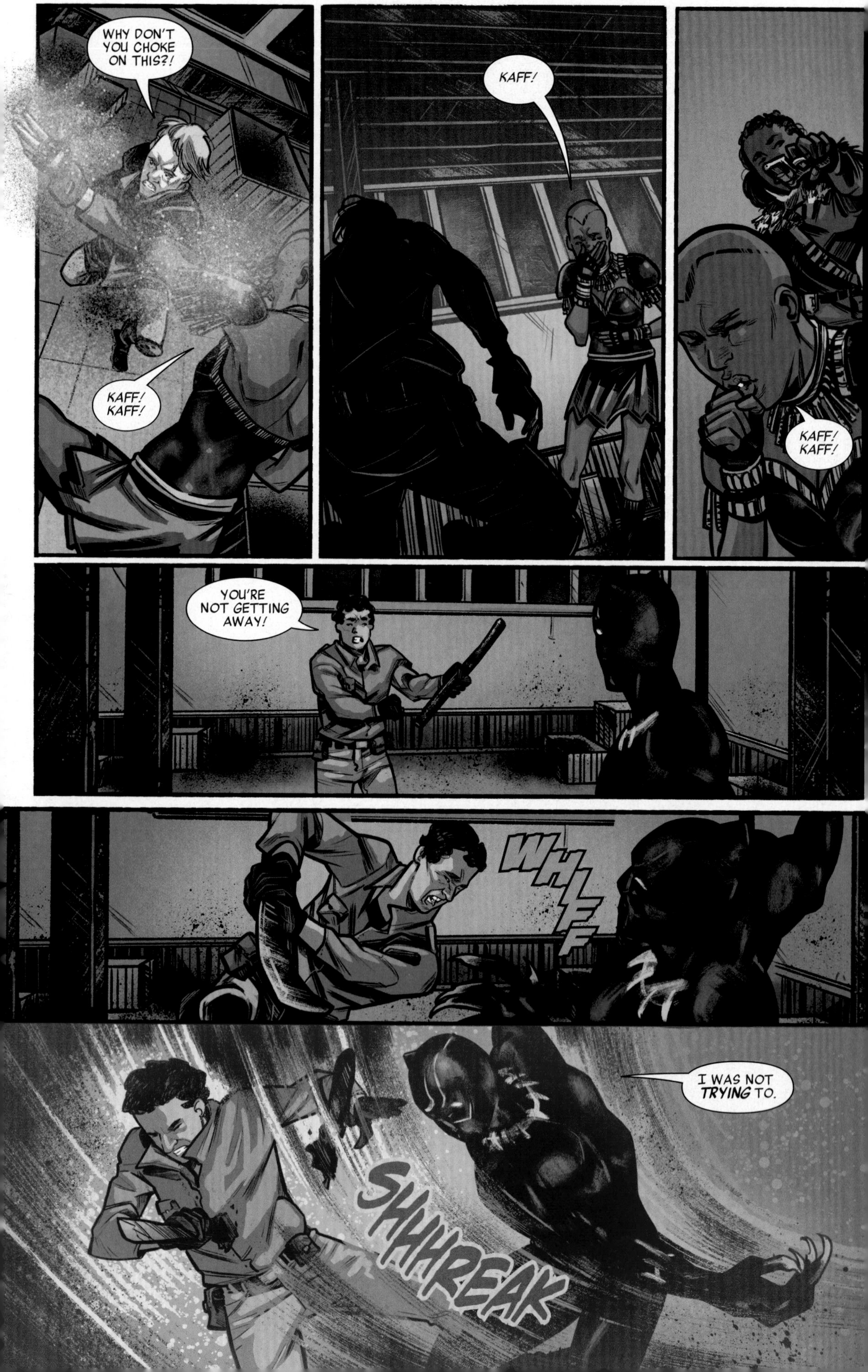
WHY DON'T YOU CHOKE ON THIS?!
KAFF! KAFF!
KAFF!
KAFF! KAFF!
YOU'RE NOT GETTING AWAY!
WHIFF
I WAS NOT *TRYING* TO.
SHHREAK

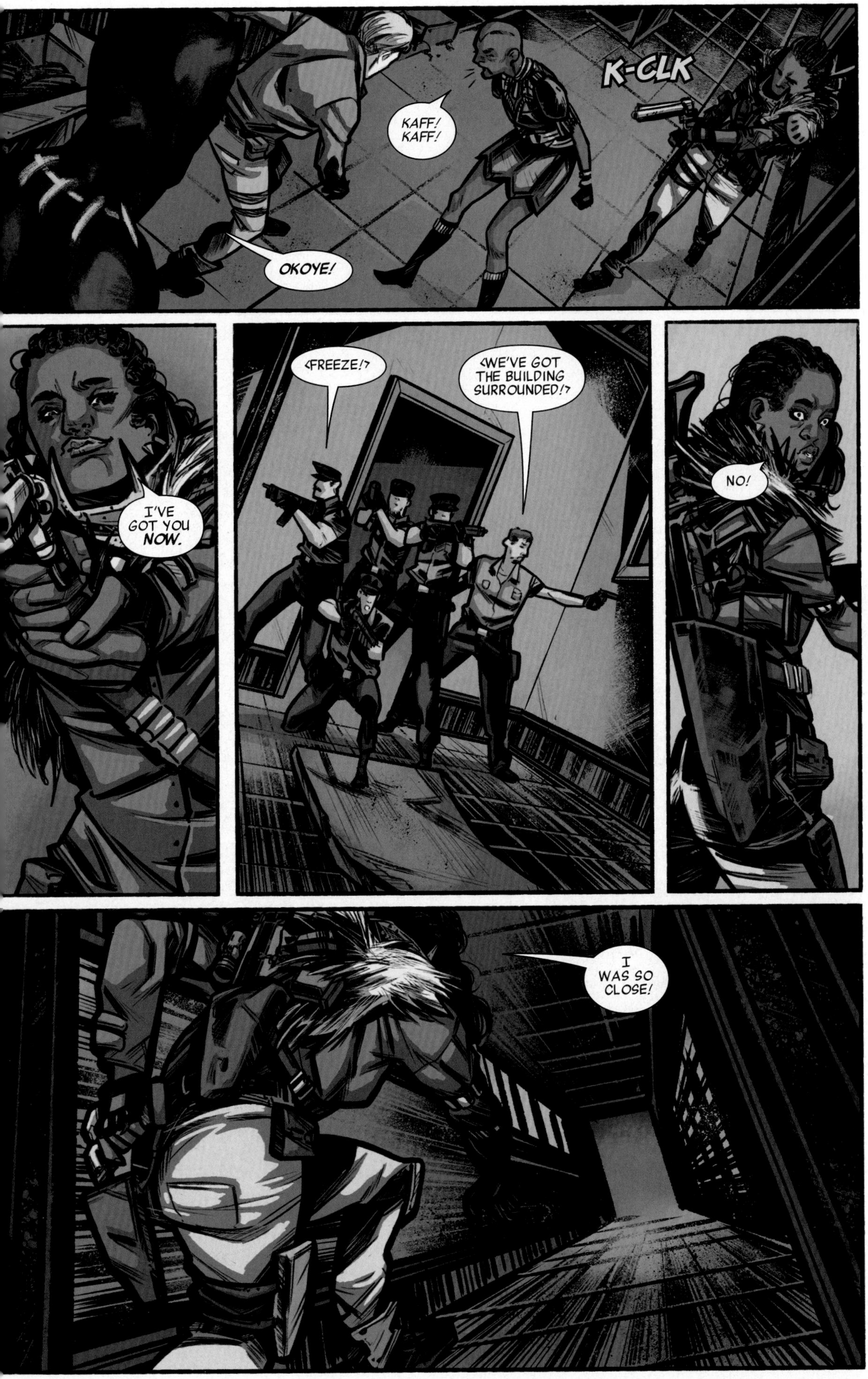
K-CLK
KAFF! KAFF!
OKOYE!
I'VE GOT YOU NOW.
<FREEZE!>
<WE'VE GOT THE BUILDING SURROUNDED!>
NO!
I WAS SO CLOSE!

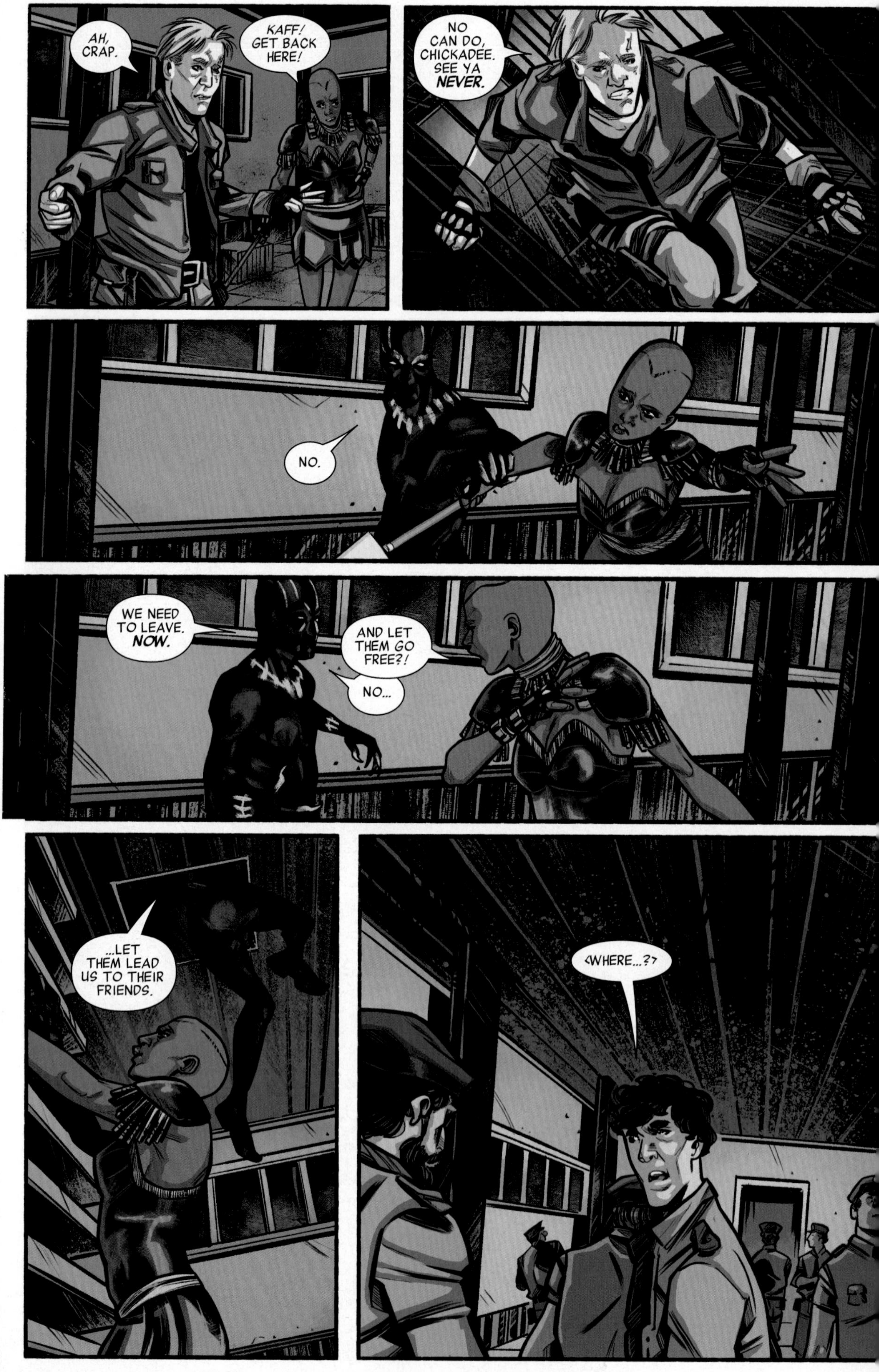
AH, CRAP.
KAFF! GET BACK HERE!
NO CAN DO, CHICKADEE. SEE YA NEVER.
NO.
WE NEED TO LEAVE. NOW.
AND LET THEM GO FREE?!
NO...
...LET THEM LEAD US TO THEIR FRIENDS.
<WHERE...?>

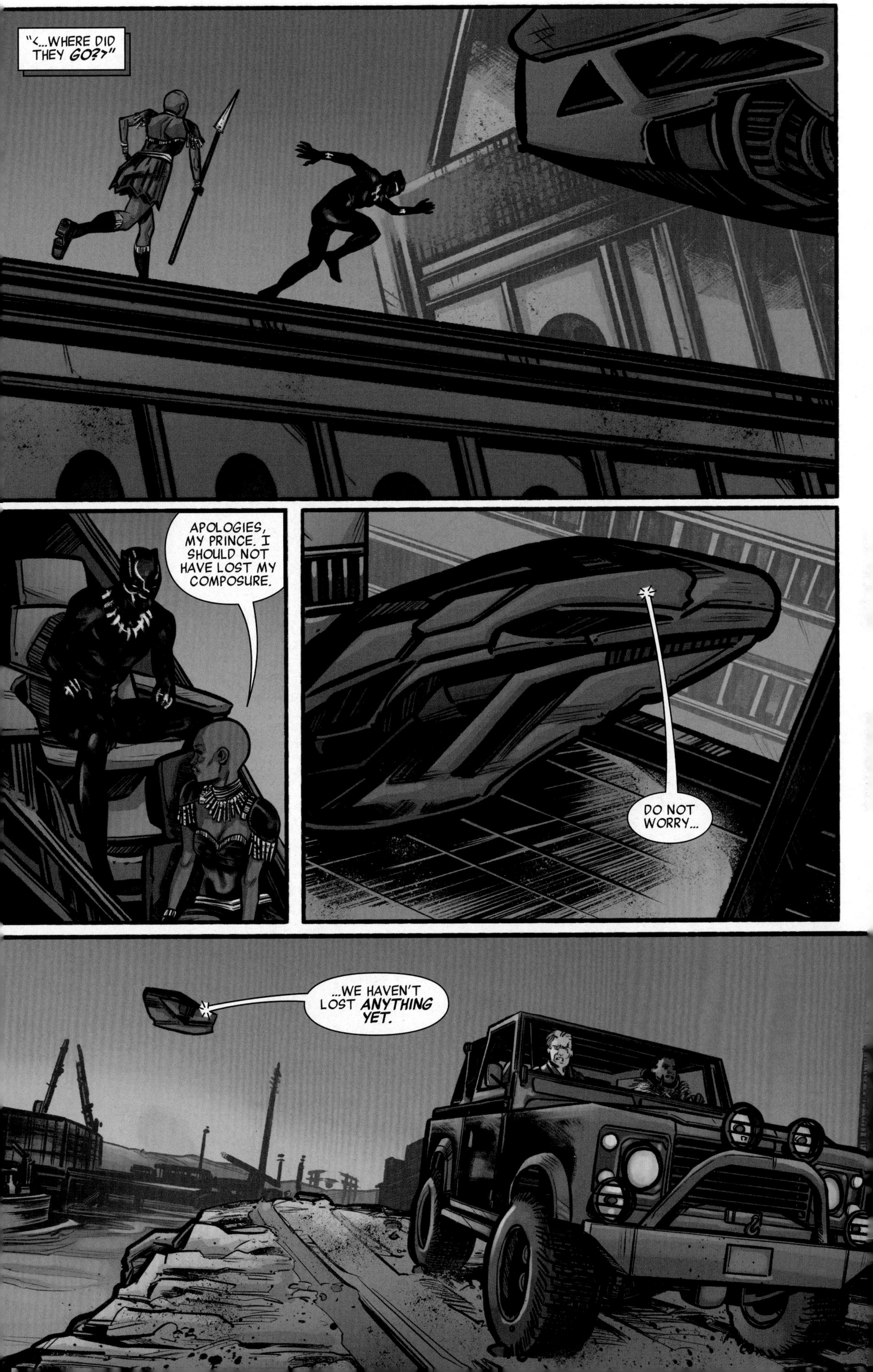
"<...WHERE DID THEY GO?>"
APOLOGIES, MY PRINCE. I SHOULD NOT HAVE LOST MY COMPOSURE.
DO NOT WORRY...
...WE HAVEN'T LOST ANYTHING YET.

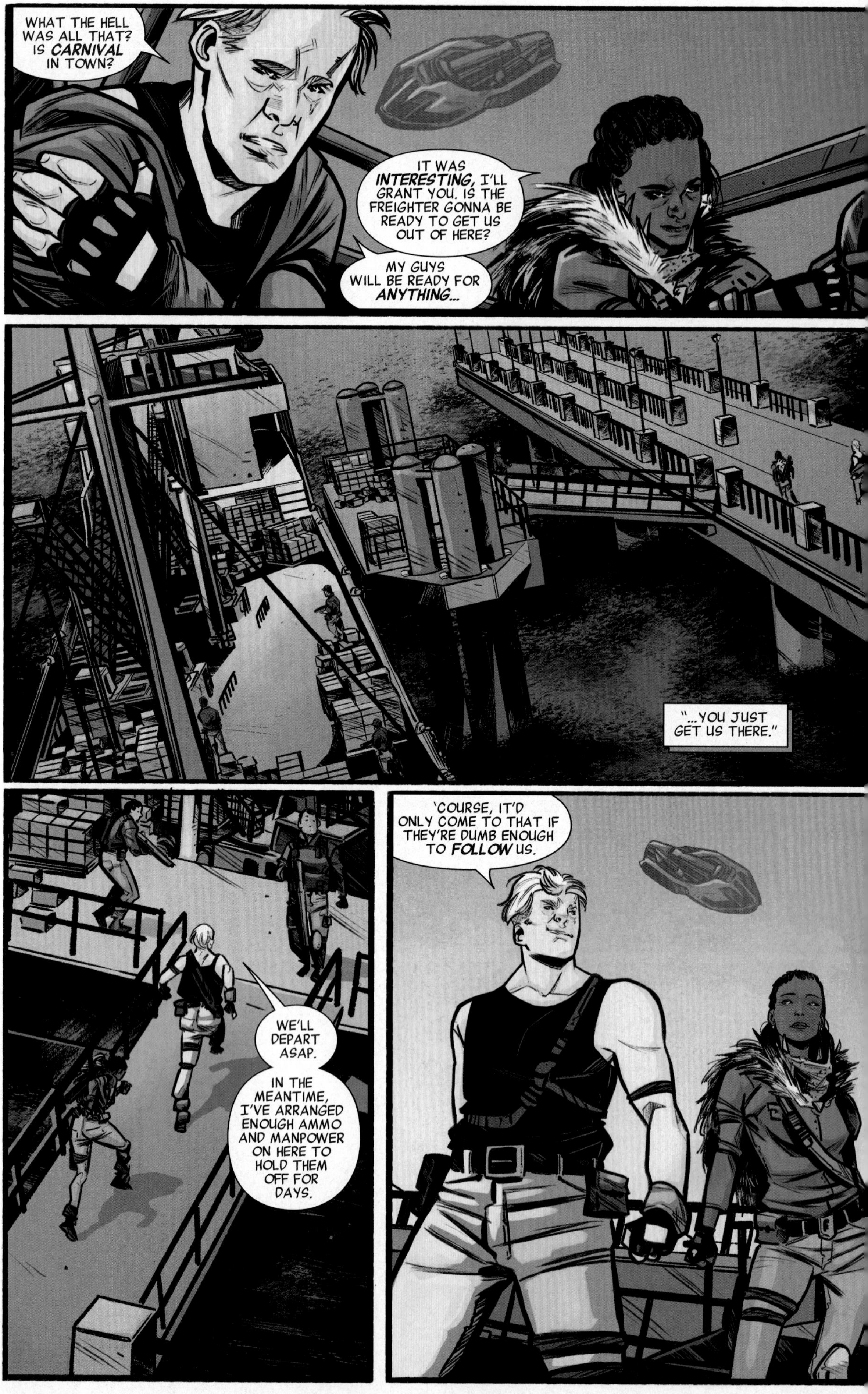
WHAT THE HELL WAS ALL THAT? IS CARNIVAL IN TOWN?
IT WAS INTERESTING, I'LL GRANT YOU. IS THE FREIGHTER GONNA BE READY TO GET US OUT OF HERE?
MY GUYS WILL BE READY FOR ANYTHING...
"...YOU JUST GET US THERE."
WE'LL DEPART ASAP.
IN THE MEANTIME, I'VE ARRANGED ENOUGH AMMO AND MANPOWER ON HERE TO HOLD THEM OFF FOR DAYS.
'COURSE, IT'D ONLY COME TO THAT IF THEY'RE DUMB ENOUGH TO FOLLOW US.

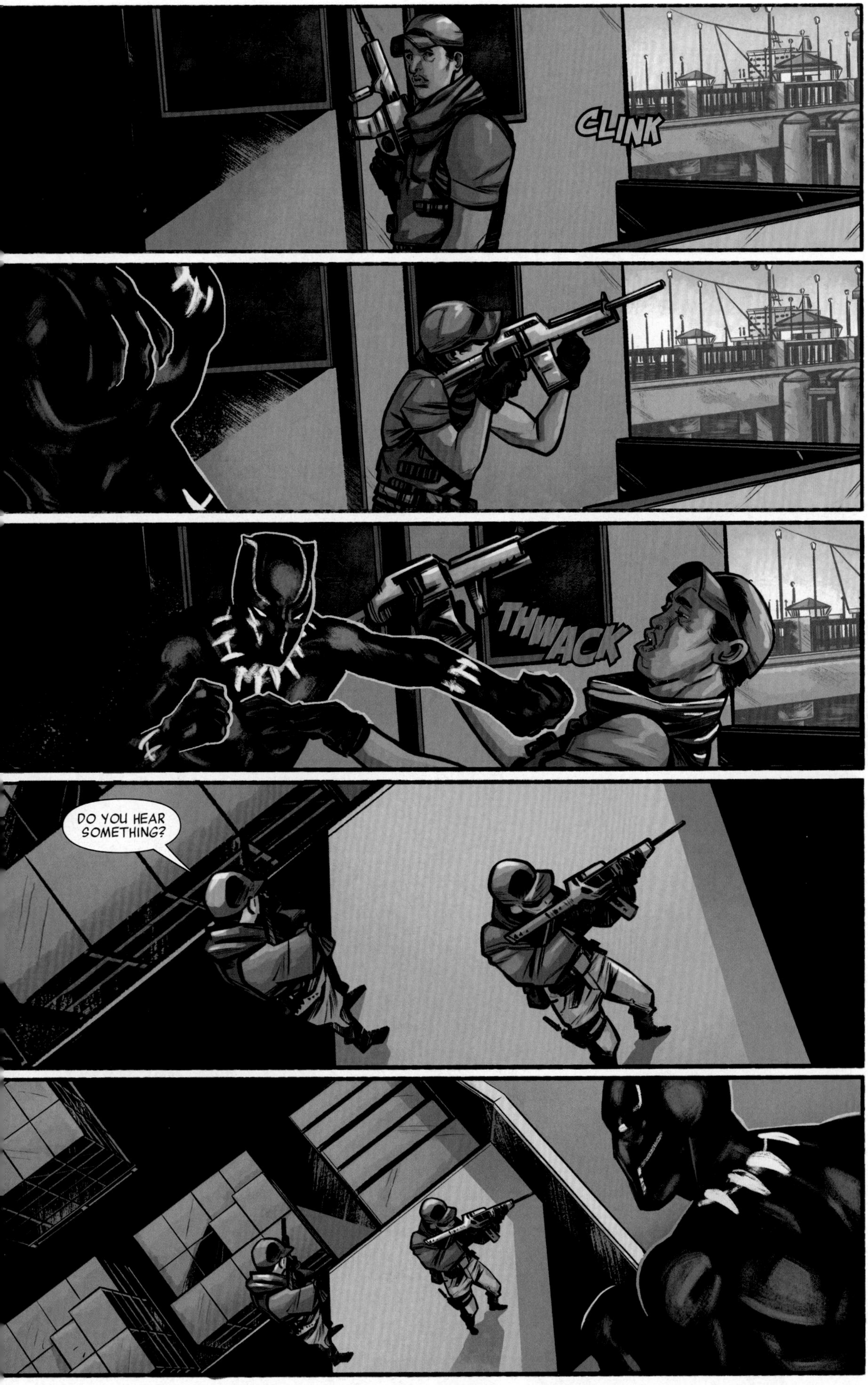
CLINK
THWACK
DO YOU HEAR SOMETHING?

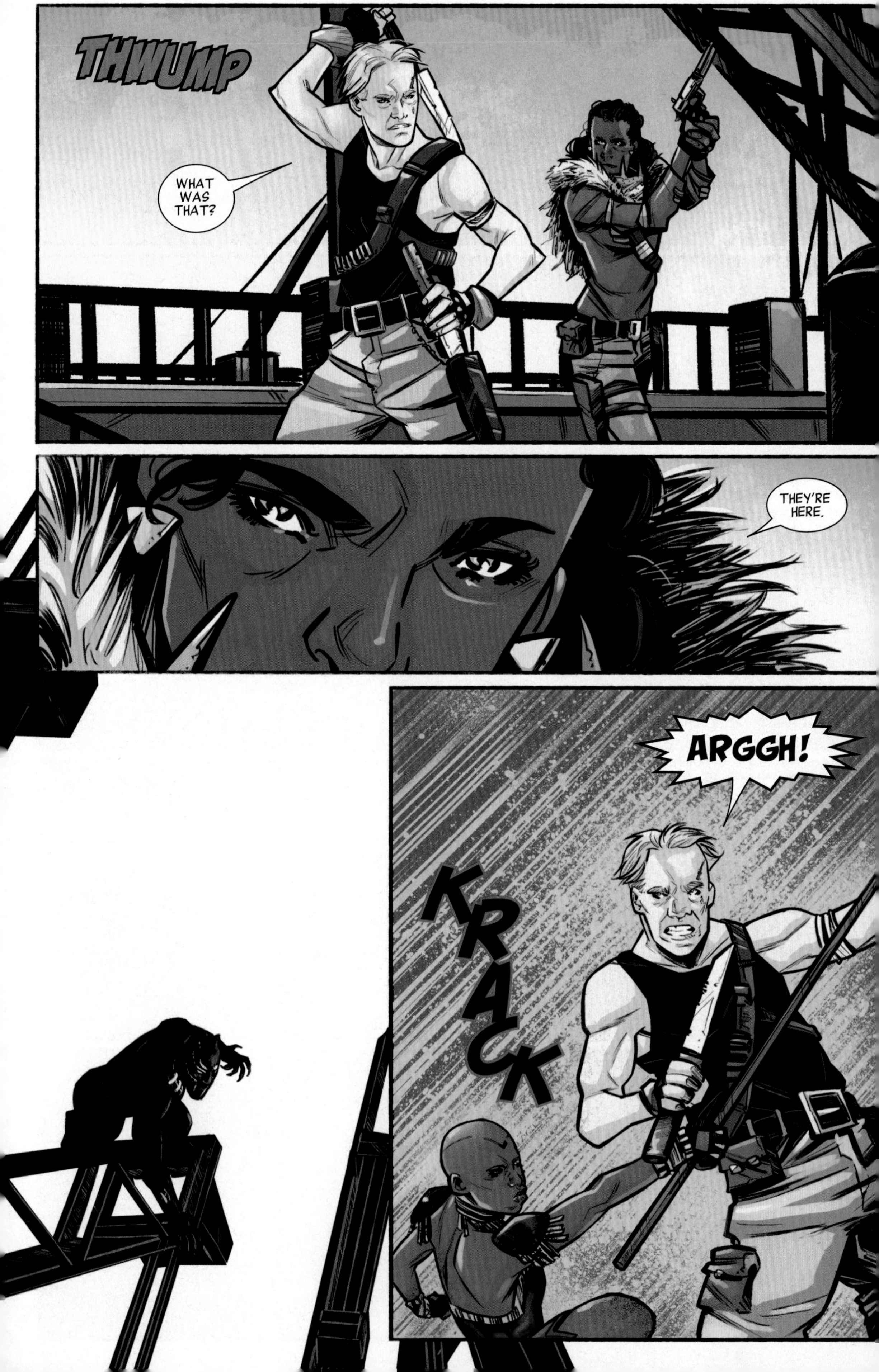
THWUMP
WHAT WAS THAT?
THEY'RE HERE.
ARGGH!
KRACK

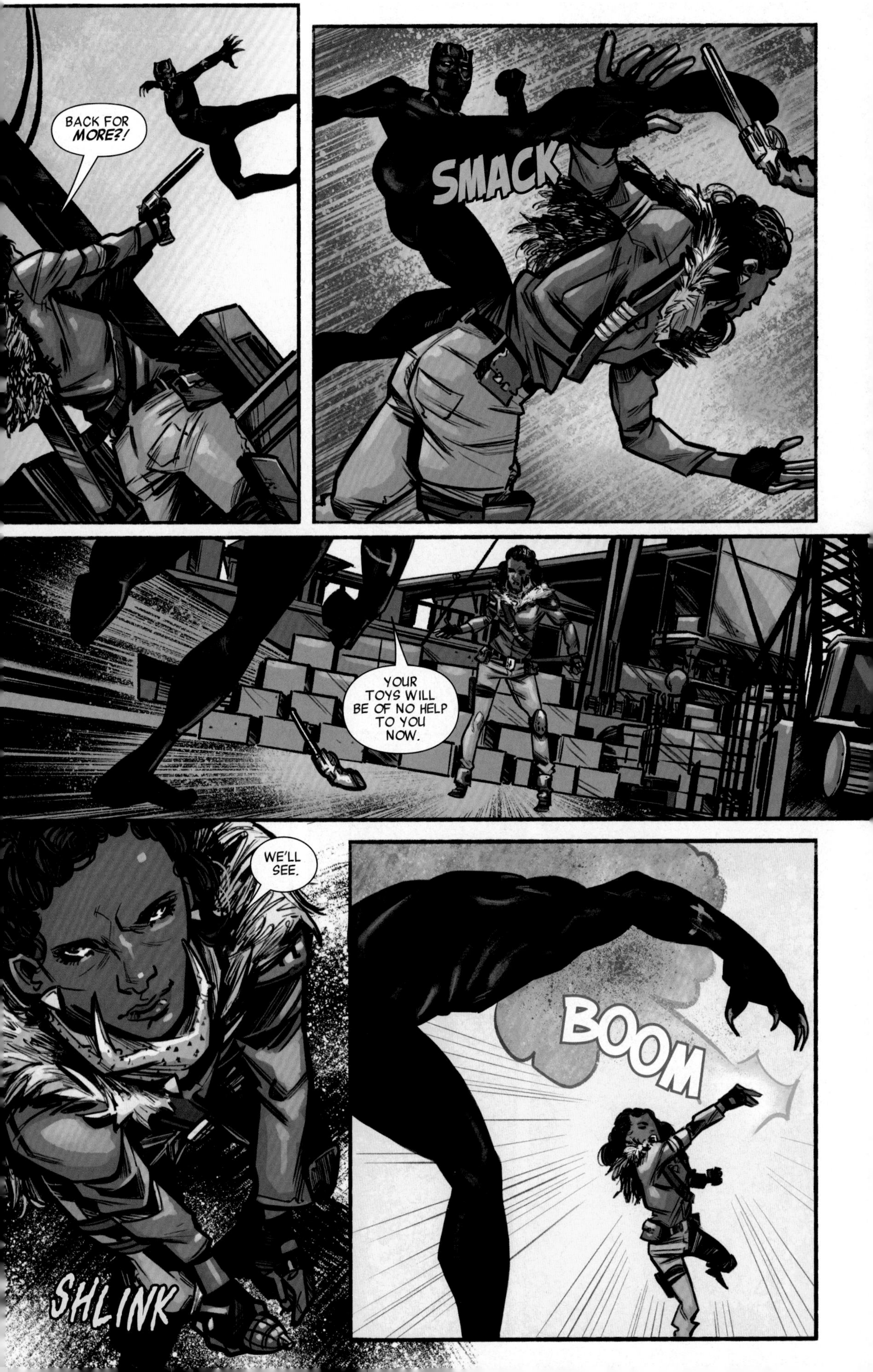
BACK FOR MORE?!
SMACK
YOUR TOYS WILL BE OF NO HELP TO YOU NOW.
WE'LL SEE.
SHLINK
BOOM

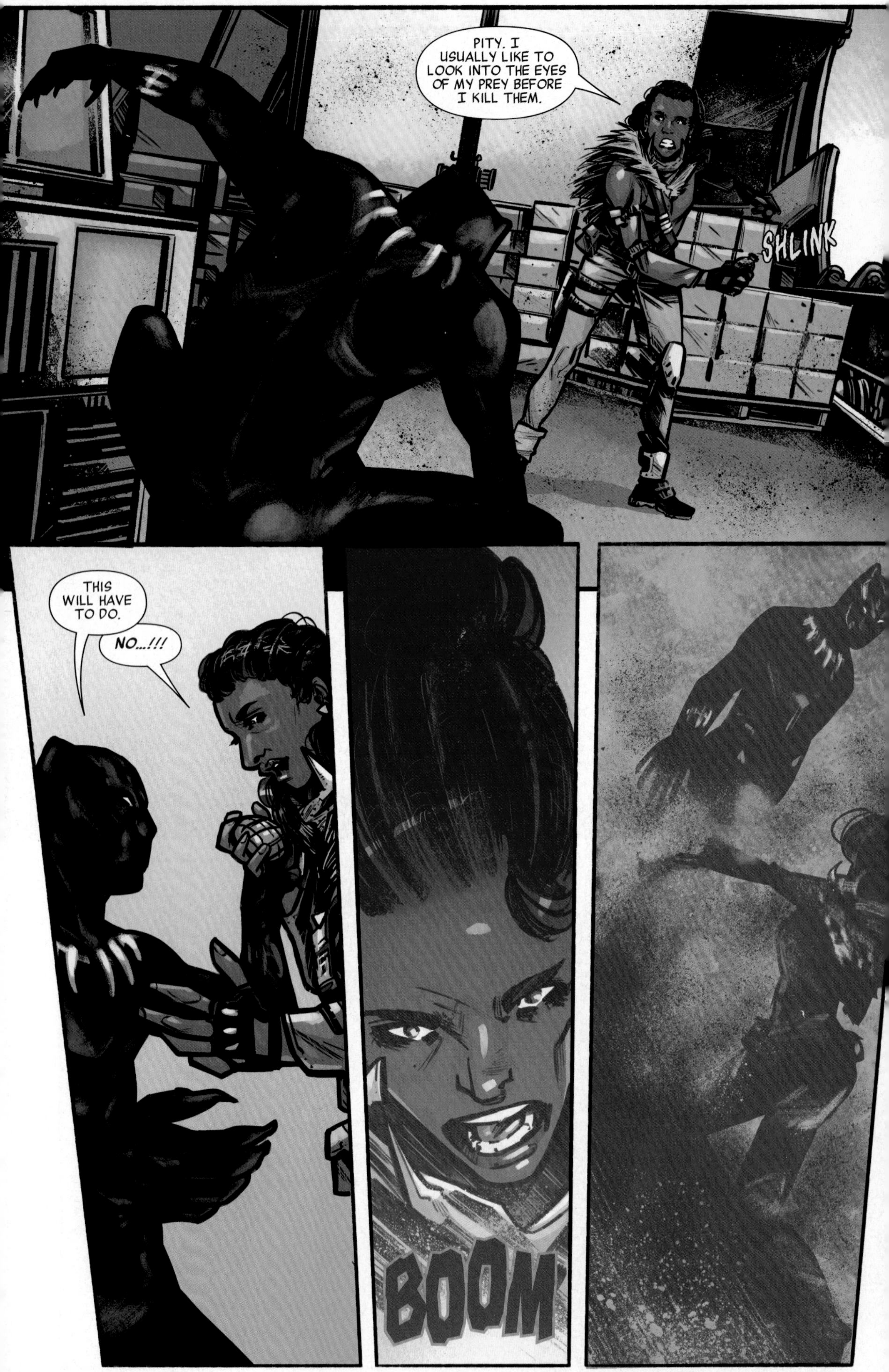
PITY. I USUALLY LIKE TO LOOK INTO THE EYES OF MY PREY BEFORE I KILL THEM.
SHLINK
THIS WILL HAVE TO DO.
NO...!!!
BOOM

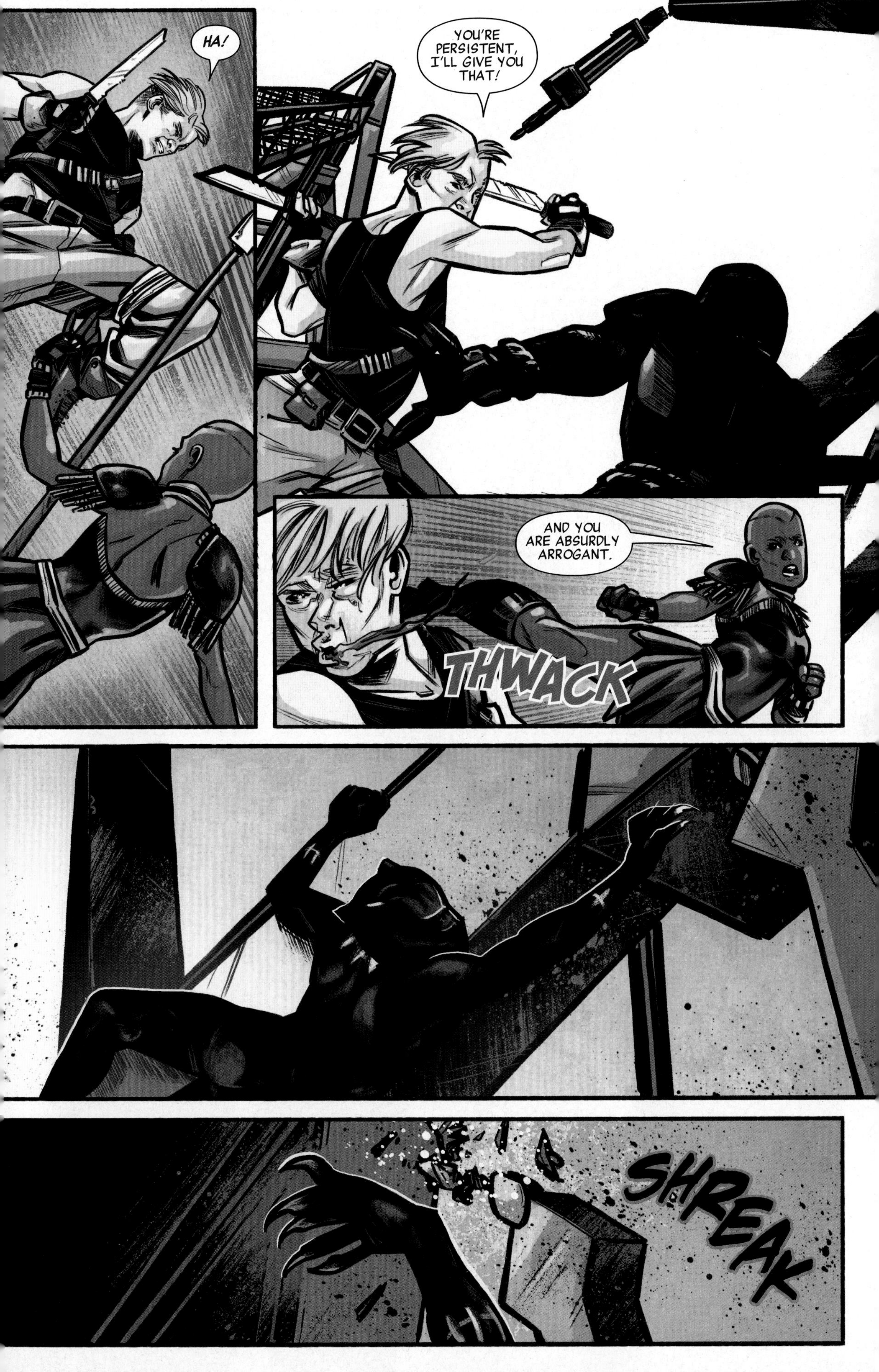
HA!
YOU'RE PERSISTENT, I'LL GIVE YOU THAT!
AND YOU ARE ABSURDLY ARROGANT.
THWACK
SHREAK

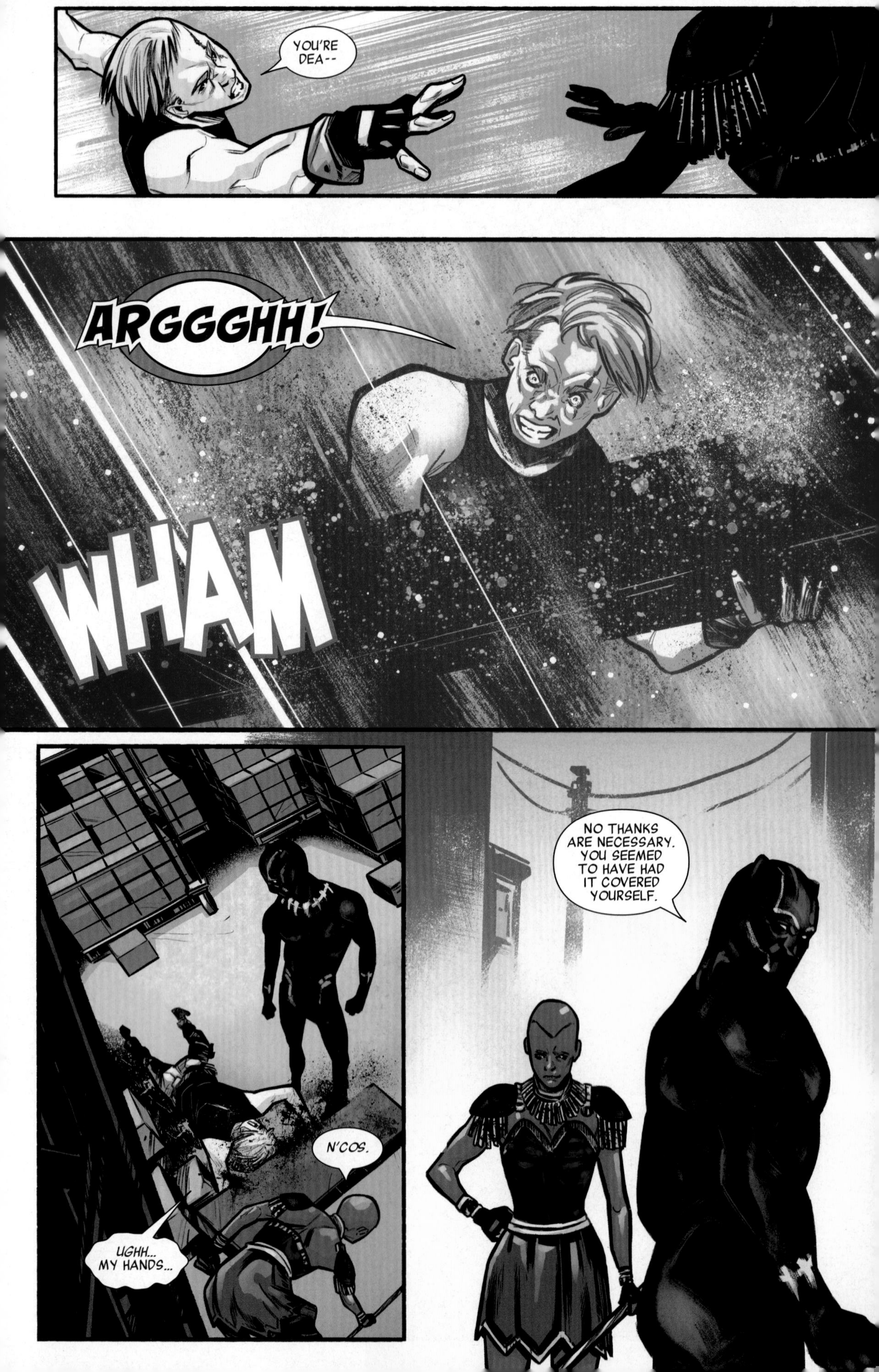

YOU'RE DEA--
ARGGGHH!
WHAM
N'COS.
UGHH... MY HANDS...
NO THANKS ARE NECESSARY. YOU SEEMED TO HAVE HAD IT COVERED YOURSELF.

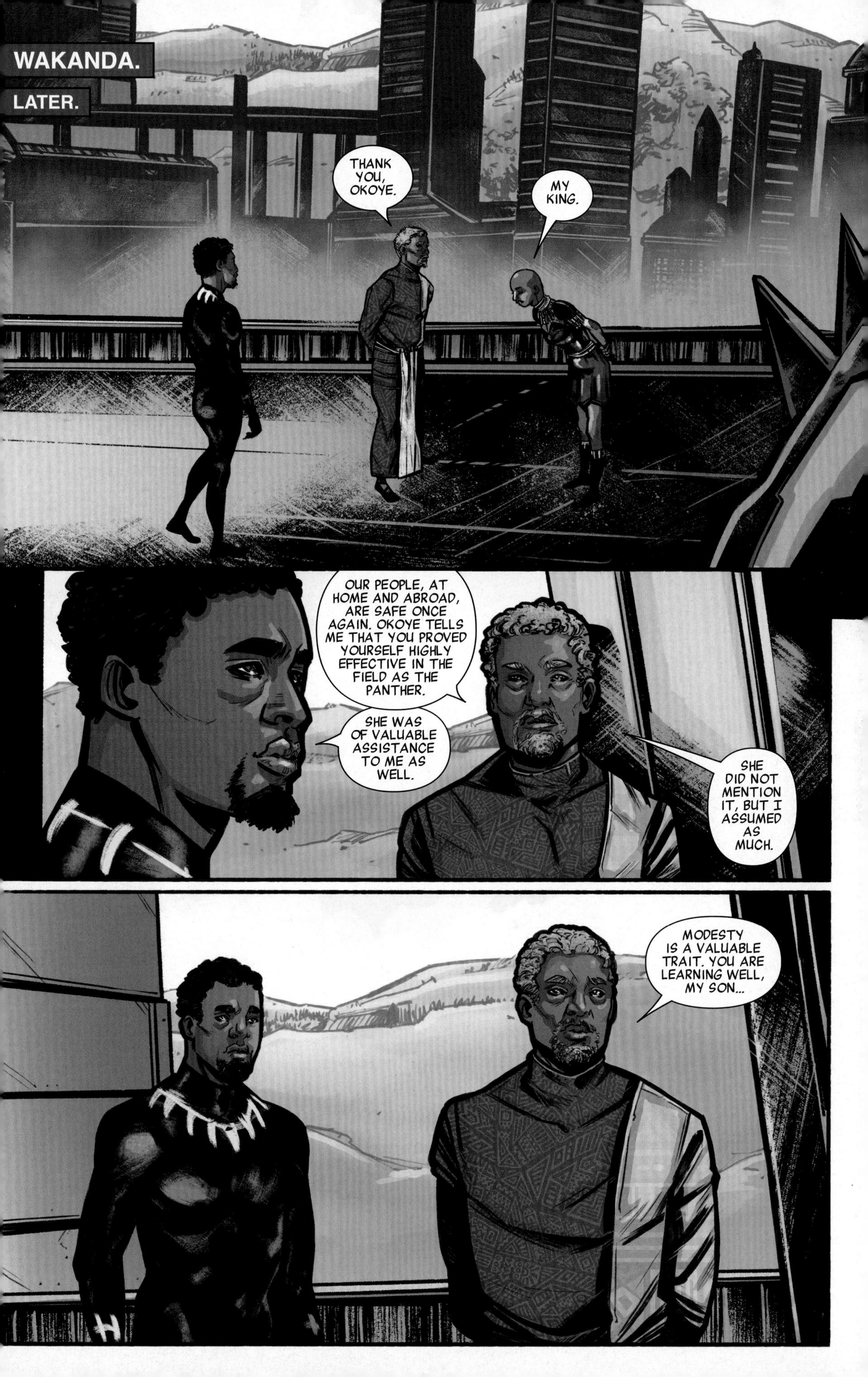
WAKANDA.
LATER.
THANK YOU, OKOYE.
MY KING.
OUR PEOPLE, AT HOME AND ABROAD, ARE SAFE ONCE AGAIN. OKOYE TELLS ME THAT YOU PROVED YOURSELF HIGHLY EFFECTIVE IN THE FIELD AS THE PANTHER.
SHE WAS OF VALUABLE ASSISTANCE TO ME AS WELL.
SHE DID NOT MENTION IT, BUT I ASSUMED AS MUCH.
MODESTY IS A VALUABLE TRAIT. YOU ARE LEARNING WELL, MY SON...

...BUT THERE IS STILL MUCH I WISH TO TEACH YOU.

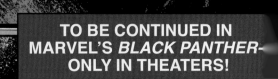

TO BE CONTINUED IN MARVEL'S *BLACK PANTHER*—ONLY IN THEATERS!

MAKING HIS FEROCIOUS FIRST APPEARANCE, ERIK KILLMONGER FUELS THE PANTHER'S RAGE IN THE OPENING CHAPTERS OF THE CLASSIC TALE BY LEGENDARY CREATORS DON McGREGOR AND RICH BUCKLER.

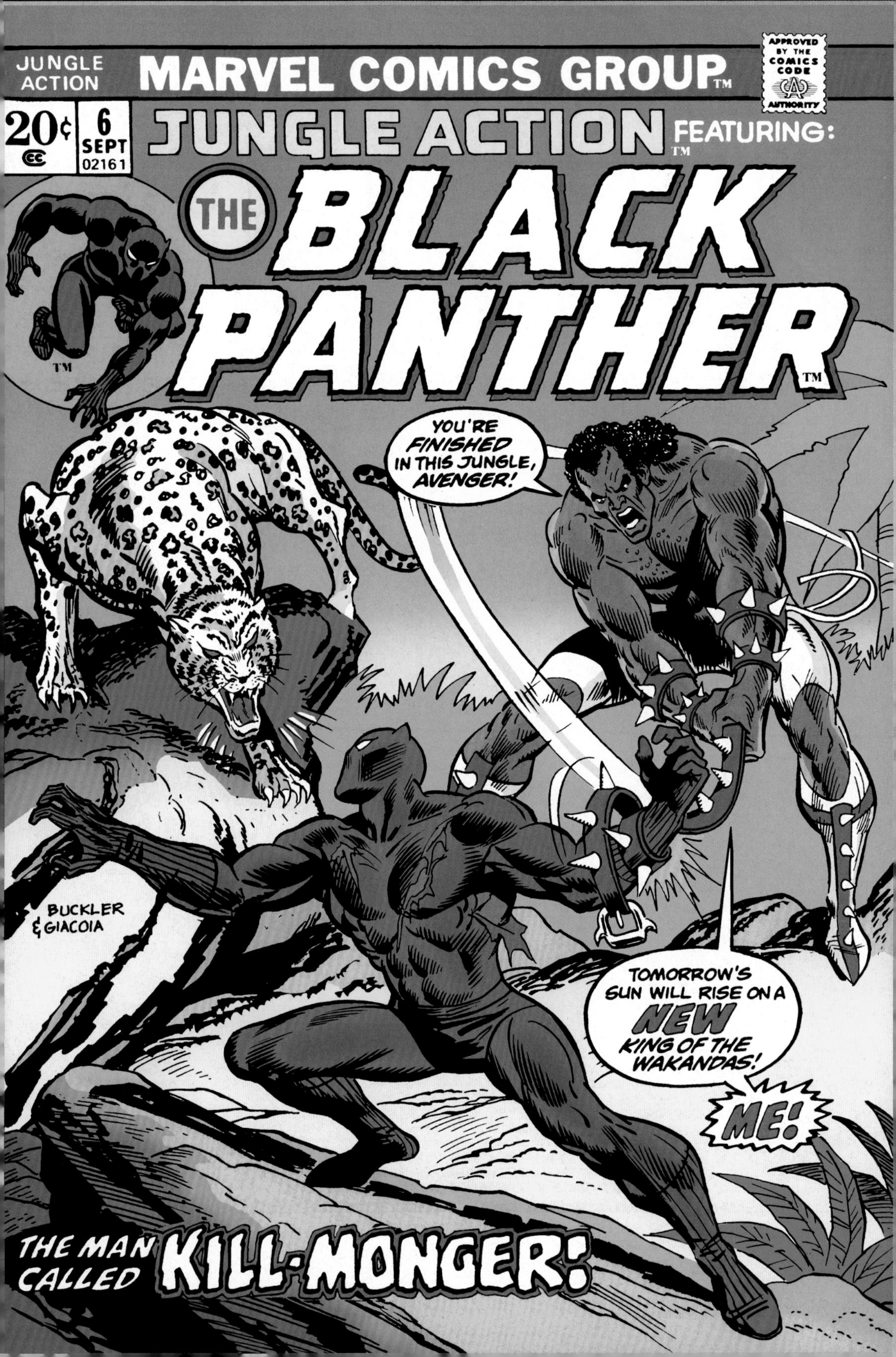

JUNGLE ACTION
MARVEL COMICS GROUP
APPROVED BY THE COMICS CODE AUTHORITY
20¢
6 SEPT 02161
JUNGLE ACTION FEATURING:
THE BLACK PANTHER
YOU'RE FINISHED IN THIS JUNGLE, AVENGER!
TOMORROW'S SUN WILL RISE ON A NEW KING OF THE WAKANDAS!
ME!
BUCKLER & GIACOIA
THE MAN CALLED KILL-MONGER!

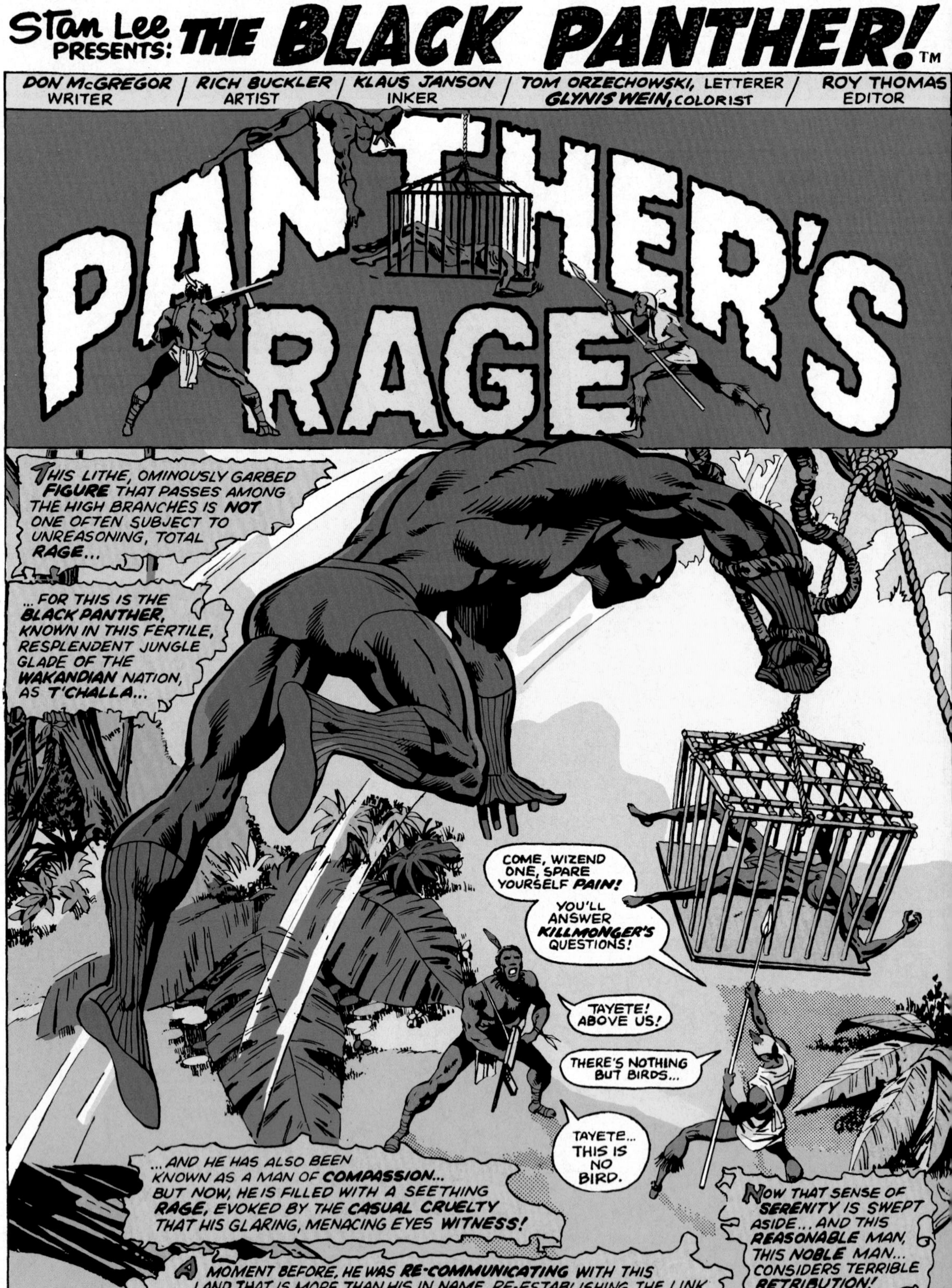
Stan Lee PRESENTS: THE BLACK PANTHER! TM
DON McGREGOR WRITER / RICH BUCKLER ARTIST / KLAUS JANSON INKER / TOM ORZECHOWSKI, LETTERER GLYNIS WEIN, COLORIST / ROY THOMAS EDITOR
PANTHER'S RAGE
THIS LITHE, OMINOUSLY GARBED FIGURE THAT PASSES AMONG THE HIGH BRANCHES IS NOT ONE OFTEN SUBJECT TO UNREASONING, TOTAL RAGE...
...FOR THIS IS THE BLACK PANTHER, KNOWN IN THIS FERTILE, RESPLENDENT JUNGLE GLADE OF THE WAKANDIAN NATION, AS T'CHALLA...
COME, WIZEND ONE, SPARE YOURSELF PAIN!
YOU'LL ANSWER KILLMONGER'S QUESTIONS!
TAYETE! ABOVE US!
THERE'S NOTHING BUT BIRDS...
TAYETE... THIS IS NO BIRD.
...AND HE HAS ALSO BEEN KNOWN AS A MAN OF COMPASSION... BUT NOW, HE IS FILLED WITH A SEETHING RAGE, EVOKED BY THE CASUAL CRUELTY THAT HIS GLARING, MENACING EYES WITNESS!
A MOMENT BEFORE, HE WAS RE-COMMUNICATING WITH THIS LAND THAT IS MORE THAN HIS IN NAME, RE-ESTABLISHING THE LINK THAT HAS WEAKENED SINCE HIS ABSENCE FROM HIS KINGDOM!
NOW THAT SENSE OF SERENITY IS SWEPT ASIDE... AND THIS REASONABLE MAN, THIS NOBLE MAN... CONSIDERS TERRIBLE RETRIBUTION!

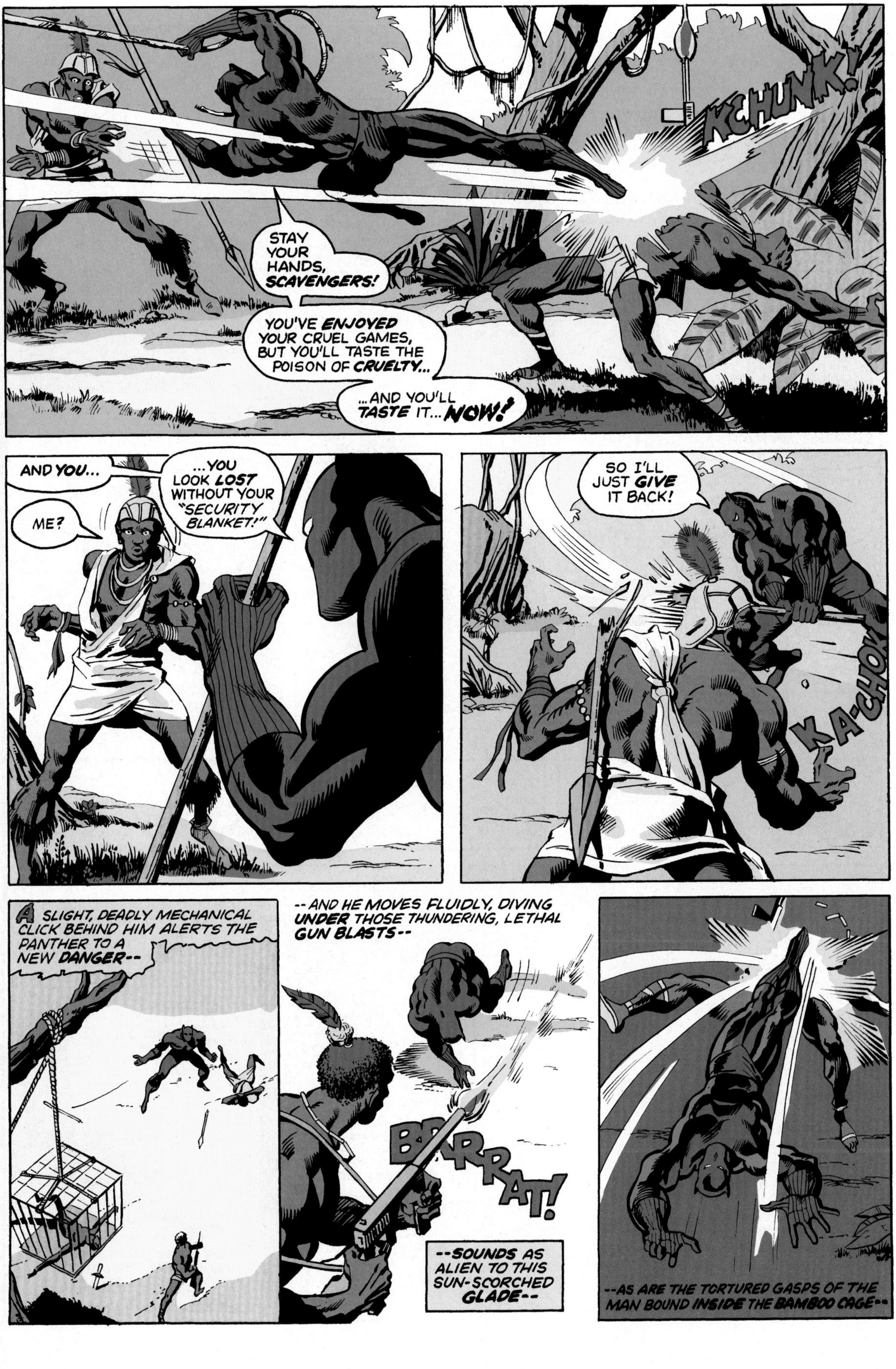
KCHUNK!
STAY YOUR HANDS, SCAVENGERS!
YOU'VE ENJOYED YOUR CRUEL GAMES, BUT YOU'LL TASTE THE POISON OF CRUELTY...
...AND YOU'LL TASTE IT... NOW!
AND YOU...
...YOU LOOK LOST WITHOUT YOUR "SECURITY BLANKET!"
ME?
SO I'LL JUST GIVE IT BACK!
KA-CHOK
A SLIGHT, DEADLY MECHANICAL CLICK BEHIND HIM ALERTS THE PANTHER TO A NEW DANGER--
--AND HE MOVES FLUIDLY, DIVING UNDER THOSE THUNDERING, LETHAL GUN BLASTS--
BRRRAT!
--SOUNDS AS ALIEN TO THIS SUN-SCORCHED GLADE--
--AS ARE THE TORTURED GASPS OF THE MAN BOUND INSIDE THE BAMBOO CAGE--

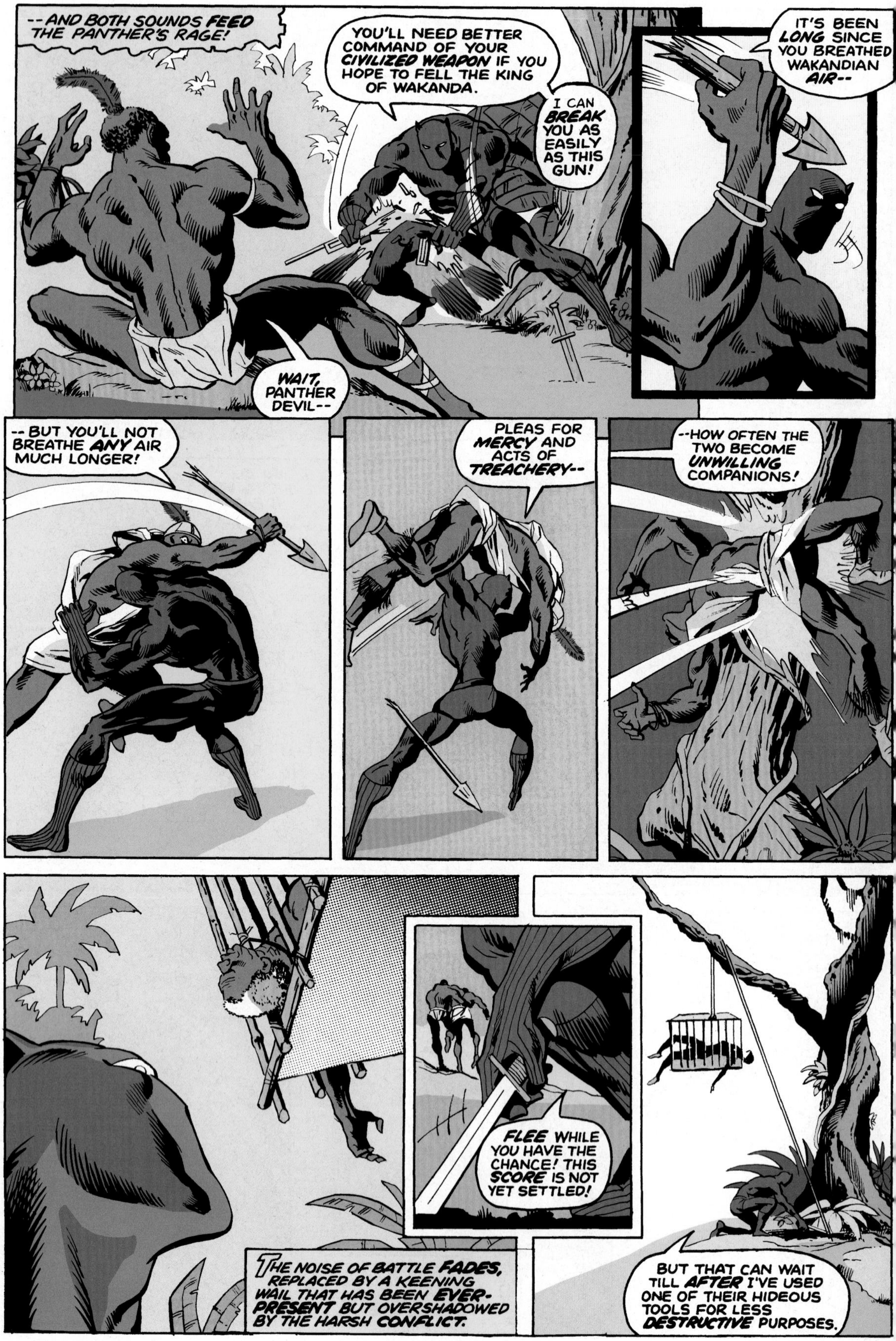
--AND BOTH SOUNDS FEED THE PANTHER'S RAGE!
YOU'LL NEED BETTER COMMAND OF YOUR CIVILIZED WEAPON IF YOU HOPE TO FELL THE KING OF WAKANDA.
I CAN BREAK YOU AS EASILY AS THIS GUN!
WAIT, PANTHER DEVIL--
IT'S BEEN LONG SINCE YOU BREATHED WAKANDIAN AIR--
--BUT YOU'LL NOT BREATHE ANY AIR MUCH LONGER!
PLEAS FOR MERCY AND ACTS OF TREACHERY--
--HOW OFTEN THE TWO BECOME UNWILLING COMPANIONS!
FLEE WHILE YOU HAVE THE CHANCE! THIS SCORE IS NOT YET SETTLED!
THE NOISE OF BATTLE FADES, REPLACED BY A KEENING WAIL THAT HAS BEEN EVER-PRESENT BUT OVERSHADOWED BY THE HARSH CONFLICT.
BUT THAT CAN WAIT TILL AFTER I'VE USED ONE OF THEIR HIDEOUS TOOLS FOR LESS DESTRUCTIVE PURPOSES.

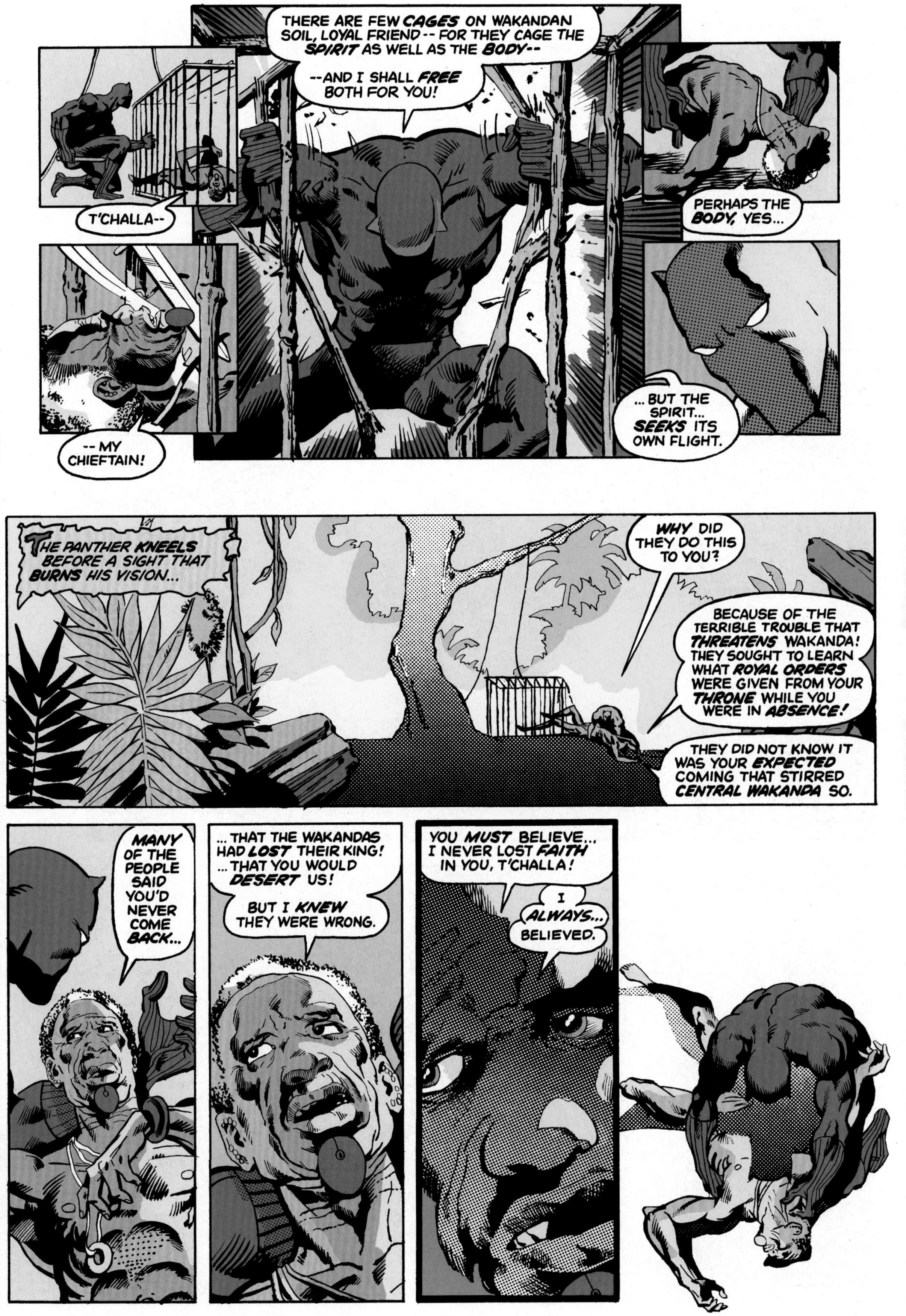

T'CHALLA--
-- MY CHIEFTAIN!
THERE ARE FEW CAGES ON WAKANDAN SOIL, LOYAL FRIEND -- FOR THEY CAGE THE SPIRIT AS WELL AS THE BODY--
--AND I SHALL FREE BOTH FOR YOU!
PERHAPS THE BODY, YES...
... BUT THE SPIRIT... SEEKS ITS OWN FLIGHT.
THE PANTHER KNEELS BEFORE A SIGHT THAT BURNS HIS VISION...
WHY DID THEY DO THIS TO YOU?
BECAUSE OF THE TERRIBLE TROUBLE THAT THREATENS WAKANDA! THEY SOUGHT TO LEARN WHAT ROYAL ORDERS WERE GIVEN FROM YOUR THRONE WHILE YOU WERE IN ABSENCE!
THEY DID NOT KNOW IT WAS YOUR EXPECTED COMING THAT STIRRED CENTRAL WAKANDA SO.
MANY OF THE PEOPLE SAID YOU'D NEVER COME BACK...
... THAT THE WAKANDAS HAD LOST THEIR KING! ... THAT YOU WOULD DESERT US!
BUT I KNEW THEY WERE WRONG.
YOU MUST BELIEVE... I NEVER LOST FAITH IN YOU, T'CHALLA!
I ALWAYS... BELIEVED.

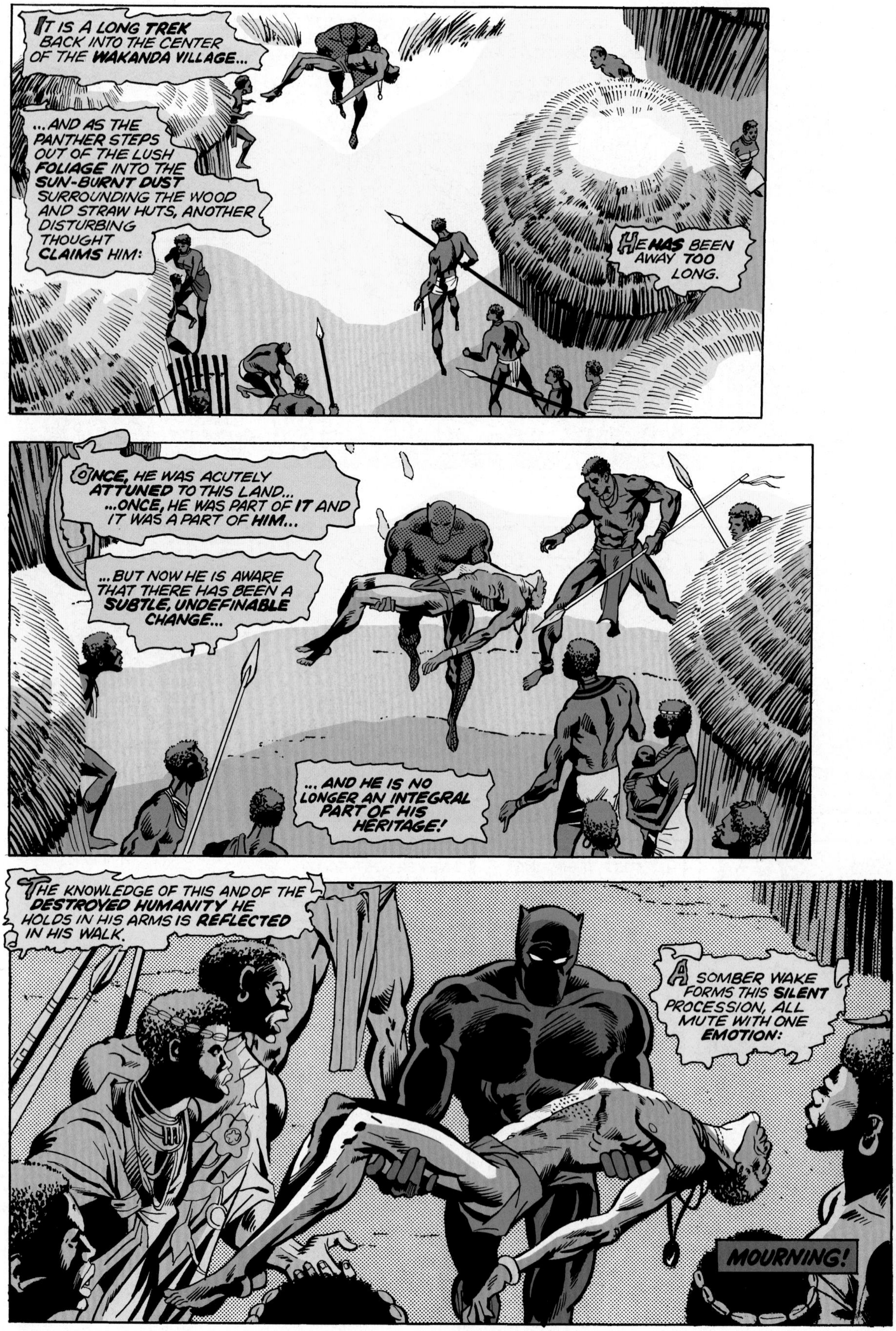
IT IS A LONG TREK BACK INTO THE CENTER OF THE WAKANDA VILLAGE...
...AND AS THE PANTHER STEPS OUT OF THE LUSH FOLIAGE INTO THE SUN-BURNT DUST SURROUNDING THE WOOD AND STRAW HUTS, ANOTHER DISTURBING THOUGHT CLAIMS HIM:
HE HAS BEEN AWAY TOO LONG.
ONCE, HE WAS ACUTELY ATTUNED TO THIS LAND... ...ONCE, HE WAS PART OF IT AND IT WAS A PART OF HIM...
...BUT NOW HE IS AWARE THAT THERE HAS BEEN A SUBTLE, UNDEFINABLE CHANGE...
...AND HE IS NO LONGER AN INTEGRAL PART OF HIS HERITAGE!
THE KNOWLEDGE OF THIS AND OF THE DESTROYED HUMANITY HE HOLDS IN HIS ARMS IS REFLECTED IN HIS WALK.
A SOMBER WAKE FORMS THIS SILENT PROCESSION, ALL MUTE WITH ONE EMOTION:
MOURNING!

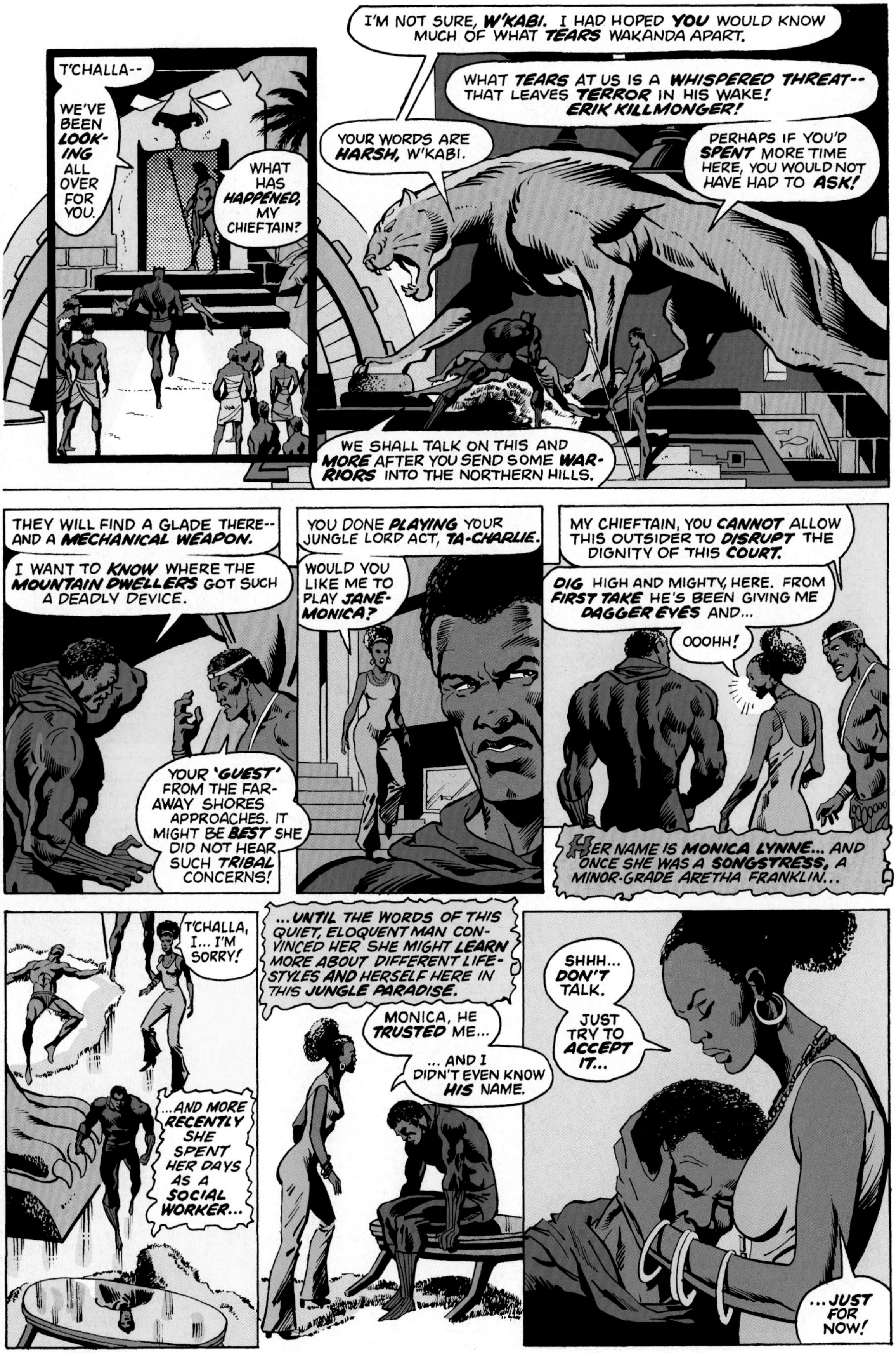
T'CHALLA--
WE'VE BEEN LOOKING ALL OVER FOR YOU.
WHAT HAS HAPPENED, MY CHIEFTAIN?
I'M NOT SURE, W'KABI. I HAD HOPED YOU WOULD KNOW MUCH OF WHAT TEARS WAKANDA APART.
WHAT TEARS AT US IS A WHISPERED THREAT-- THAT LEAVES TERROR IN HIS WAKE! ERIK KILLMONGER!
YOUR WORDS ARE HARSH, W'KABI.
PERHAPS IF YOU'D SPENT MORE TIME HERE, YOU WOULD NOT HAVE HAD TO ASK!
WE SHALL TALK ON THIS AND MORE AFTER YOU SEND SOME WARRIORS INTO THE NORTHERN HILLS.
THEY WILL FIND A GLADE THERE-- AND A MECHANICAL WEAPON.
I WANT TO KNOW WHERE THE MOUNTAIN DWELLERS GOT SUCH A DEADLY DEVICE.
YOUR 'GUEST' FROM THE FAR-AWAY SHORES APPROACHES. IT MIGHT BE BEST SHE DID NOT HEAR SUCH TRIBAL CONCERNS!
YOU DONE PLAYING YOUR JUNGLE LORD ACT, TA-CHARLIE.
WOULD YOU LIKE ME TO PLAY JANE-MONICA?
MY CHIEFTAIN, YOU CANNOT ALLOW THIS OUTSIDER TO DISRUPT THE DIGNITY OF THIS COURT.
DIG HIGH AND MIGHTY, HERE. FROM FIRST TAKE HE'S BEEN GIVING ME DAGGER EYES AND...
OOOHH!
HER NAME IS MONICA LYNNE... AND ONCE SHE WAS A SONGSTRESS, A MINOR-GRADE ARETHA FRANKLIN...
T'CHALLA, I... I'M SORRY!
...AND MORE RECENTLY SHE SPENT HER DAYS AS A SOCIAL WORKER...
...UNTIL THE WORDS OF THIS QUIET, ELOQUENT MAN CONVINCED HER SHE MIGHT LEARN MORE ABOUT DIFFERENT LIFE-STYLES AND HERSELF HERE IN THIS JUNGLE PARADISE.
MONICA, HE TRUSTED ME...
... AND I DIDN'T EVEN KNOW HIS NAME.
SHHH... DON'T TALK.
JUST TRY TO ACCEPT IT...
... JUST FOR NOW!

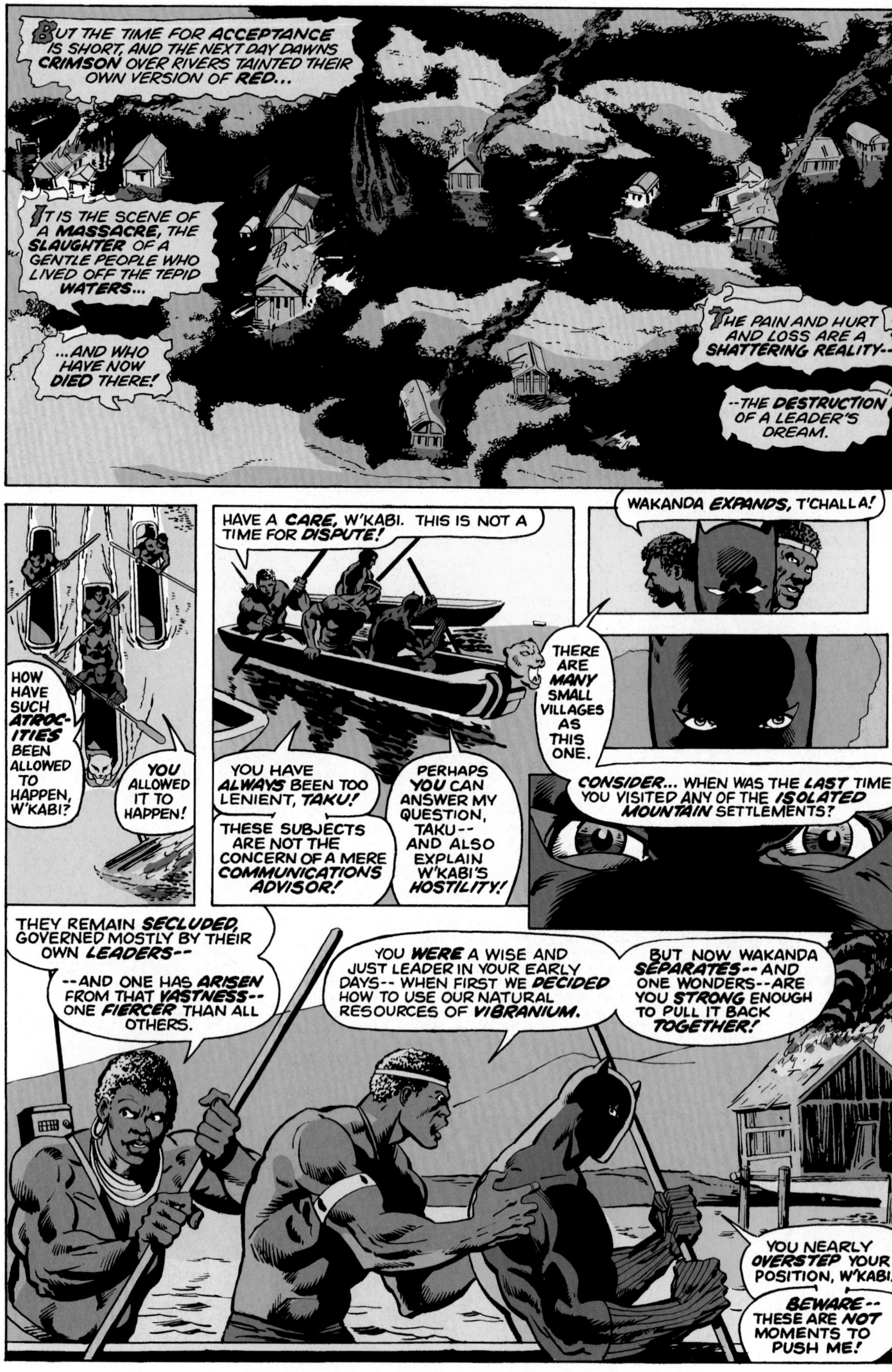
BUT THE TIME FOR ACCEPTANCE IS SHORT, AND THE NEXT DAY DAWNS CRIMSON OVER RIVERS TAINTED THEIR OWN VERSION OF RED...
IT IS THE SCENE OF A MASSACRE, THE SLAUGHTER OF A GENTLE PEOPLE WHO LIVED OFF THE TEPID WATERS...
...AND WHO HAVE NOW DIED THERE!
THE PAIN AND HURT AND LOSS ARE A SHATTERING REALITY--
--THE DESTRUCTION OF A LEADER'S DREAM.
HOW HAVE SUCH ATROCITIES BEEN ALLOWED TO HAPPEN, W'KABI?
YOU ALLOWED IT TO HAPPEN!
HAVE A CARE, W'KABI. THIS IS NOT A TIME FOR DISPUTE!
YOU HAVE ALWAYS BEEN TOO LENIENT, TAKU!
THESE SUBJECTS ARE NOT THE CONCERN OF A MERE COMMUNICATIONS ADVISOR!
PERHAPS YOU CAN ANSWER MY QUESTION, TAKU-- AND ALSO EXPLAIN W'KABI'S HOSTILITY!
WAKANDA EXPANDS, T'CHALLA!
THERE ARE MANY SMALL VILLAGES AS THIS ONE.
CONSIDER... WHEN WAS THE LAST TIME YOU VISITED ANY OF THE ISOLATED MOUNTAIN SETTLEMENTS?
THEY REMAIN SECLUDED, GOVERNED MOSTLY BY THEIR OWN LEADERS--
--AND ONE HAS ARISEN FROM THAT VASTNESS-- ONE FIERCER THAN ALL OTHERS.
YOU WERE A WISE AND JUST LEADER IN YOUR EARLY DAYS-- WHEN FIRST WE DECIDED HOW TO USE OUR NATURAL RESOURCES OF VIBRANIUM.
BUT NOW WAKANDA SEPARATES-- AND ONE WONDERS--ARE YOU STRONG ENOUGH TO PULL IT BACK TOGETHER!
YOU NEARLY OVERSTEP YOUR POSITION, W'KABI!
BEWARE-- THESE ARE NOT MOMENTS TO PUSH ME!

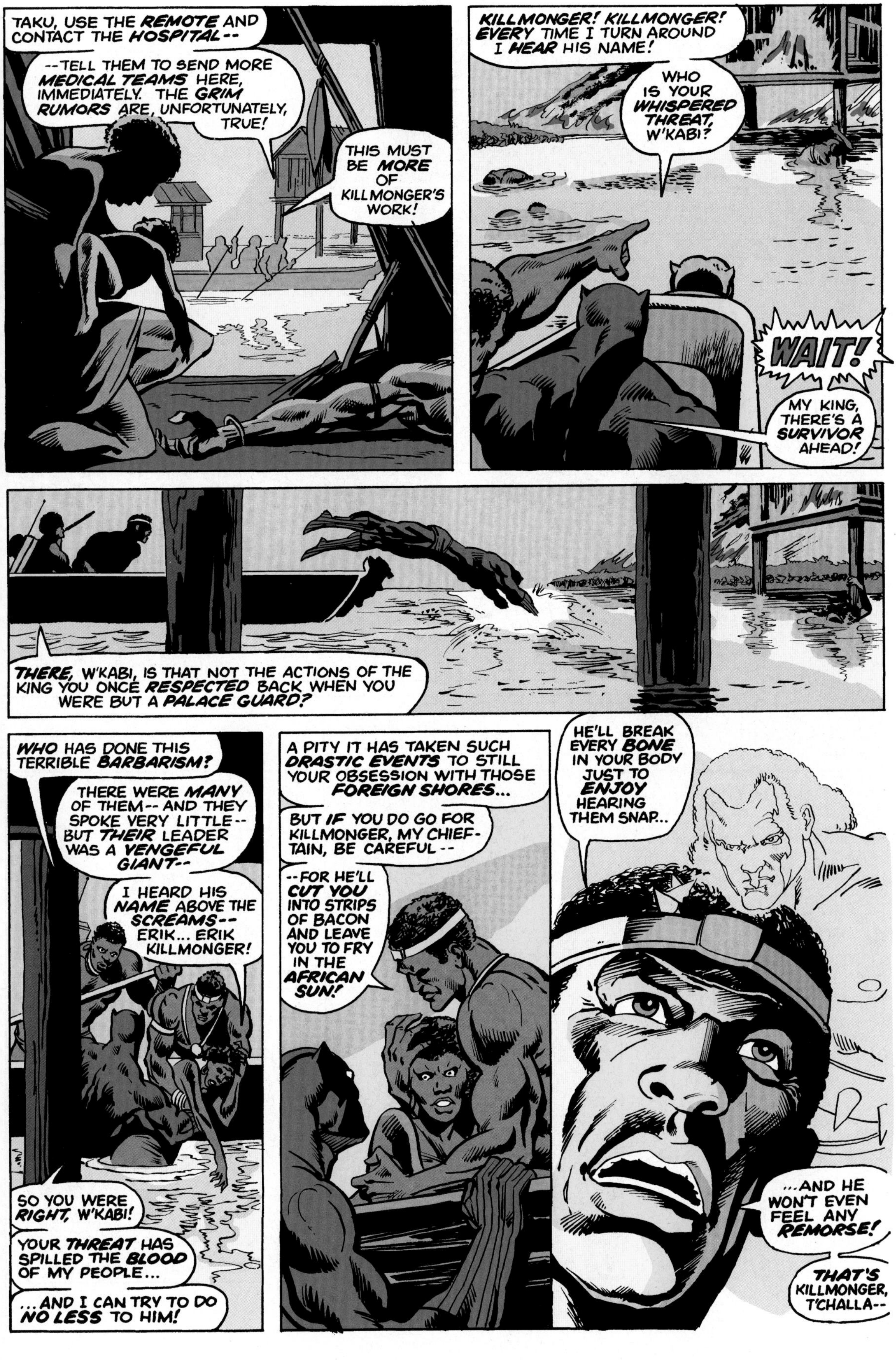
TAKU, USE THE REMOTE AND CONTACT THE HOSPITAL--
--TELL THEM TO SEND MORE MEDICAL TEAMS HERE, IMMEDIATELY. THE GRIM RUMORS ARE, UNFORTUNATELY, TRUE!
THIS MUST BE MORE OF KILLMONGER'S WORK!
KILLMONGER! KILLMONGER! EVERY TIME I TURN AROUND I HEAR HIS NAME!
WHO IS YOUR WHISPERED THREAT, W'KABI?
WAIT!
MY KING, THERE'S A SURVIVOR AHEAD!
THERE, W'KABI, IS THAT NOT THE ACTIONS OF THE KING YOU ONCE RESPECTED BACK WHEN YOU WERE BUT A PALACE GUARD?
WHO HAS DONE THIS TERRIBLE BARBARISM?
THERE WERE MANY OF THEM-- AND THEY SPOKE VERY LITTLE-- BUT THEIR LEADER WAS A VENGEFUL GIANT--
I HEARD HIS NAME ABOVE THE SCREAMS-- ERIK... ERIK KILLMONGER!
SO YOU WERE RIGHT, W'KABI!
YOUR THREAT HAS SPILLED THE BLOOD OF MY PEOPLE...
...AND I CAN TRY TO DO NO LESS TO HIM!
A PITY IT HAS TAKEN SUCH DRASTIC EVENTS TO STILL YOUR OBSESSION WITH THOSE FOREIGN SHORES...
BUT IF YOU DO GO FOR KILLMONGER, MY CHIEFTAIN, BE CAREFUL--
--FOR HE'LL CUT YOU INTO STRIPS OF BACON AND LEAVE YOU TO FRY IN THE AFRICAN SUN!
HE'LL BREAK EVERY BONE IN YOUR BODY JUST TO ENJOY HEARING THEM SNAP...
...AND HE WON'T EVEN FEEL ANY REMORSE!
THAT'S KILLMONGER, T'CHALLA--

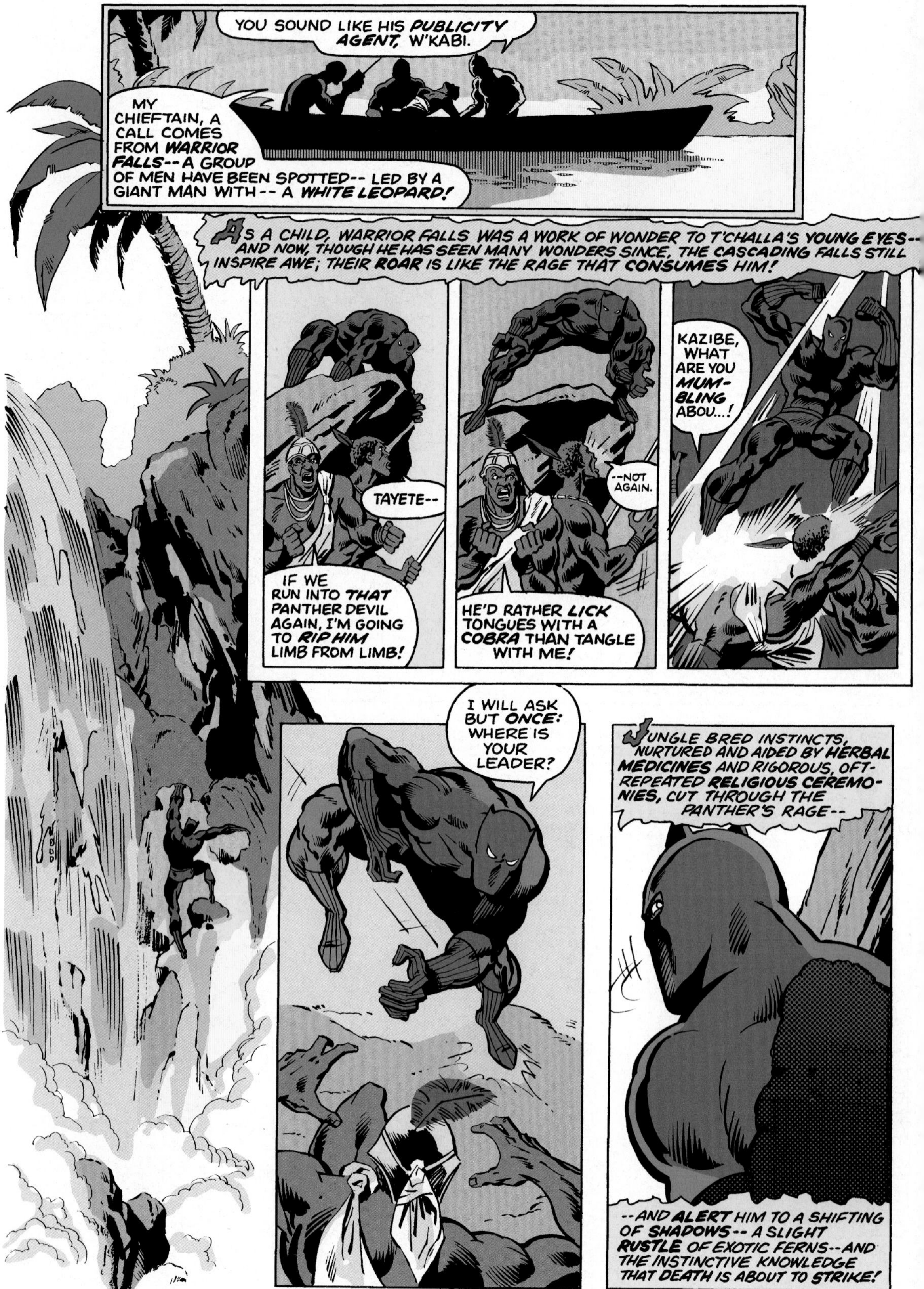
YOU SOUND LIKE HIS PUBLICITY AGENT, W'KABI.
MY CHIEFTAIN, A CALL COMES FROM WARRIOR FALLS-- A GROUP OF MEN HAVE BEEN SPOTTED-- LED BY A GIANT MAN WITH -- A WHITE LEOPARD!
AS A CHILD, WARRIOR FALLS WAS A WORK OF WONDER TO T'CHALLA'S YOUNG EYES-- AND NOW, THOUGH HE HAS SEEN MANY WONDERS SINCE, THE CASCADING FALLS STILL INSPIRE AWE; THEIR ROAR IS LIKE THE RAGE THAT CONSUMES HIM!
TAYETE--
IF WE RUN INTO THAT PANTHER DEVIL AGAIN, I'M GOING TO RIP HIM LIMB FROM LIMB!
--NOT AGAIN.
HE'D RATHER LICK TONGUES WITH A COBRA THAN TANGLE WITH ME!
KAZIBE, WHAT ARE YOU MUMBLING ABOU...!
I WILL ASK BUT ONCE: WHERE IS YOUR LEADER?
JUNGLE BRED INSTINCTS, NURTURED AND AIDED BY HERBAL MEDICINES AND RIGOROUS, OFT-REPEATED RELIGIOUS CEREMONIES, CUT THROUGH THE PANTHER'S RAGE--
--AND ALERT HIM TO A SHIFTING OF SHADOWS-- A SLIGHT RUSTLE OF EXOTIC FERNS--AND THE INSTINCTIVE KNOWLEDGE THAT DEATH IS ABOUT TO STRIKE!

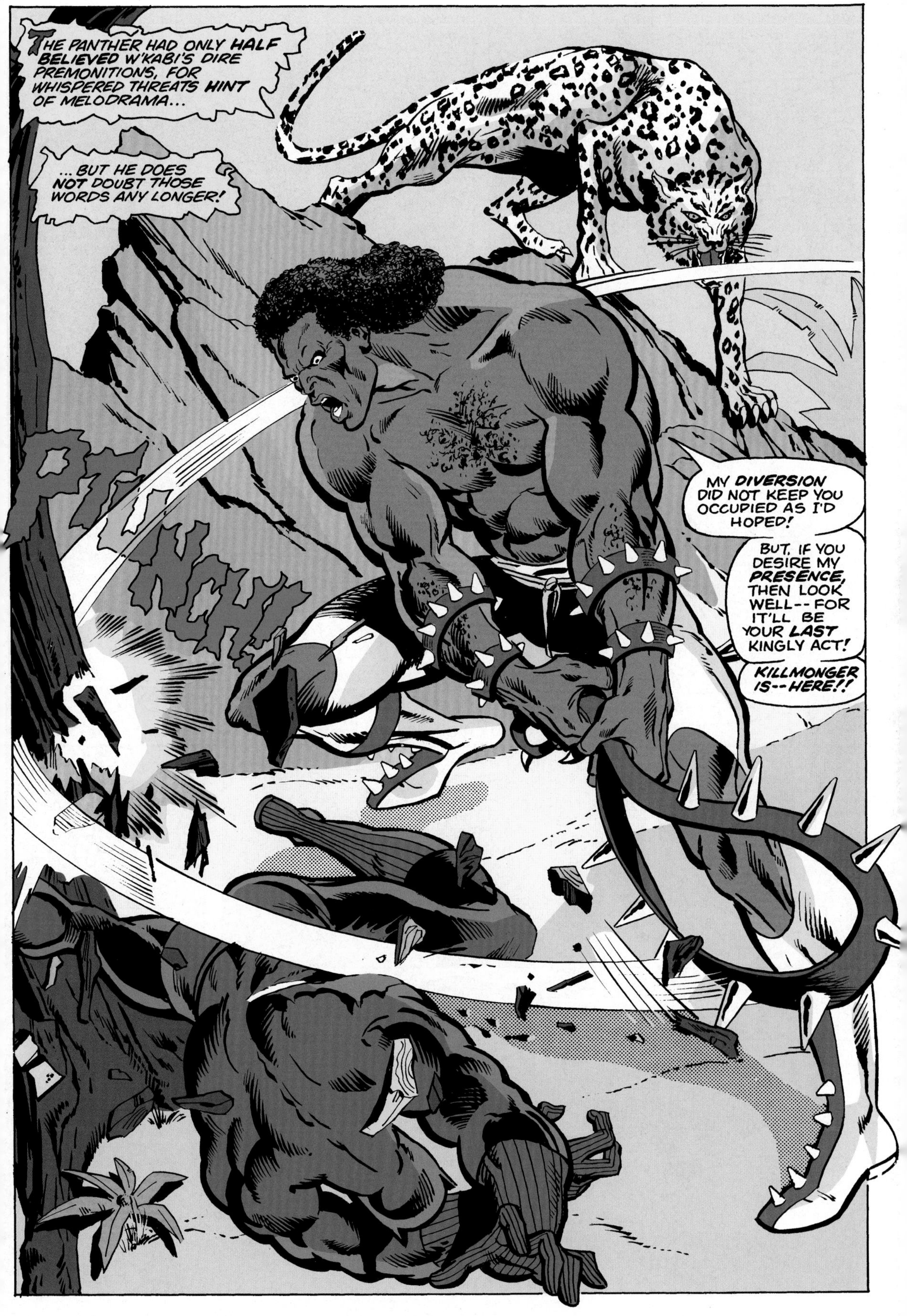
THE PANTHER HAD ONLY HALF BELIEVED W'KABI'S DIRE PREMONITIONS, FOR WHISPERED THREATS HINT OF MELODRAMA...
...BUT HE DOES NOT DOUBT THOSE WORDS ANY LONGER!
PTNCH!
MY DIVERSION DID NOT KEEP YOU OCCUPIED AS I'D HOPED!
BUT, IF YOU DESIRE MY PRESENCE, THEN LOOK WELL--FOR IT'LL BE YOUR LAST KINGLY ACT!
KILLMONGER IS--HERE!!

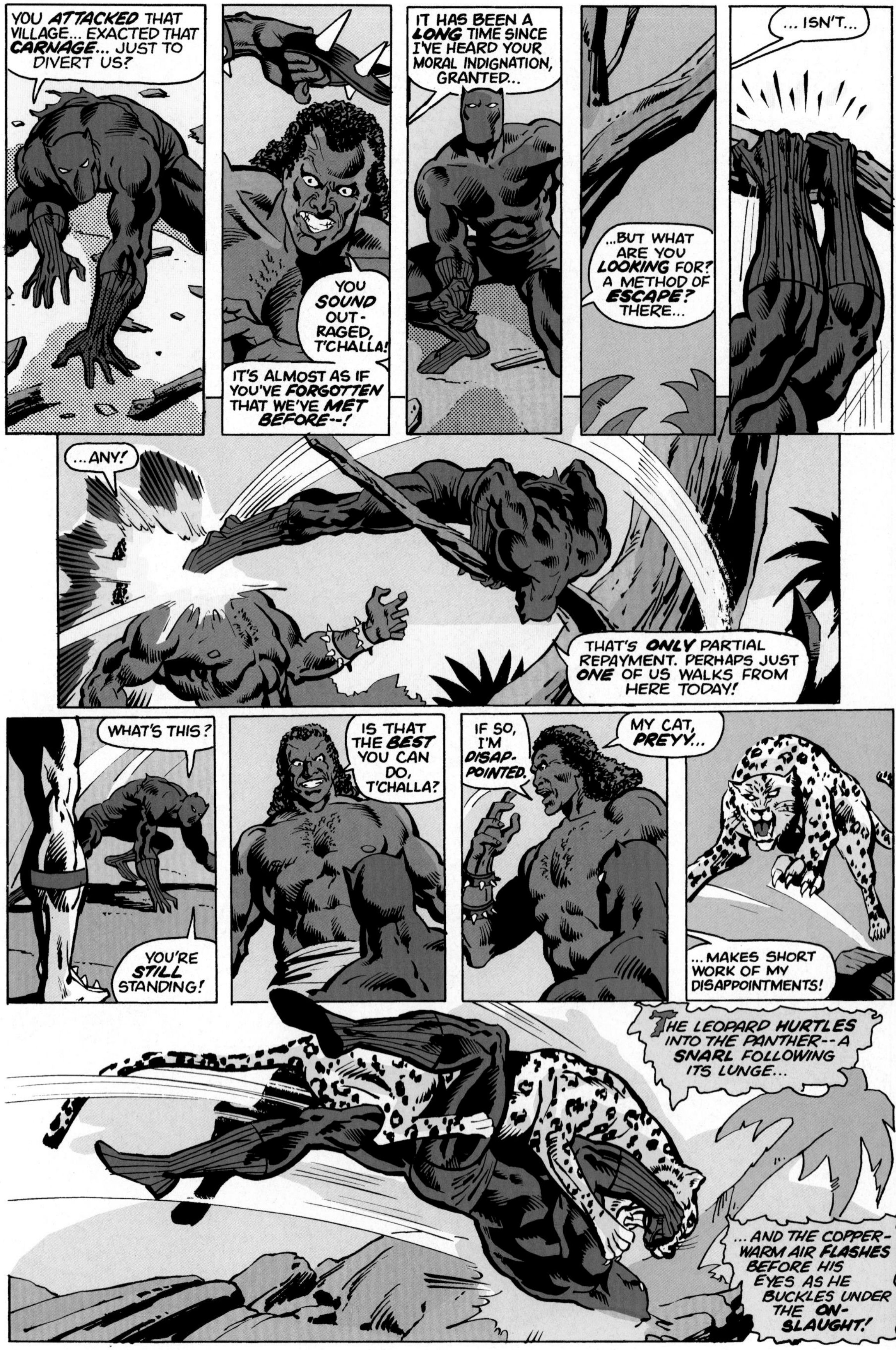

YOU ATTACKED THAT VILLAGE... EXACTED THAT CARNAGE... JUST TO DIVERT US?
YOU SOUND OUT-RAGED, T'CHALLA!
IT'S ALMOST AS IF YOU'VE FORGOTTEN THAT WE'VE MET BEFORE--!
IT HAS BEEN A LONG TIME SINCE I'VE HEARD YOUR MORAL INDIGNATION, GRANTED...
...BUT WHAT ARE YOU LOOKING FOR? A METHOD OF ESCAPE? THERE...
... ISN'T...
...ANY!
THAT'S ONLY PARTIAL REPAYMENT. PERHAPS JUST ONE OF US WALKS FROM HERE TODAY!
WHAT'S THIS?
YOU'RE STILL STANDING!
IS THAT THE BEST YOU CAN DO, T'CHALLA?
IF SO, I'M DISAP-POINTED.
MY CAT, PREYY...
...MAKES SHORT WORK OF MY DISAPPOINTMENTS!
THE LEOPARD HURTLES INTO THE PANTHER--A SNARL FOLLOWING ITS LUNGE...
...AND THE COPPER-WARM AIR FLASHES BEFORE HIS EYES AS HE BUCKLES UNDER THE ON-SLAUGHT!

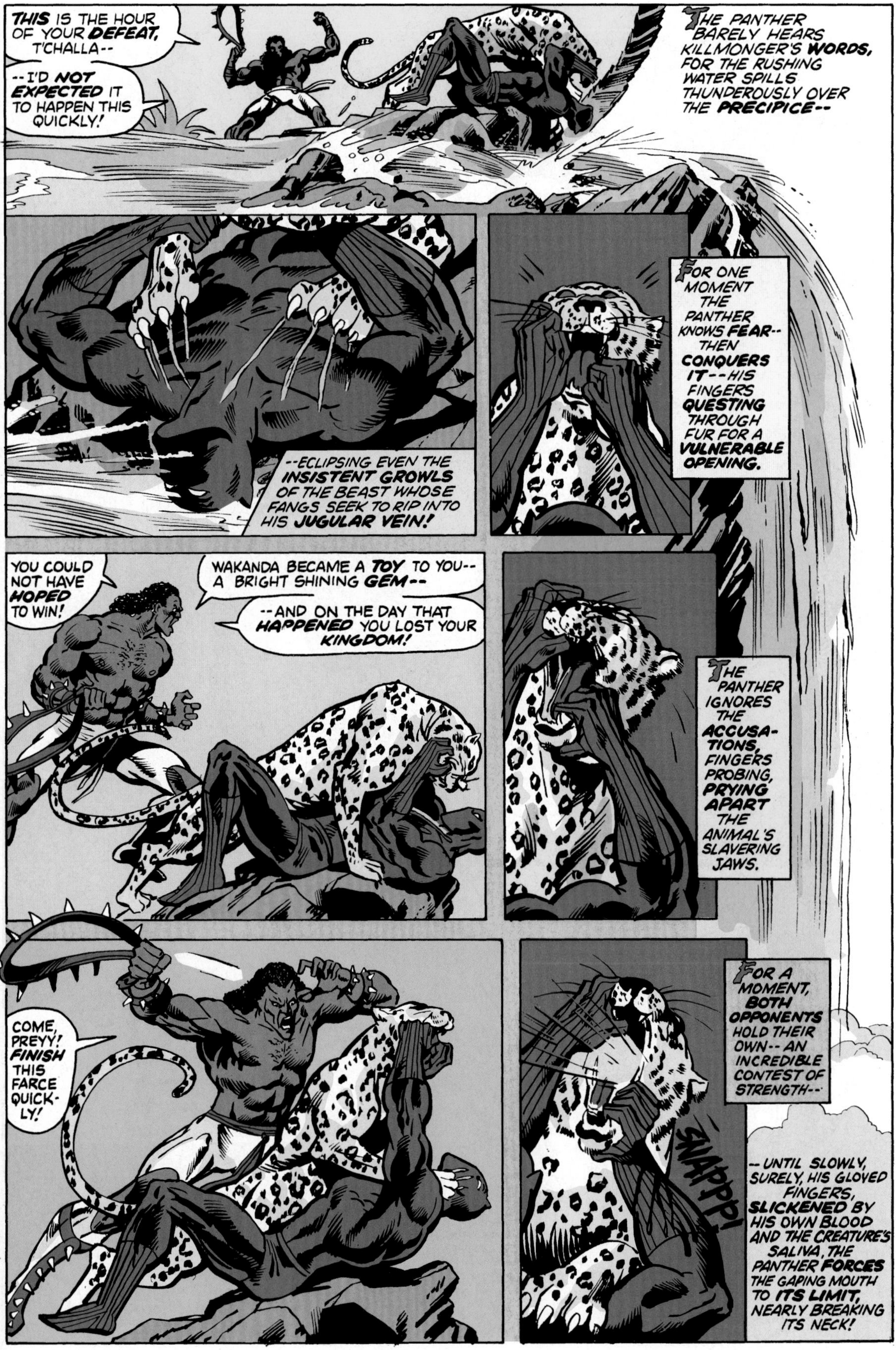
THIS IS THE HOUR OF YOUR DEFEAT, T'CHALLA--
--I'D NOT EXPECTED IT TO HAPPEN THIS QUICKLY!
THE PANTHER BARELY HEARS KILLMONGER'S WORDS, FOR THE RUSHING WATER SPILLS THUNDEROUSLY OVER THE PRECIPICE--
--ECLIPSING EVEN THE INSISTENT GROWLS OF THE BEAST WHOSE FANGS SEEK TO RIP INTO HIS JUGULAR VEIN!
FOR ONE MOMENT THE PANTHER KNOWS FEAR-- THEN CONQUERS IT--HIS FINGERS QUESTING THROUGH FUR FOR A VULNERABLE OPENING.
YOU COULD NOT HAVE HOPED TO WIN!
WAKANDA BECAME A TOY TO YOU-- A BRIGHT SHINING GEM--
--AND ON THE DAY THAT HAPPENED YOU LOST YOUR KINGDOM!
THE PANTHER IGNORES THE ACCUSA-TIONS, FINGERS PROBING, PRYING APART THE ANIMAL'S SLAVERING JAWS.
COME, PREYY! FINISH THIS FARCE QUICK-LY!
FOR A MOMENT, BOTH OPPONENTS HOLD THEIR OWN-- AN INCREDIBLE CONTEST OF STRENGTH--
SNAPPP!
--UNTIL SLOWLY, SURELY, HIS GLOVED FINGERS, SLICKENED BY HIS OWN BLOOD AND THE CREATURE'S SALIVA, THE PANTHER FORCES THE GAPING MOUTH TO ITS LIMIT, NEARLY BREAKING ITS NECK!

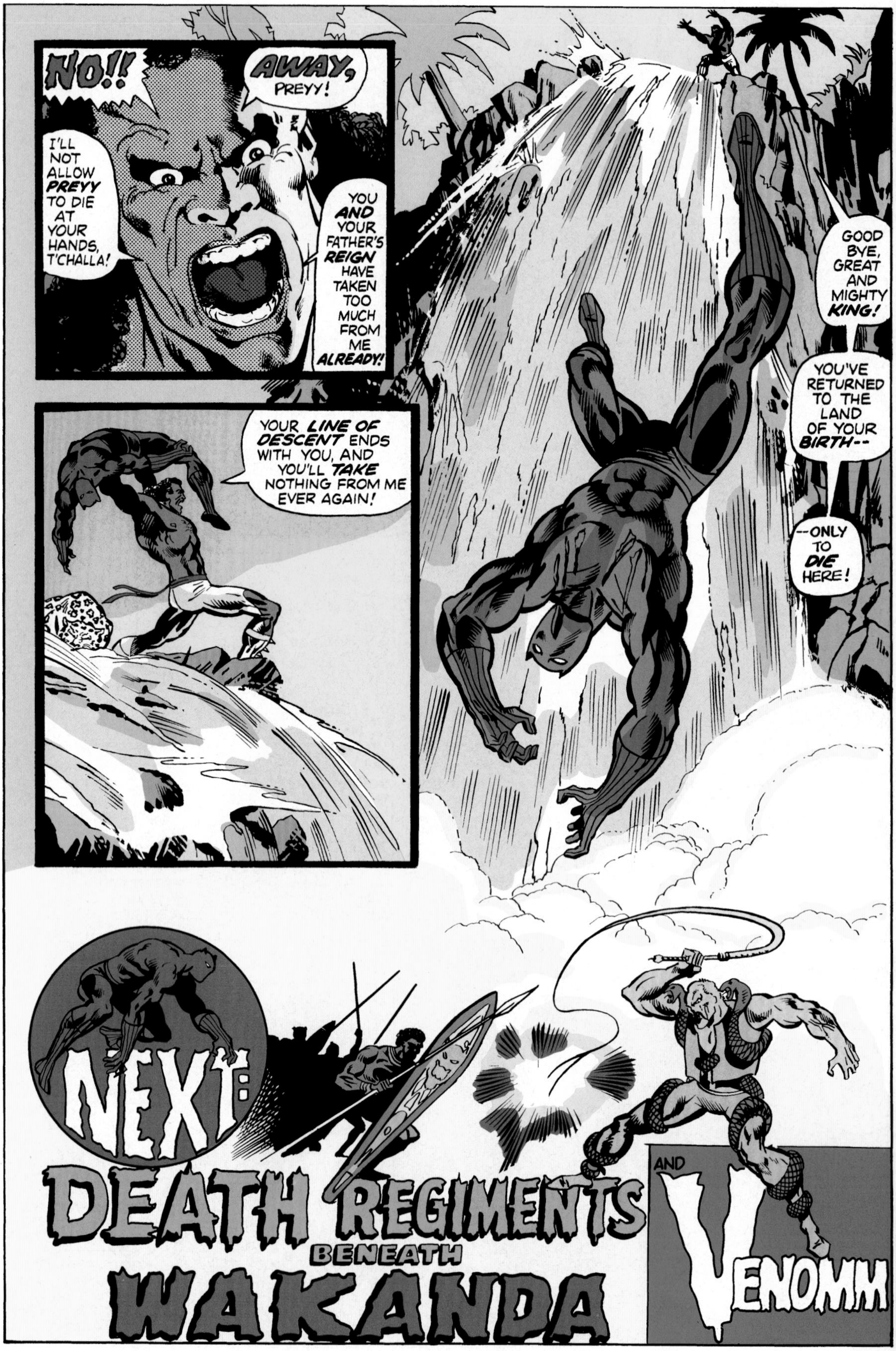
NO!!
AWAY, PREYY!
I'LL NOT ALLOW PREYY TO DIE AT YOUR HANDS, T'CHALLA!
YOU AND YOUR FATHER'S REIGN HAVE TAKEN TOO MUCH FROM ME ALREADY!
YOUR LINE OF DESCENT ENDS WITH YOU, AND YOU'LL TAKE NOTHING FROM ME EVER AGAIN!
GOOD BYE, GREAT AND MIGHTY KING!
YOU'VE RETURNED TO THE LAND OF YOUR BIRTH--
--ONLY TO DIE HERE!
NEXT:
DEATH REGIMENTS BENEATH WAKANDA
AND VENOMM

MAP OF THE LAND OF THE WAKANDA

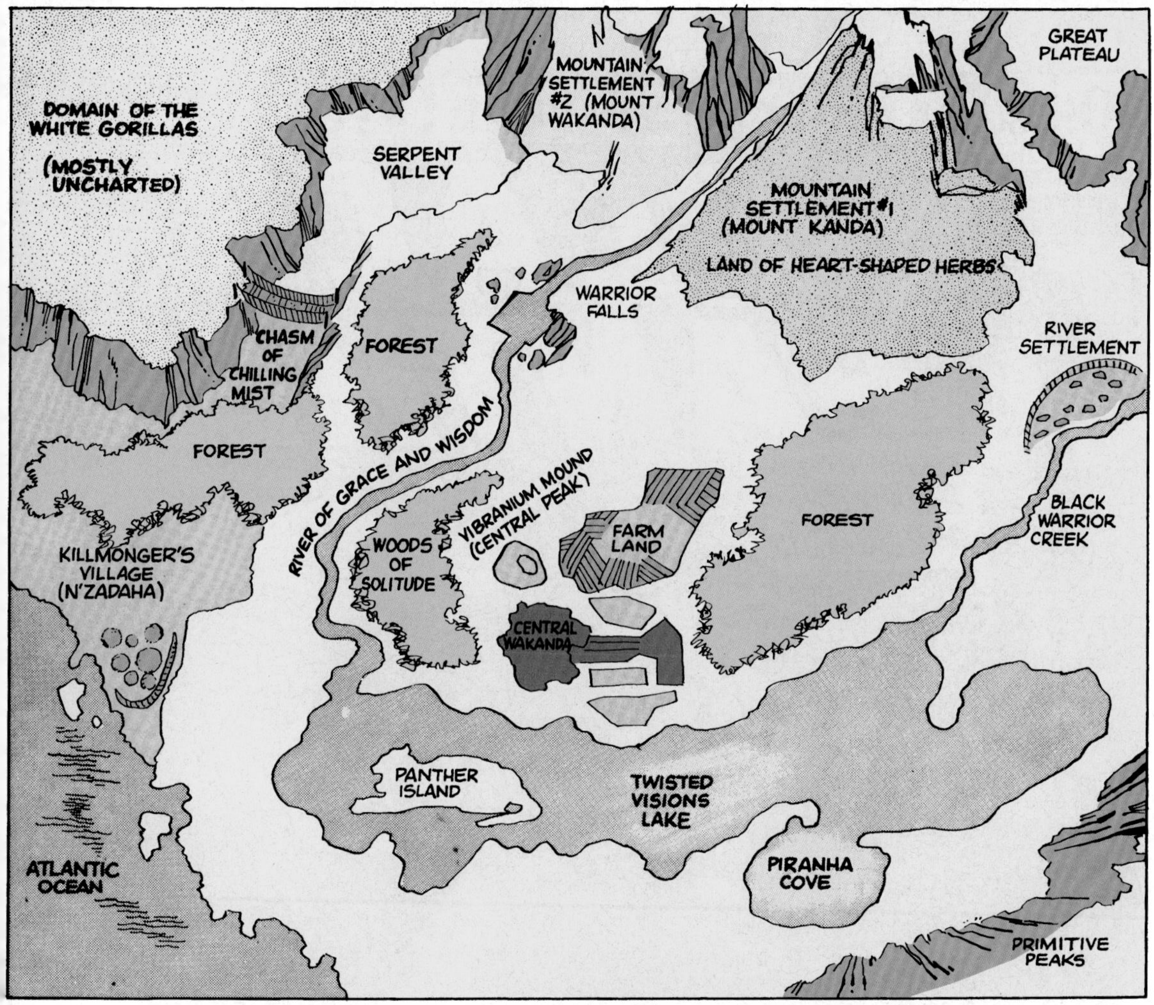

DOMAIN OF THE WHITE GORILLAS
(MOSTLY UNCHARTED)
SERPENT VALLEY
MOUNTAIN SETTLEMENT #2 (MOUNT WAKANDA)
GREAT PLATEAU
MOUNTAIN SETTLEMENT #1 (MOUNT KANDA)
LAND OF HEART-SHAPED HERBS
WARRIOR FALLS
CHASM OF CHILLING MIST
FOREST
RIVER SETTLEMENT
FOREST
RIVER OF GRACE AND WISDOM
VIBRANIUM MOUND (CENTRAL PEAK)
FARM LAND
FOREST
BLACK WARRIOR CREEK
KILLMONGER'S VILLAGE (N'ZADAHA)
WOODS OF SOLITUDE
CENTRAL WAKANDA
PANTHER ISLAND
TWISTED VISIONS LAKE
ATLANTIC OCEAN
PIRANHA COVE
PRIMITIVE PEAKS

CENTRAL WAKANDA

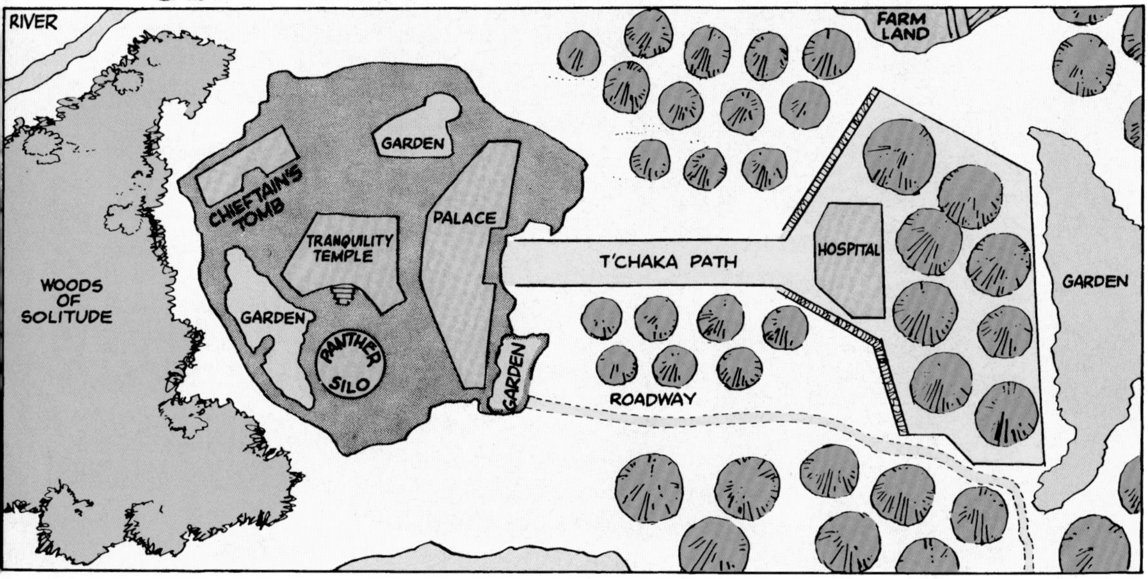

RIVER
FARM LAND
GARDEN
CHIEFTAIN'S TOMB
PALACE
TRANQUILITY TEMPLE
T'CHAKA PATH
HOSPITAL
WOODS OF SOLITUDE
GARDEN
GARDEN
PANTHER SILO
GARDEN
ROADWAY

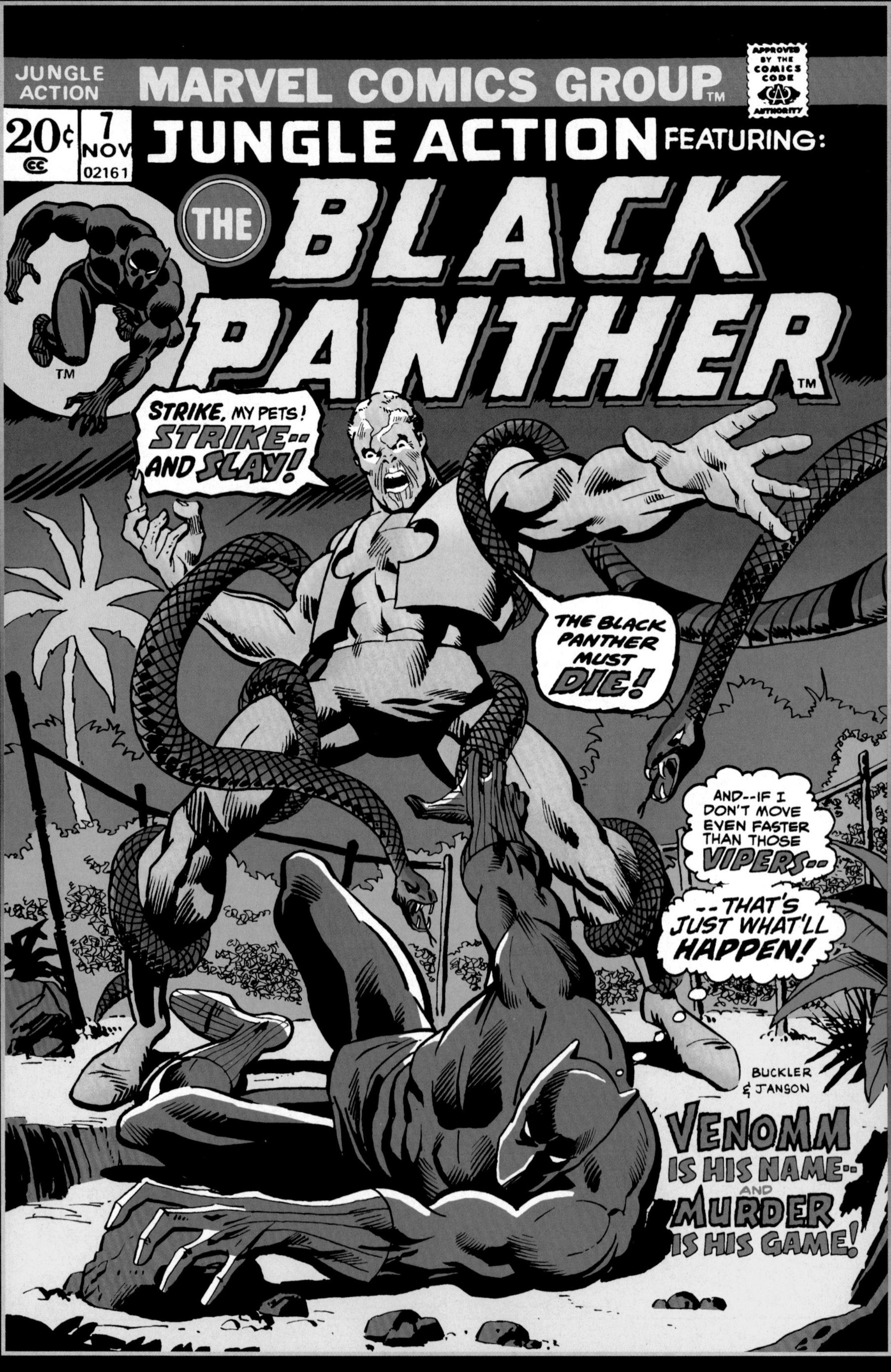
JUNGLE ACTION
MARVEL COMICS GROUP TM
APPROVED BY THE COMICS CODE AUTHORITY
20¢
7 NOV
02161
JUNGLE ACTION FEATURING:
THE BLACK PANTHER TM
TM
STRIKE, MY PETS! STRIKE.. AND SLAY!
THE BLACK PANTHER MUST DIE!
AND--IF I DON'T MOVE EVEN FASTER THAN THOSE VIPERS..
--THAT'S JUST WHAT'LL HAPPEN!
BUCKLER & JANSON
VENOMM IS HIS NAME.. AND MURDER IS HIS GAME!

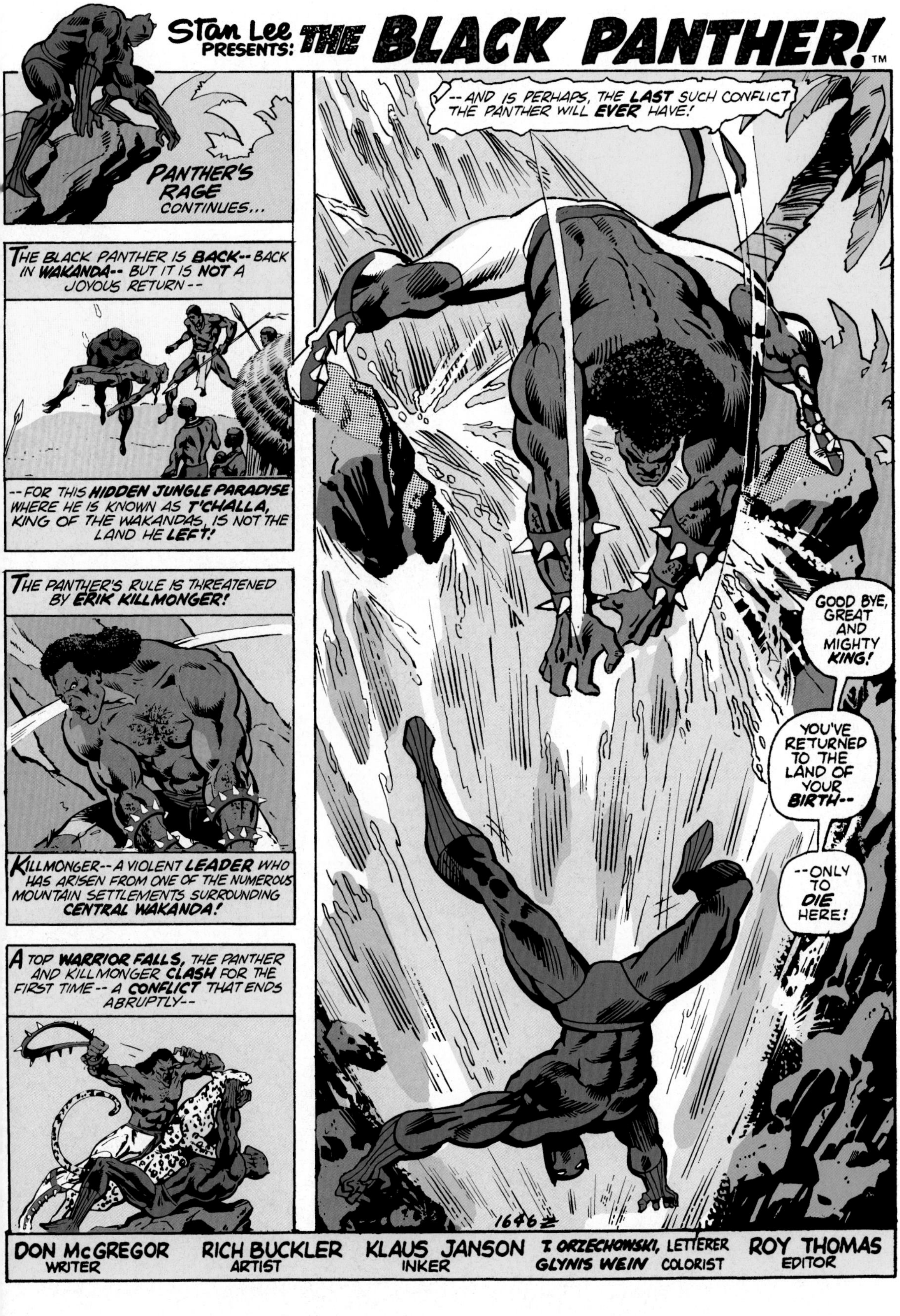
Stan Lee PRESENTS: THE BLACK PANTHER! TM
PANTHER'S RAGE CONTINUES...
THE BLACK PANTHER IS BACK-- BACK IN WAKANDA-- BUT IT IS NOT A JOYOUS RETURN--
--FOR THIS HIDDEN JUNGLE PARADISE WHERE HE IS KNOWN AS T'CHALLA, KING OF THE WAKANDAS, IS NOT THE LAND HE LEFT!
THE PANTHER'S RULE IS THREATENED BY ERIK KILLMONGER!
KILLMONGER-- A VIOLENT LEADER WHO HAS ARISEN FROM ONE OF THE NUMEROUS MOUNTAIN SETTLEMENTS SURROUNDING CENTRAL WAKANDA!
A TOP WARRIOR FALLS, THE PANTHER AND KILLMONGER CLASH FOR THE FIRST TIME-- A CONFLICT THAT ENDS ABRUPTLY--
--AND IS PERHAPS, THE LAST SUCH CONFLICT THE PANTHER WILL EVER HAVE!
GOOD BYE, GREAT AND MIGHTY KING!
YOU'VE RETURNED TO THE LAND OF YOUR BIRTH--
--ONLY TO DIE HERE!
DON McGREGOR WRITER
RICH BUCKLER ARTIST
KLAUS JANSON INKER
T. ORZECHOWSKI, LETTERER
GLYNIS WEIN COLORIST
ROY THOMAS EDITOR

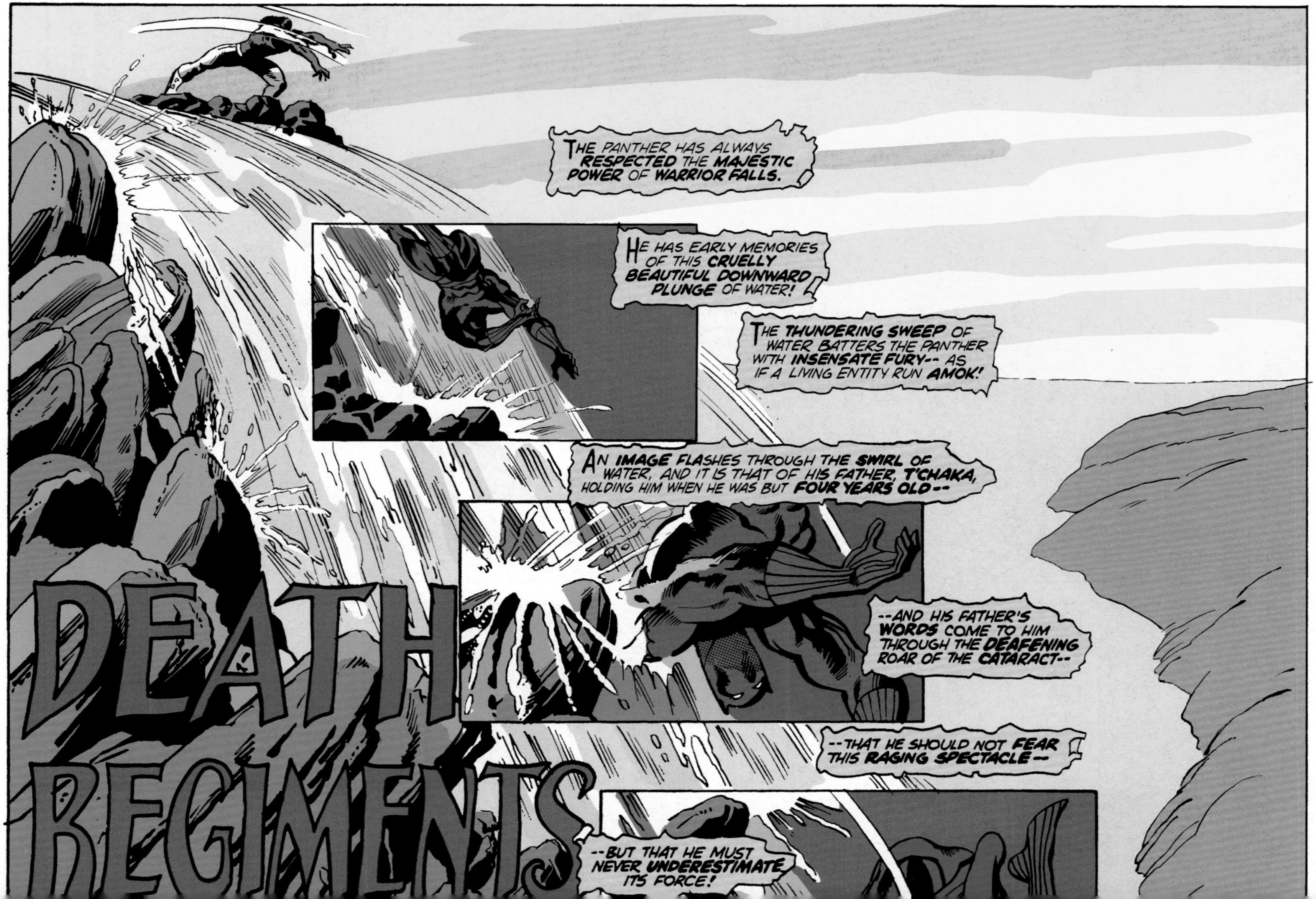

THE PANTHER HAS ALWAYS RESPECTED THE MAJESTIC POWER OF WARRIOR FALLS.
HE HAS EARLY MEMORIES OF THIS CRUELLY BEAUTIFUL DOWNWARD PLUNGE OF WATER!
THE THUNDERING SWEEP OF WATER BATTERS THE PANTHER WITH INSENSATE FURY-- AS IF A LIVING ENTITY RUN AMOK!
AN IMAGE FLASHES THROUGH THE SWIRL OF WATER, AND IT IS THAT OF HIS FATHER, T'CHAKA, HOLDING HIM WHEN HE WAS BUT FOUR YEARS OLD--
DEATH REGIMENTS
--AND HIS FATHER'S WORDS COME TO HIM THROUGH THE DEAFENING ROAR OF THE CATARACT--
--THAT HE SHOULD NOT FEAR THIS RAGING SPECTACLE--
--BUT THAT HE MUST NEVER UNDERESTIMATE ITS FORCE!

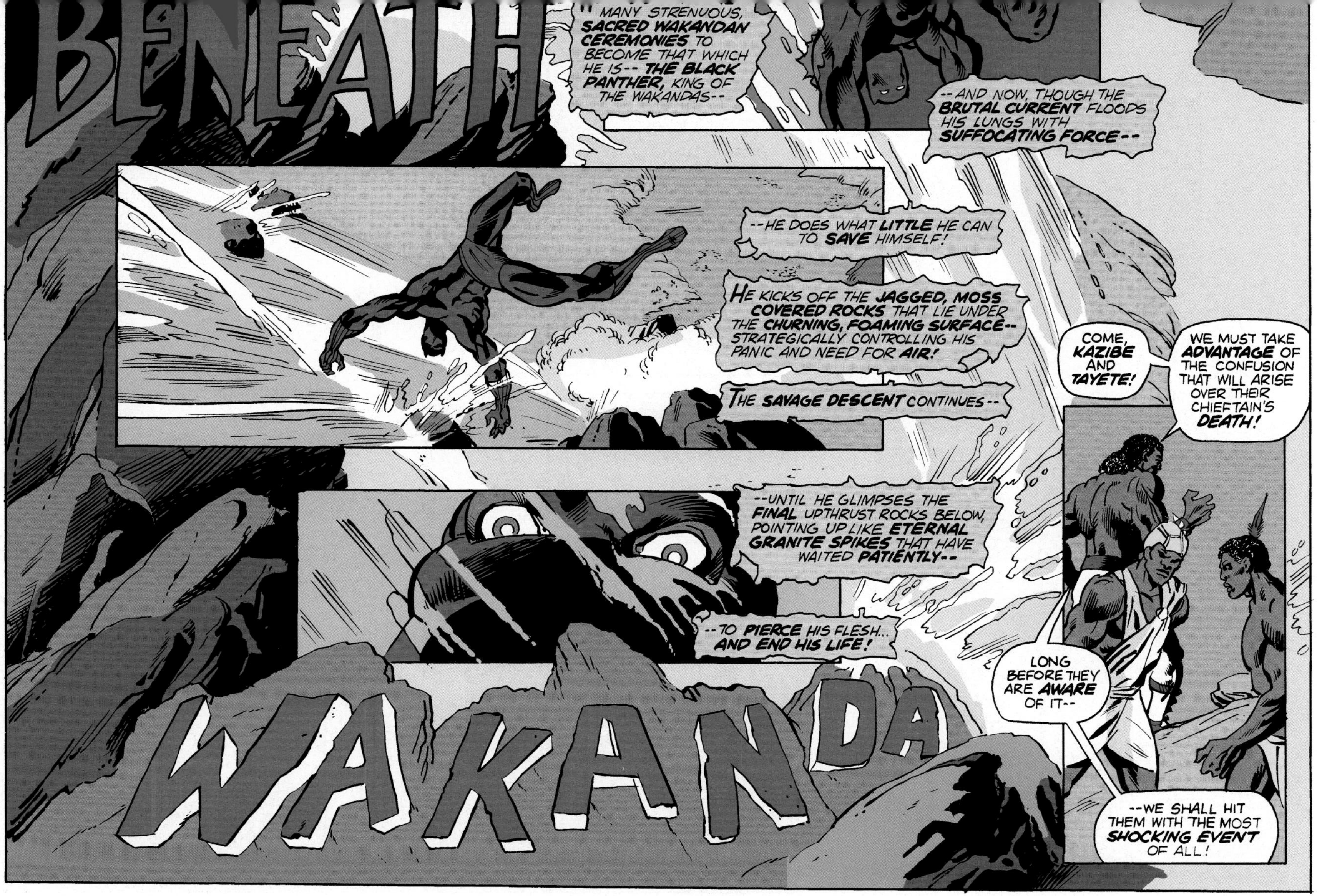
BENEATH
"MANY STRENUOUS, SACRED WAKANDAN CEREMONIES TO BECOME THAT WHICH HE IS-- THE BLACK PANTHER, KING OF THE WAKANDAS--
--AND NOW, THOUGH THE BRUTAL CURRENT FLOODS HIS LUNGS WITH SUFFOCATING FORCE--
--HE DOES WHAT LITTLE HE CAN TO SAVE HIMSELF!
HE KICKS OFF THE JAGGED, MOSS COVERED ROCKS THAT LIE UNDER THE CHURNING, FOAMING SURFACE-- STRATEGICALLY CONTROLLING HIS PANIC AND NEED FOR AIR!
THE SAVAGE DESCENT CONTINUES--
--UNTIL HE GLIMPSES THE FINAL UPTHRUST ROCKS BELOW, POINTING UP LIKE ETERNAL GRANITE SPIKES THAT HAVE WAITED PATIENTLY--
--TO PIERCE HIS FLESH... AND END HIS LIFE!
WAKANDA
COME, KAZIBE AND TAYETE!
WE MUST TAKE ADVANTAGE OF THE CONFUSION THAT WILL ARISE OVER THEIR CHIEFTAIN'S DEATH!
LONG BEFORE THEY ARE AWARE OF IT--
--WE SHALL HIT THEM WITH THE MOST SHOCKING EVENT OF ALL!

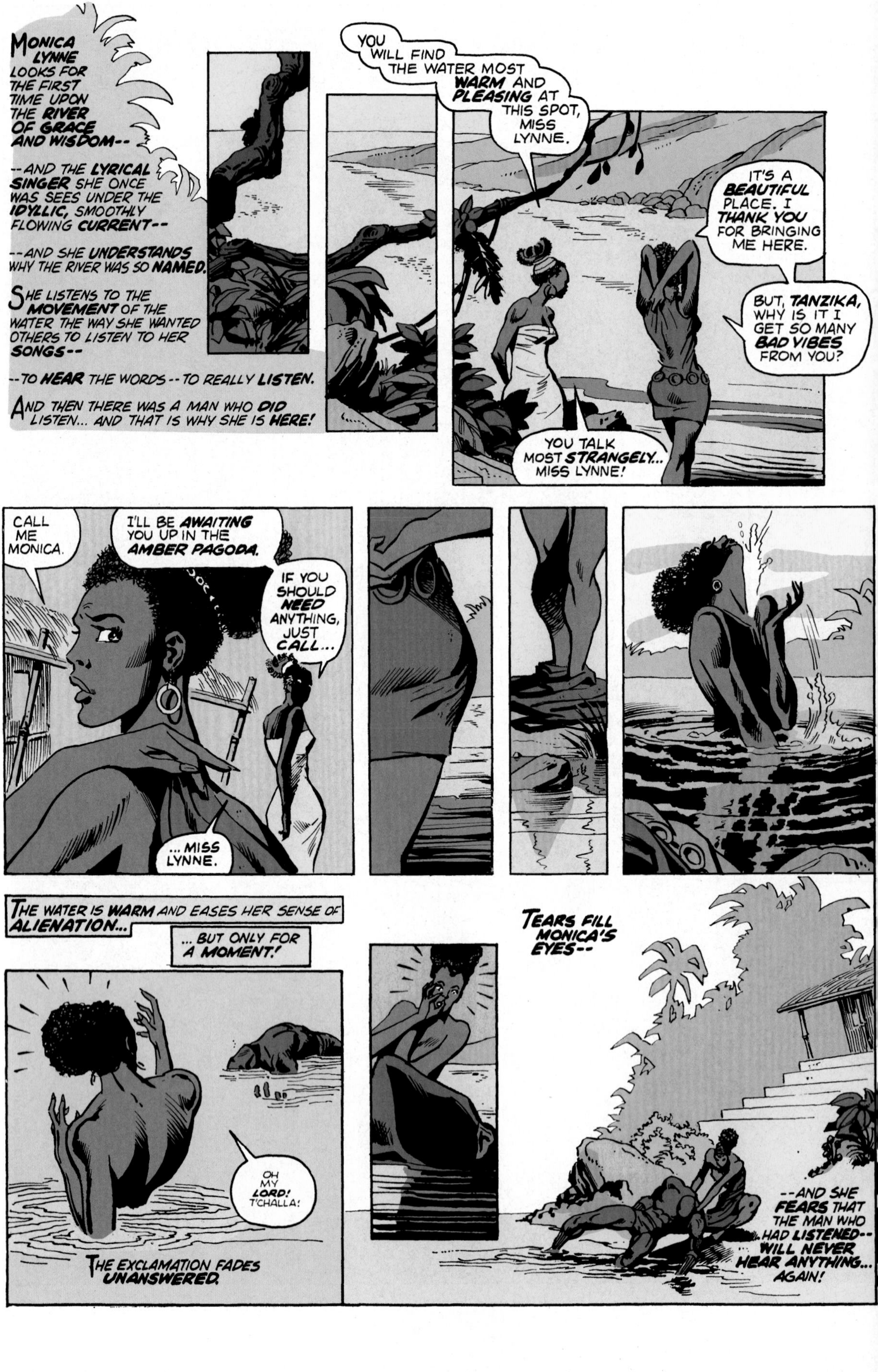
MONICA LYNNE LOOKS FOR THE FIRST TIME UPON THE RIVER OF GRACE AND WISDOM--
--AND THE LYRICAL SINGER SHE ONCE WAS SEES UNDER THE IDYLLIC, SMOOTHLY FLOWING CURRENT--
--AND SHE UNDERSTANDS WHY THE RIVER WAS SO NAMED.
SHE LISTENS TO THE MOVEMENT OF THE WATER THE WAY SHE WANTED OTHERS TO LISTEN TO HER SONGS--
--TO HEAR THE WORDS--TO REALLY LISTEN.
AND THEN THERE WAS A MAN WHO DID LISTEN... AND THAT IS WHY SHE IS HERE!
YOU WILL FIND THE WATER MOST WARM AND PLEASING AT THIS SPOT, MISS LYNNE.
IT'S A BEAUTIFUL PLACE. I THANK YOU FOR BRINGING ME HERE.
BUT, TANZIKA, WHY IS IT I GET SO MANY BAD VIBES FROM YOU?
YOU TALK MOST STRANGELY... MISS LYNNE!
CALL ME MONICA.
I'LL BE AWAITING YOU UP IN THE AMBER PAGODA.
IF YOU SHOULD NEED ANYTHING, JUST CALL...
...MISS LYNNE.
THE WATER IS WARM AND EASES HER SENSE OF ALIENATION...
...BUT ONLY FOR A MOMENT!
OH MY LORD! T'CHALLA!
THE EXCLAMATION FADES UNANSWERED.
TEARS FILL MONICA'S EYES--
--AND SHE FEARS THAT THE MAN WHO HAD LISTENED--WILL NEVER HEAR ANYTHING... AGAIN!

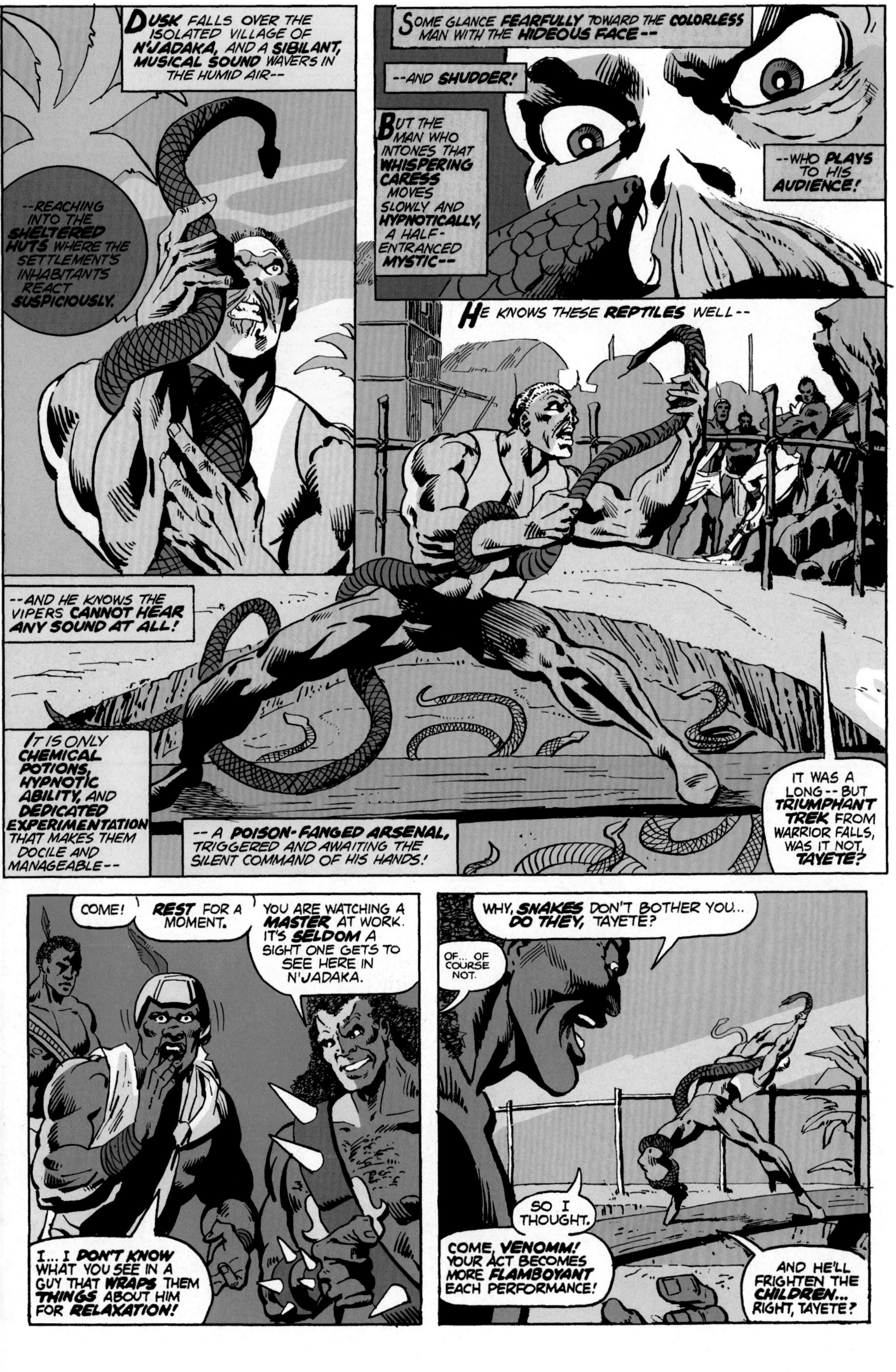
DUSK FALLS OVER THE ISOLATED VILLAGE OF N'JADAKA, AND A SIBILANT, MUSICAL SOUND WAVERS IN THE HUMID AIR--
--REACHING INTO THE SHELTERED HUTS WHERE THE SETTLEMENT'S INHABITANTS REACT SUSPICIOUSLY.
SOME GLANCE FEARFULLY TOWARD THE COLORLESS MAN WITH THE HIDEOUS FACE--
--AND SHUDDER!
BUT THE MAN WHO INTONES THAT WHISPERING CARESS MOVES SLOWLY AND HYPNOTICALLY, A HALF-ENTRANCED MYSTIC--
--WHO PLAYS TO HIS AUDIENCE!
HE KNOWS THESE REPTILES WELL--
--AND HE KNOWS THE VIPERS CANNOT HEAR ANY SOUND AT ALL!
IT IS ONLY CHEMICAL POTIONS, HYPNOTIC ABILITY, AND DEDICATED EXPERIMENTATION THAT MAKES THEM DOCILE AND MANAGEABLE--
--A POISON-FANGED ARSENAL, TRIGGERED AND AWAITING THE SILENT COMMAND OF HIS HANDS!
IT WAS A LONG--BUT TRIUMPHANT TREK FROM WARRIOR FALLS, WAS IT NOT, TAYETE?
COME!
REST FOR A MOMENT.
YOU ARE WATCHING A MASTER AT WORK. IT'S SELDOM A SIGHT ONE GETS TO SEE HERE IN N'JADAKA.
I... I DON'T KNOW WHAT YOU SEE IN A GUY THAT WRAPS THEM THINGS ABOUT HIM FOR RELAXATION!
WHY, SNAKES DON'T BOTHER YOU... DO THEY, TAYETE?
OF... OF COURSE NOT.
SO I THOUGHT.
COME, VENOMM! YOUR ACT BECOMES MORE FLAMBOYANT EACH PERFORMANCE!
AND HE'LL FRIGHTEN THE CHILDREN... RIGHT, TAYETE?

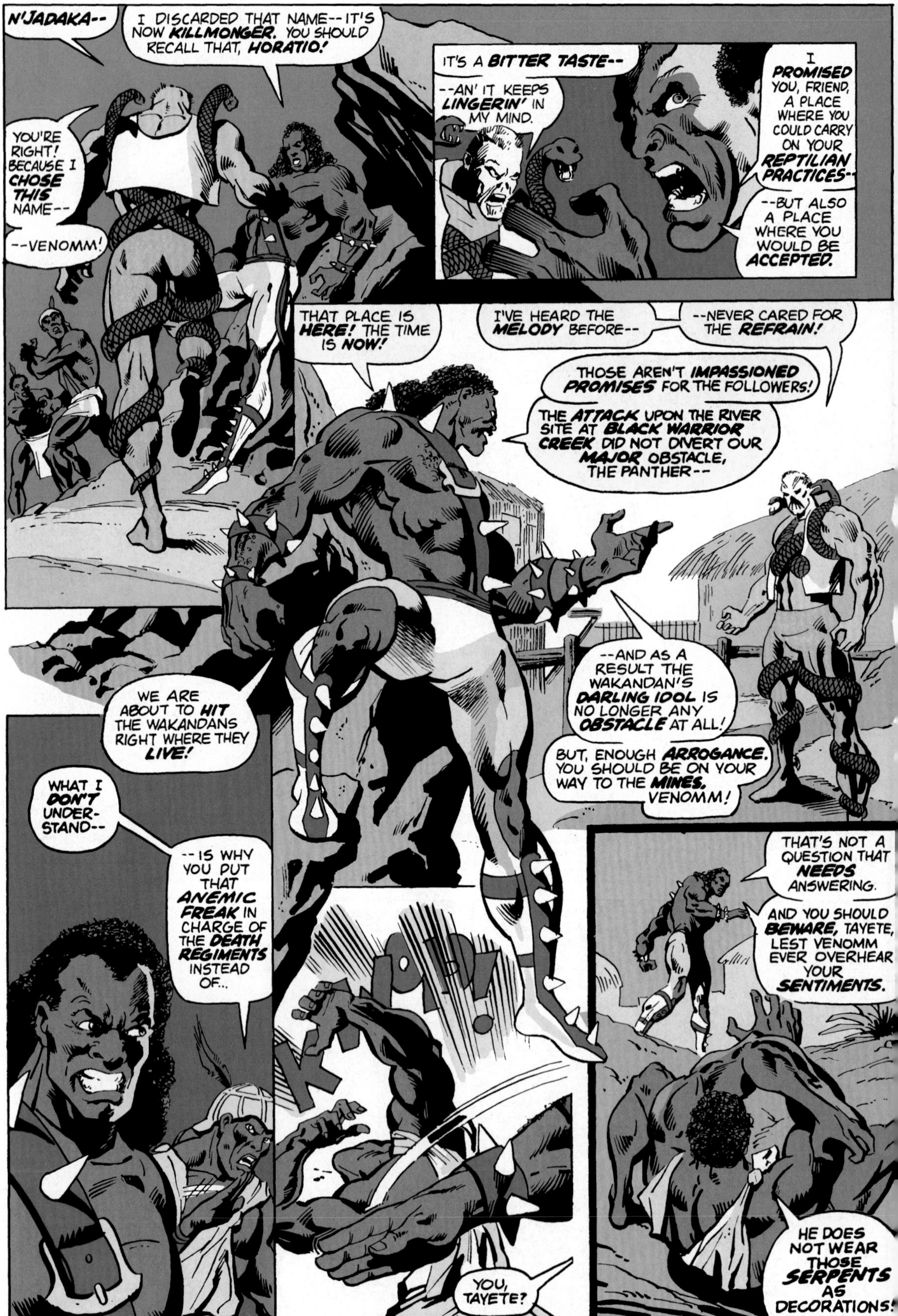
N'JADAKA--
I DISCARDED THAT NAME--IT'S NOW KILLMONGER. YOU SHOULD RECALL THAT, HORATIO!
YOU'RE RIGHT! BECAUSE I CHOSE THIS NAME--
--VENOMM!
IT'S A BITTER TASTE--
--AN' IT KEEPS LINGERIN' IN MY MIND.
I PROMISED YOU, FRIEND, A PLACE WHERE YOU COULD CARRY ON YOUR REPTILIAN PRACTICES--
--BUT ALSO A PLACE WHERE YOU WOULD BE ACCEPTED.
THAT PLACE IS HERE! THE TIME IS NOW!
I'VE HEARD THE MELODY BEFORE--
--NEVER CARED FOR THE REFRAIN!
THOSE AREN'T IMPASSIONED PROMISES FOR THE FOLLOWERS!
THE ATTACK UPON THE RIVER SITE AT BLACK WARRIOR CREEK DID NOT DIVERT OUR MAJOR OBSTACLE, THE PANTHER--
--AND AS A RESULT THE WAKANDAN'S DARLING IDOL IS NO LONGER ANY OBSTACLE AT ALL!
BUT, ENOUGH ARROGANCE. YOU SHOULD BE ON YOUR WAY TO THE MINES, VENOMM!
WE ARE ABOUT TO HIT THE WAKANDANS RIGHT WHERE THEY LIVE!
WHAT I DON'T UNDER-STAND--
--IS WHY YOU PUT THAT ANEMIC FREAK IN CHARGE OF THE DEATH REGIMENTS INSTEAD OF..
YOU, TAYETE?
THAT'S NOT A QUESTION THAT NEEDS ANSWERING.
AND YOU SHOULD BEWARE, TAYETE, LEST VENOMM EVER OVERHEAR YOUR SENTIMENTS.
HE DOES NOT WEAR THOSE SERPENTS AS DECORATIONS!

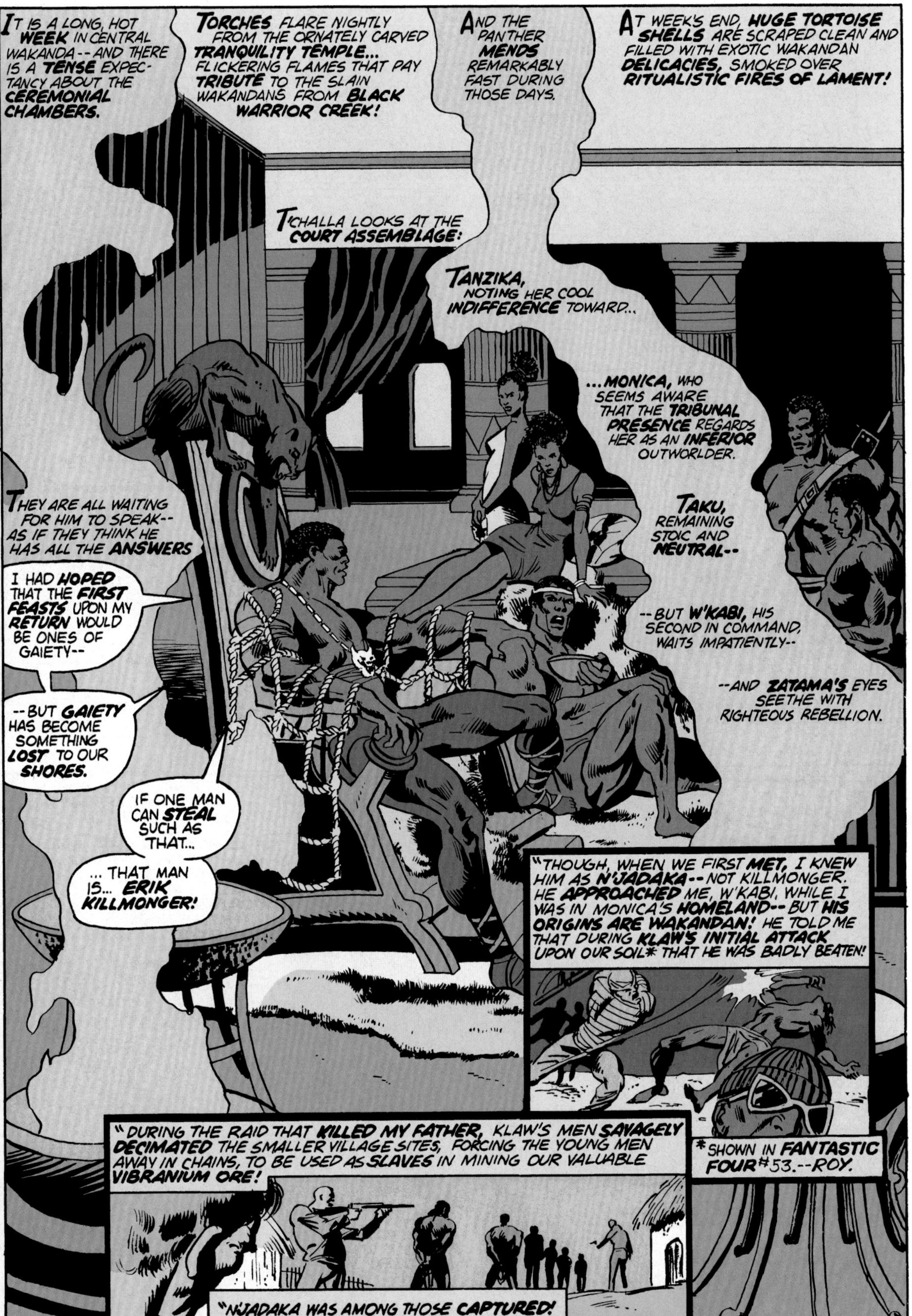
IT IS A LONG, HOT WEEK IN CENTRAL WAKANDA -- AND THERE IS A TENSE EXPECTANCY ABOUT THE CEREMONIAL CHAMBERS.
TORCHES FLARE NIGHTLY FROM THE ORNATELY CARVED TRANQUILITY TEMPLE... FLICKERING FLAMES THAT PAY TRIBUTE TO THE SLAIN WAKANDANS FROM BLACK WARRIOR CREEK!
AND THE PANTHER MENDS REMARKABLY FAST DURING THOSE DAYS.
AT WEEK'S END, HUGE TORTOISE SHELLS ARE SCRAPED CLEAN AND FILLED WITH EXOTIC WAKANDAN DELICACIES, SMOKED OVER RITUALISTIC FIRES OF LAMENT!
T'CHALLA LOOKS AT THE COURT ASSEMBLAGE:
TANZIKA, NOTING HER COOL INDIFFERENCE TOWARD...
...MONICA, WHO SEEMS AWARE THAT THE TRIBUNAL PRESENCE REGARDS HER AS AN INFERIOR OUTWORLDER.
TAKU, REMAINING STOIC AND NEUTRAL--
--BUT W'KABI, HIS SECOND IN COMMAND, WAITS IMPATIENTLY--
--AND ZATAMA'S EYES SEETHE WITH RIGHTEOUS REBELLION.
THEY ARE ALL WAITING FOR HIM TO SPEAK-- AS IF THEY THINK HE HAS ALL THE ANSWERS
I HAD HOPED THAT THE FIRST FEASTS UPON MY RETURN WOULD BE ONES OF GAIETY--
--BUT GAIETY HAS BECOME SOMETHING LOST TO OUR SHORES.
IF ONE MAN CAN STEAL SUCH AS THAT...
... THAT MAN IS... ERIK KILLMONGER!
"THOUGH, WHEN WE FIRST MET, I KNEW HIM AS N'JADAKA -- NOT KILLMONGER. HE APPROACHED ME, W'KABI, WHILE I WAS IN MONICA'S HOMELAND -- BUT HIS ORIGINS ARE WAKANDAN! HE TOLD ME THAT DURING KLAW'S INITIAL ATTACK UPON OUR SOIL* THAT HE WAS BADLY BEATEN!
"DURING THE RAID THAT KILLED MY FATHER, KLAW'S MEN SAVAGELY DECIMATED THE SMALLER VILLAGE SITES, FORCING THE YOUNG MEN AWAY IN CHAINS, TO BE USED AS SLAVES IN MINING OUR VALUABLE VIBRANIUM ORE!
*SHOWN IN FANTASTIC FOUR #53.--ROY.
"N'JADAKA WAS AMONG THOSE CAPTURED!

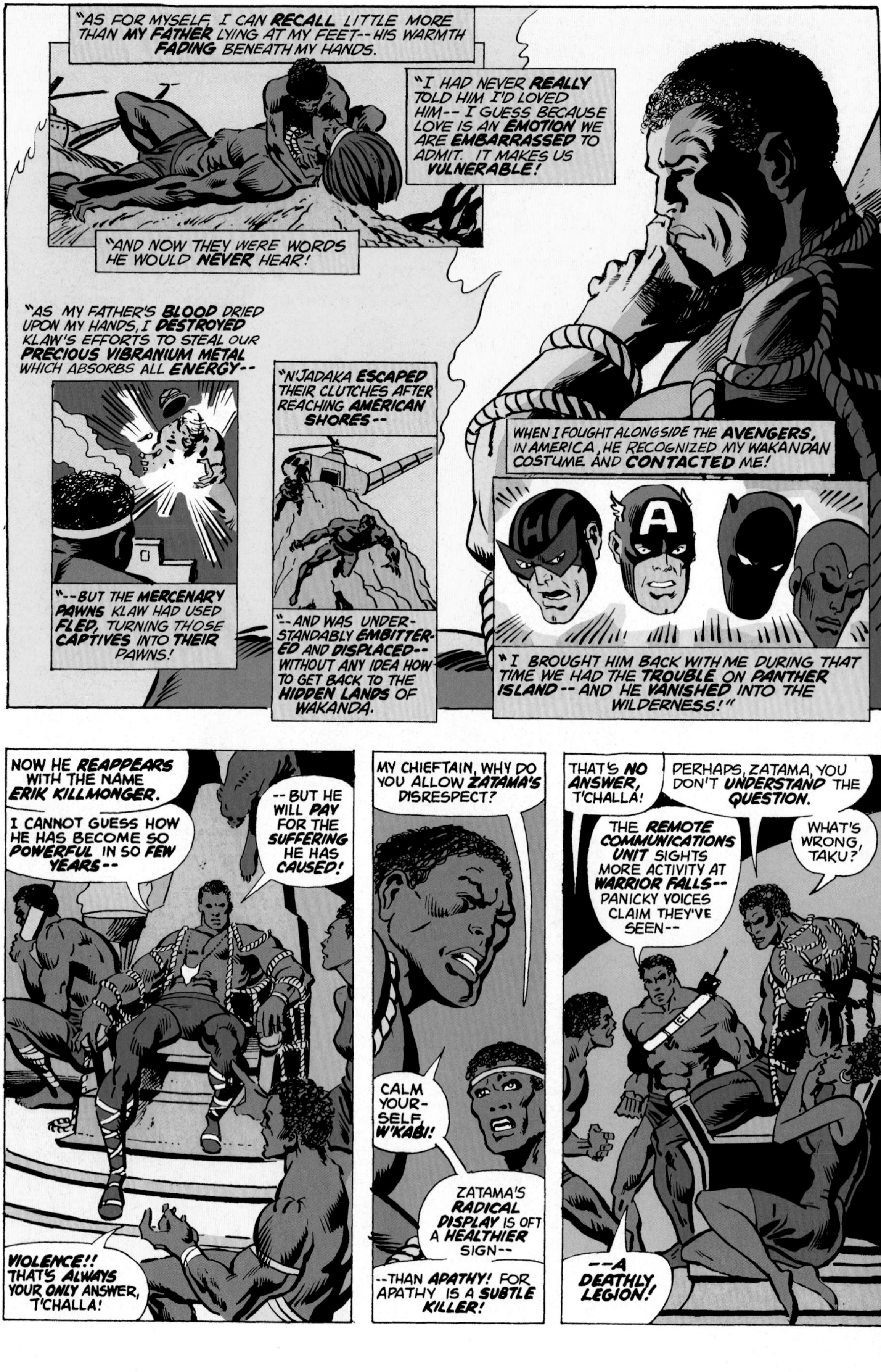
"AS FOR MYSELF, I CAN RECALL LITTLE MORE THAN MY FATHER LYING AT MY FEET-- HIS WARMTH FADING BENEATH MY HANDS.
"I HAD NEVER REALLY TOLD HIM I'D LOVED HIM-- I GUESS BECAUSE LOVE IS AN EMOTION WE ARE EMBARRASSED TO ADMIT. IT MAKES US VULNERABLE!
"AND NOW THEY WERE WORDS HE WOULD NEVER HEAR!
"AS MY FATHER'S BLOOD DRIED UPON MY HANDS, I DESTROYED KLAW'S EFFORTS TO STEAL OUR PRECIOUS VIBRANIUM METAL WHICH ABSORBS ALL ENERGY--
"--BUT THE MERCENARY PAWNS KLAW HAD USED FLED, TURNING THOSE CAPTIVES INTO THEIR PAWNS!
"N'JADAKA ESCAPED THEIR CLUTCHES AFTER REACHING AMERICAN SHORES--
"--AND WAS UNDERSTANDABLY EMBITTERED AND DISPLACED-- WITHOUT ANY IDEA HOW TO GET BACK TO THE HIDDEN LANDS OF WAKANDA.
WHEN I FOUGHT ALONGSIDE THE AVENGERS, IN AMERICA, HE RECOGNIZED MY WAKANDAN COSTUME AND CONTACTED ME!
"I BROUGHT HIM BACK WITH ME DURING THAT TIME WE HAD THE TROUBLE ON PANTHER ISLAND -- AND HE VANISHED INTO THE WILDERNESS!"
NOW HE REAPPEARS WITH THE NAME ERIK KILLMONGER.
I CANNOT GUESS HOW HE HAS BECOME SO POWERFUL IN SO FEW YEARS--
-- BUT HE WILL PAY FOR THE SUFFERING HE HAS CAUSED!
VIOLENCE!! THAT'S ALWAYS YOUR ONLY ANSWER, T'CHALLA!
MY CHIEFTAIN, WHY DO YOU ALLOW ZATAMA'S DISRESPECT?
CALM YOURSELF, W'KABI!
ZATAMA'S RADICAL DISPLAY IS OFT A HEALTHIER SIGN--
--THAN APATHY! FOR APATHY IS A SUBTLE KILLER!
THAT'S NO ANSWER, T'CHALLA!
PERHAPS, ZATAMA, YOU DON'T UNDERSTAND THE QUESTION.
WHAT'S WRONG, TAKU?
THE REMOTE COMMUNICATIONS UNIT SIGHTS MORE ACTIVITY AT WARRIOR FALLS-- PANICKY VOICES CLAIM THEY'VE SEEN--
--A DEATHLY LEGION!

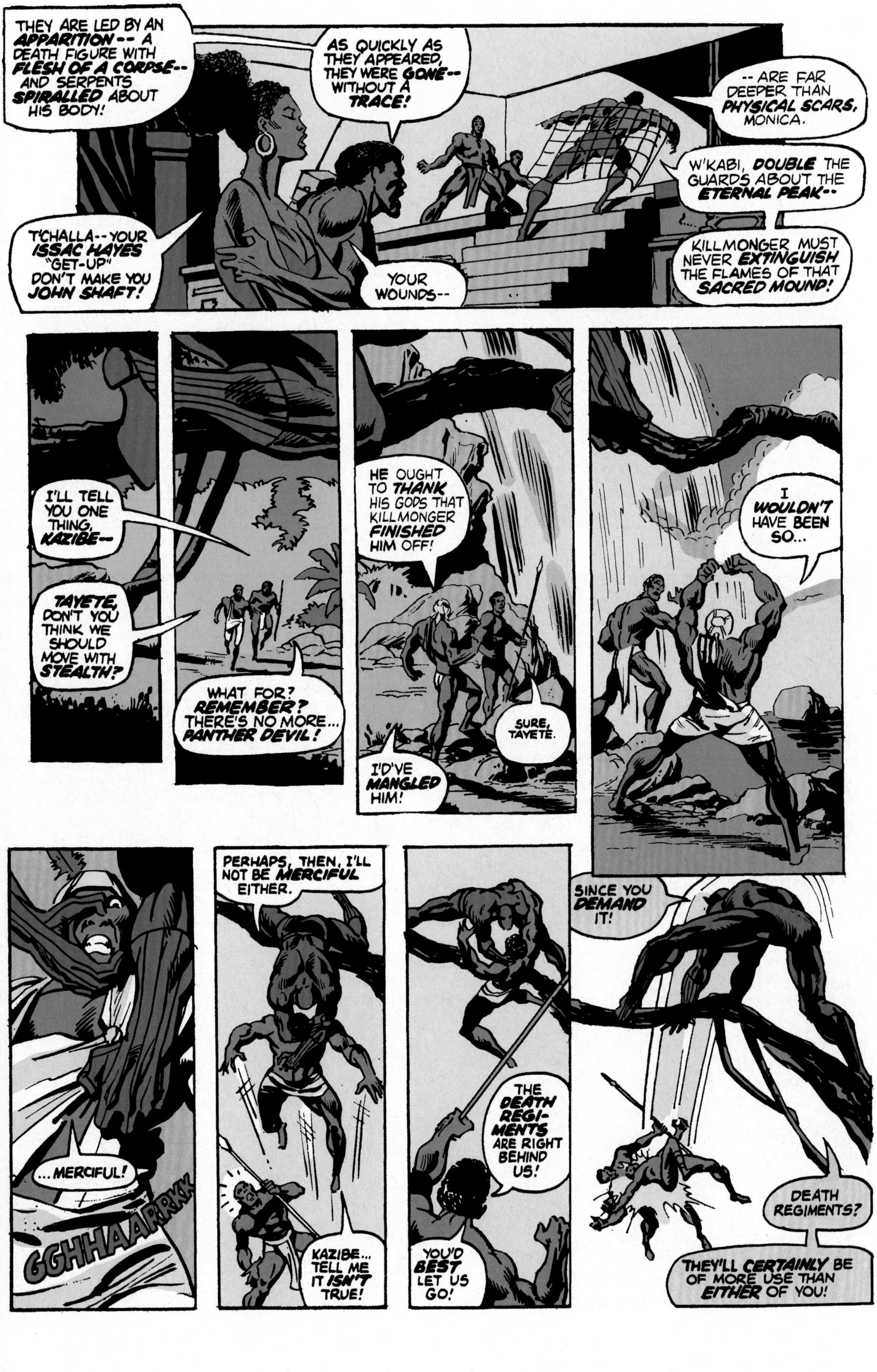
THEY ARE LED BY AN APPARITION -- A DEATH FIGURE WITH FLESH OF A CORPSE -- AND SERPENTS SPIRALLED ABOUT HIS BODY!
AS QUICKLY AS THEY APPEARED, THEY WERE GONE -- WITHOUT A TRACE!
T'CHALLA -- YOUR ISSAC HAYES "GET-UP" DON'T MAKE YOU JOHN SHAFT!
YOUR WOUNDS--
-- ARE FAR DEEPER THAN PHYSICAL SCARS, MONICA.
W'KABI, DOUBLE THE GUARDS ABOUT THE ETERNAL PEAK --
KILLMONGER MUST NEVER EXTINGUISH THE FLAMES OF THAT SACRED MOUND!
I'LL TELL YOU ONE THING, KAZIBE--
TAYETE, DON'T YOU THINK WE SHOULD MOVE WITH STEALTH?
WHAT FOR? REMEMBER? THERE'S NO MORE... PANTHER DEVIL!
HE OUGHT TO THANK HIS GODS THAT KILLMONGER FINISHED HIM OFF!
SURE, TAYETE.
I'D'VE MANGLED HIM!
I WOULDN'T HAVE BEEN SO...
...MERCIFUL!
GGHHAAARRKK
PERHAPS, THEN, I'LL NOT BE MERCIFUL EITHER.
KAZIBE... TELL ME IT ISN'T TRUE!
THE DEATH REGIMENTS ARE RIGHT BEHIND US!
YOU'D BEST LET US GO!
SINCE YOU DEMAND IT!
DEATH REGIMENTS?
THEY'LL CERTAINLY BE OF MORE USE THAN EITHER OF YOU!

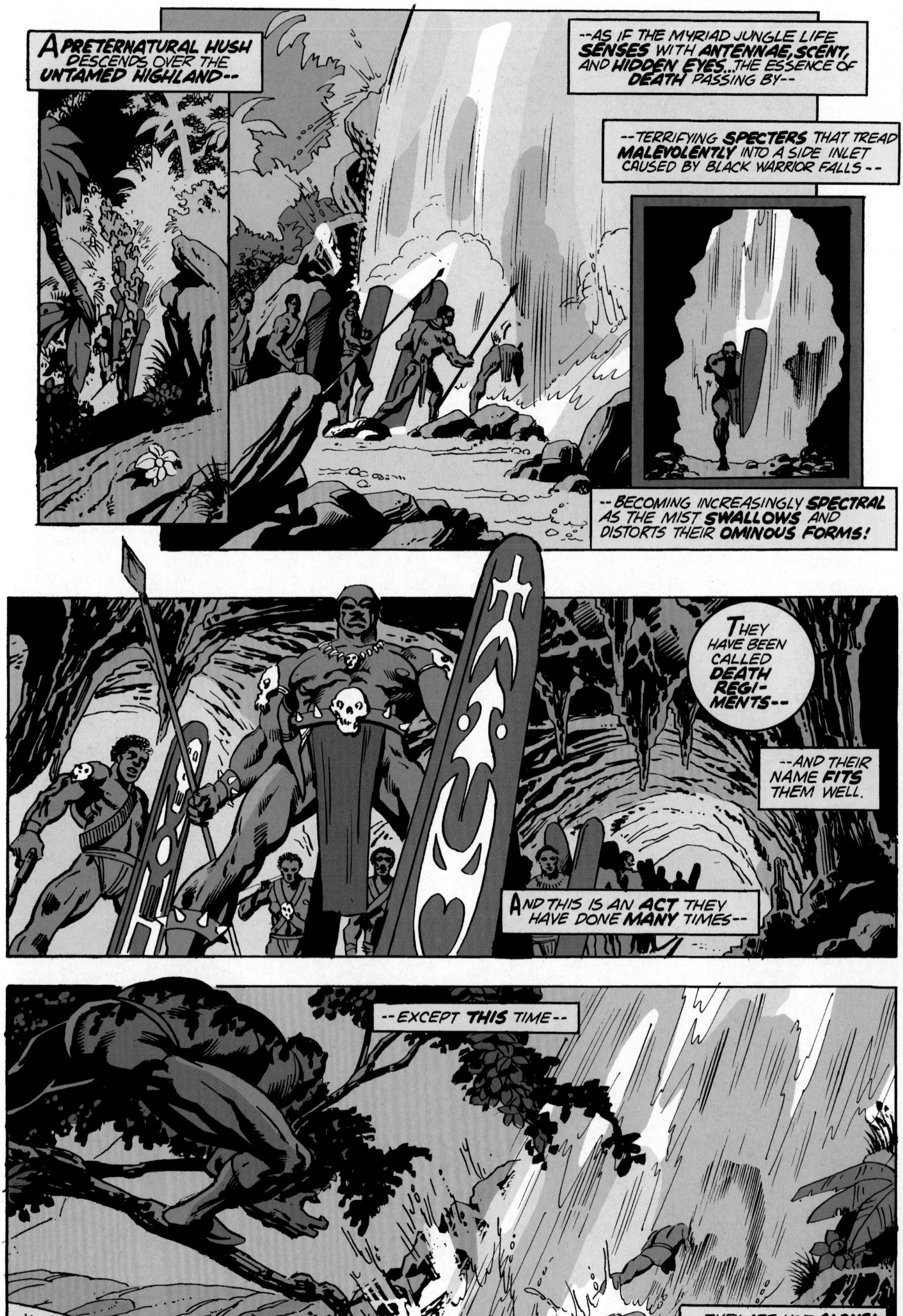
A PRETERNATURAL HUSH DESCENDS OVER THE UNTAMED HIGHLAND--
--AS IF THE MYRIAD JUNGLE LIFE SENSES WITH ANTENNAE, SCENT, AND HIDDEN EYES... THE ESSENCE OF DEATH PASSING BY--
--TERRIFYING SPECTERS THAT TREAD MALEVOLENTLY INTO A SIDE INLET CAUSED BY BLACK WARRIOR FALLS--
--BECOMING INCREASINGLY SPECTRAL AS THE MIST SWALLOWS AND DISTORTS THEIR OMINOUS FORMS!
THEY HAVE BEEN CALLED DEATH REGIMENTS--
--AND THEIR NAME FITS THEM WELL.
AND THIS IS AN ACT THEY HAVE DONE MANY TIMES--
--EXCEPT THIS TIME--
--THEY ARE NOT ALONE!

DESPITE THE FACT THAT **TORN LIGAMENTS** AND **BRUISED MUSCLES** SIGNAL THEIR **ACHE**--

--THE PANTHER **FOLLOWS!**

HIS **CAT-LIKE EYES** REGISTER THE **ROCK HEWN** WALLS--

--AND A **STARTLING PREMONITION** TELLS HIM WHERE THIS **SHADOW-FRAUGHT PASSAGE** LEADS!

THE PANTHER **MOVES OUT,** MUCH LIKE HIS NAMESAKE --

--AND THOUGH THESE **CAVERN WALLS** WOULD NORMALLY **MAGNIFY** ALL SOUND--

-- HIS PURSUIT IS **ABSOLUTELY SILENT!**

BUT AT THE TRAIL'S END, THE SIGHT THAT **SEARS** HIS EYES--

--IS EVEN MORE **STAGGERING** THAN HIS **EARLIER FEAR!**

IT IS AN **IMMENSE MINING OPERATION**--

--BATHED IN **EERIE ILLUMINOSITY,** THE VALUABLE **ORE** STREAKING THROUGH THE STONE WALLS RADIATING A **BLUISH OVERCAST!**

THE PANTHER KNOWS HE IS DIRECTLY **UNDER** THE **SACRED MOUND OF VIBRANIUM**--

--AND THAT ALL THE **GUARDS** THAT STAND **VIGILANCE** OVER THIS SUBSTANCE WHICH **ABSORBS ALL VIBRATIONS**--

-- WILL NEVER REALIZE THAT THE VERY MOUND UPON WHICH THEY **STAND**--

--IS BEING **HOLLOWED OUT** BENEATH THEIR **FEET!**

WHIIIIRRRRRRRRRRR

CRACK!

AND THEN THERE IS A **SINISTER SOUND**-- JUST BEFORE A **DOUBLE-PRONGED BULLWHIP** RIPS ABOUT HIS **THROAT** AND **CHEST!**

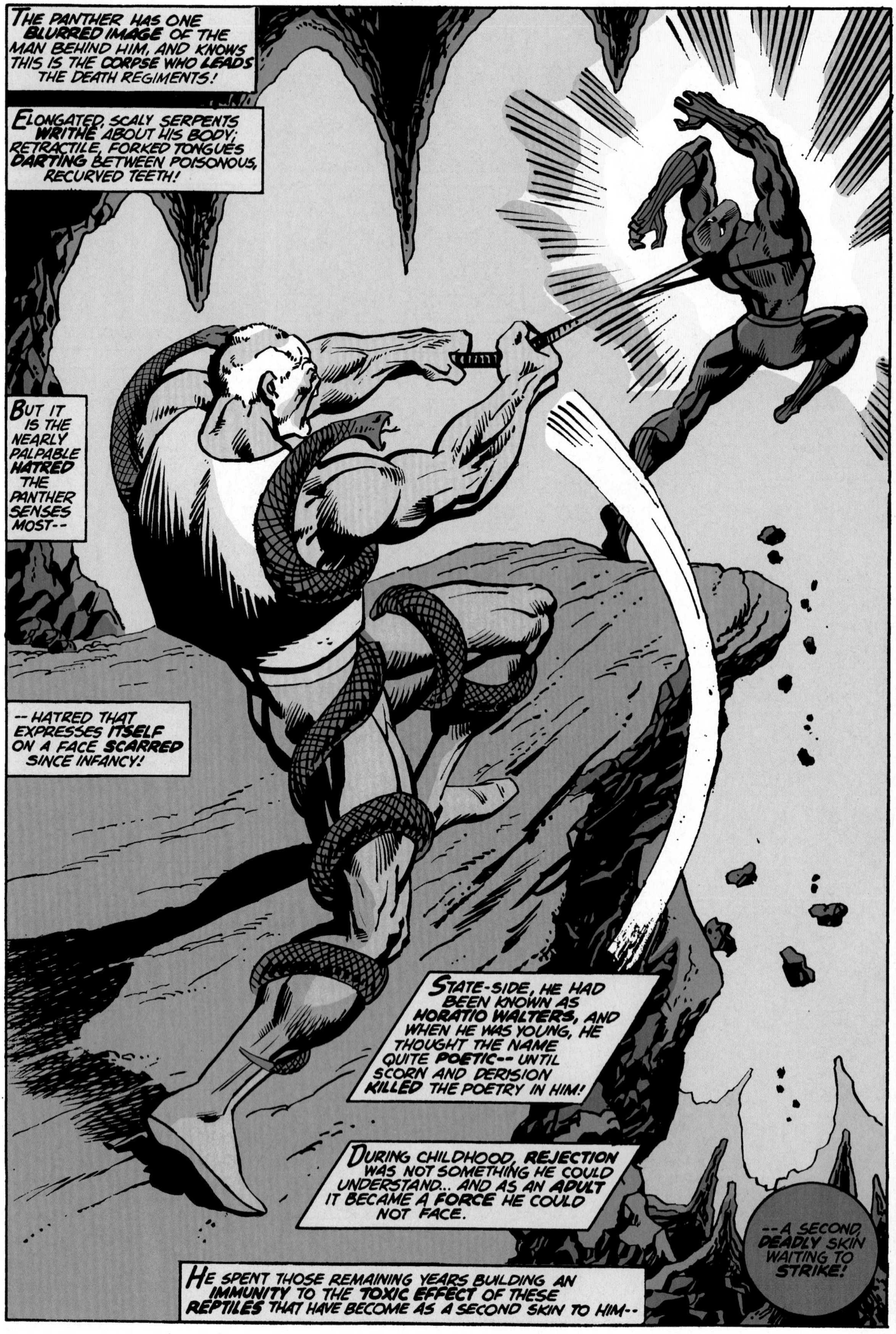
THE PANTHER HAS ONE BLURRED IMAGE OF THE MAN BEHIND HIM, AND KNOWS THIS IS THE CORPSE WHO LEADS THE DEATH REGIMENTS!
ELONGATED, SCALY SERPENTS WRITHE ABOUT HIS BODY; RETRACTILE, FORKED TONGUES DARTING BETWEEN POISONOUS, RECURVED TEETH!
BUT IT IS THE NEARLY PALPABLE HATRED THE PANTHER SENSES MOST--
--HATRED THAT EXPRESSES ITSELF ON A FACE SCARRED SINCE INFANCY!
STATE-SIDE, HE HAD BEEN KNOWN AS HORATIO WALTERS, AND WHEN HE WAS YOUNG, HE THOUGHT THE NAME QUITE POETIC-- UNTIL SCORN AND DERISION KILLED THE POETRY IN HIM!
DURING CHILDHOOD, REJECTION WAS NOT SOMETHING HE COULD UNDERSTAND... AND AS AN ADULT IT BECAME A FORCE HE COULD NOT FACE.
HE SPENT THOSE REMAINING YEARS BUILDING AN IMMUNITY TO THE TOXIC EFFECT OF THESE REPTILES THAT HAVE BECOME AS A SECOND SKIN TO HIM--
--A SECOND, DEADLY SKIN WAITING TO STRIKE!

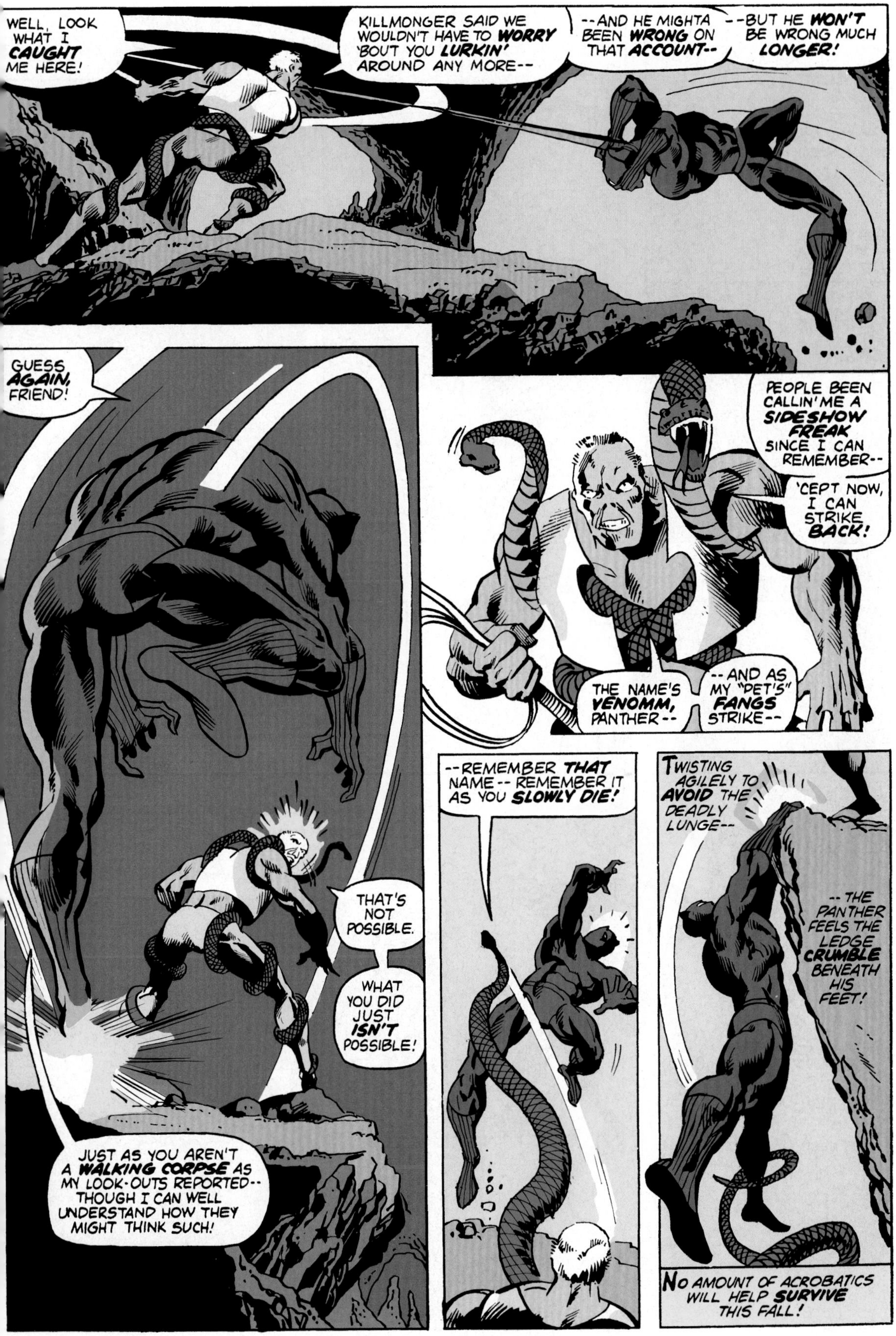
WELL, LOOK WHAT I CAUGHT ME HERE!
KILLMONGER SAID WE WOULDN'T HAVE TO WORRY 'BOUT YOU LURKIN' AROUND ANY MORE--
--AND HE MIGHTA BEEN WRONG ON THAT ACCOUNT--
--BUT HE WON'T BE WRONG MUCH LONGER!
GUESS AGAIN, FRIEND!
THAT'S NOT POSSIBLE.
WHAT YOU DID JUST ISN'T POSSIBLE!
JUST AS YOU AREN'T A WALKING CORPSE AS MY LOOK-OUTS REPORTED-- THOUGH I CAN WELL UNDERSTAND HOW THEY MIGHT THINK SUCH!
PEOPLE BEEN CALLIN' ME A SIDESHOW FREAK SINCE I CAN REMEMBER--
'CEPT NOW, I CAN STRIKE BACK!
THE NAME'S VENOMM, PANTHER--
--AND AS MY "PET'S" FANGS STRIKE--
--REMEMBER THAT NAME-- REMEMBER IT AS YOU SLOWLY DIE!
TWISTING AGILELY TO AVOID THE DEADLY LUNGE--
--THE PANTHER FEELS THE LEDGE CRUMBLE BENEATH HIS FEET!
NO AMOUNT OF ACROBATICS WILL HELP SURVIVE THIS FALL!

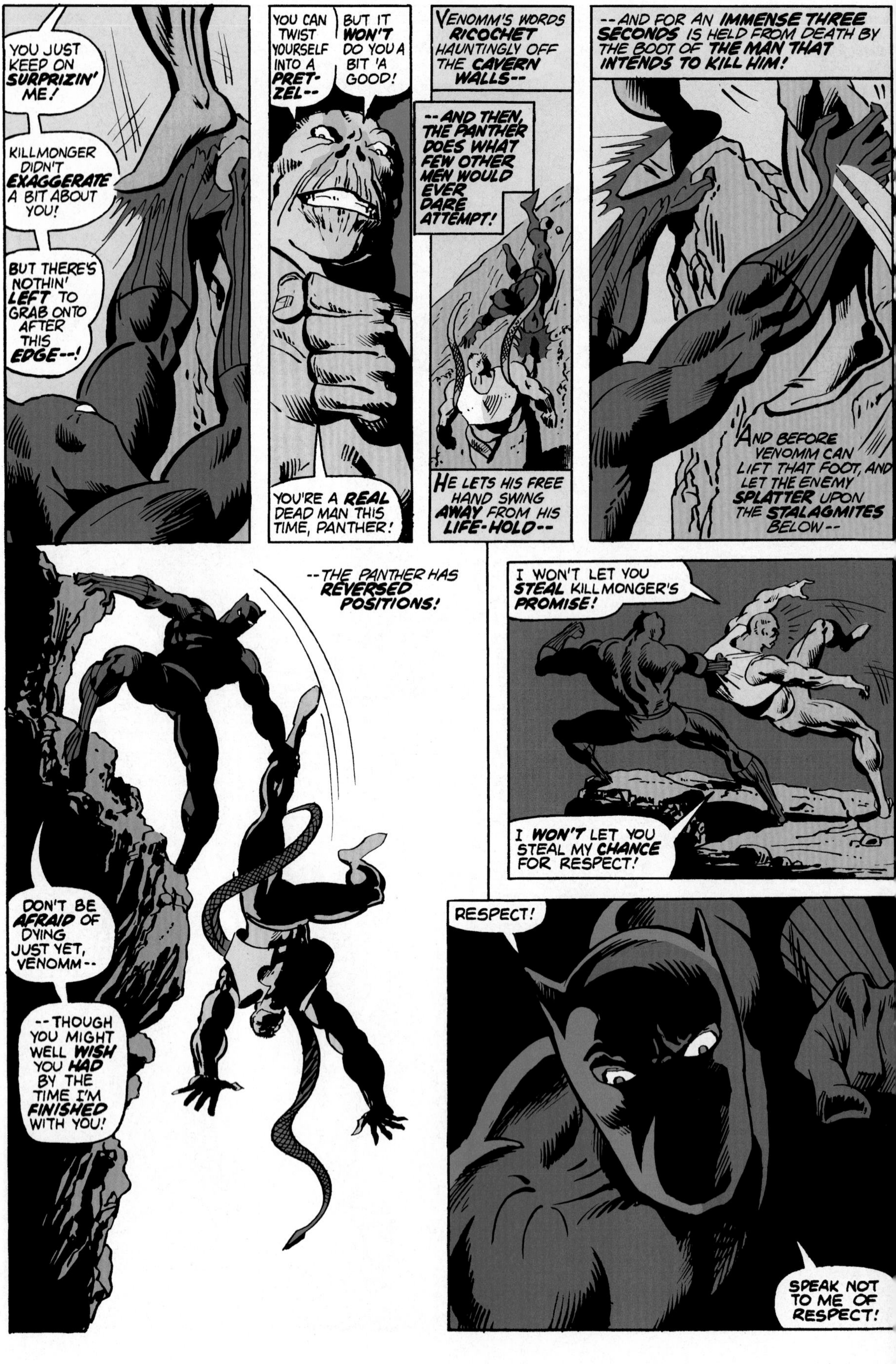
YOU JUST KEEP ON SURPRIZIN' ME!
KILLMONGER DIDN'T EXAGGERATE A BIT ABOUT YOU!
BUT THERE'S NOTHIN' LEFT TO GRAB ONTO AFTER THIS EDGE--!
YOU CAN TWIST YOURSELF INTO A PRETZEL--
BUT IT WON'T DO YOU A BIT 'A GOOD!
YOU'RE A REAL DEAD MAN THIS TIME, PANTHER!
VENOMM'S WORDS RICOCHET HAUNTINGLY OFF THE CAVERN WALLS--
--AND THEN, THE PANTHER DOES WHAT FEW OTHER MEN WOULD EVER DARE ATTEMPT!
HE LETS HIS FREE HAND SWING AWAY FROM HIS LIFE-HOLD--
--AND FOR AN IMMENSE THREE SECONDS IS HELD FROM DEATH BY THE BOOT OF THE MAN THAT INTENDS TO KILL HIM!
AND BEFORE VENOMM CAN LIFT THAT FOOT, AND LET THE ENEMY SPLATTER UPON THE STALAGMITES BELOW--
--THE PANTHER HAS REVERSED POSITIONS!
DON'T BE AFRAID OF DYING JUST YET, VENOMM--
--THOUGH YOU MIGHT WELL WISH YOU HAD BY THE TIME I'M FINISHED WITH YOU!
I WON'T LET YOU STEAL KILLMONGER'S PROMISE!
I WON'T LET YOU STEAL MY CHANCE FOR RESPECT!
RESPECT!
SPEAK NOT TO ME OF RESPECT!

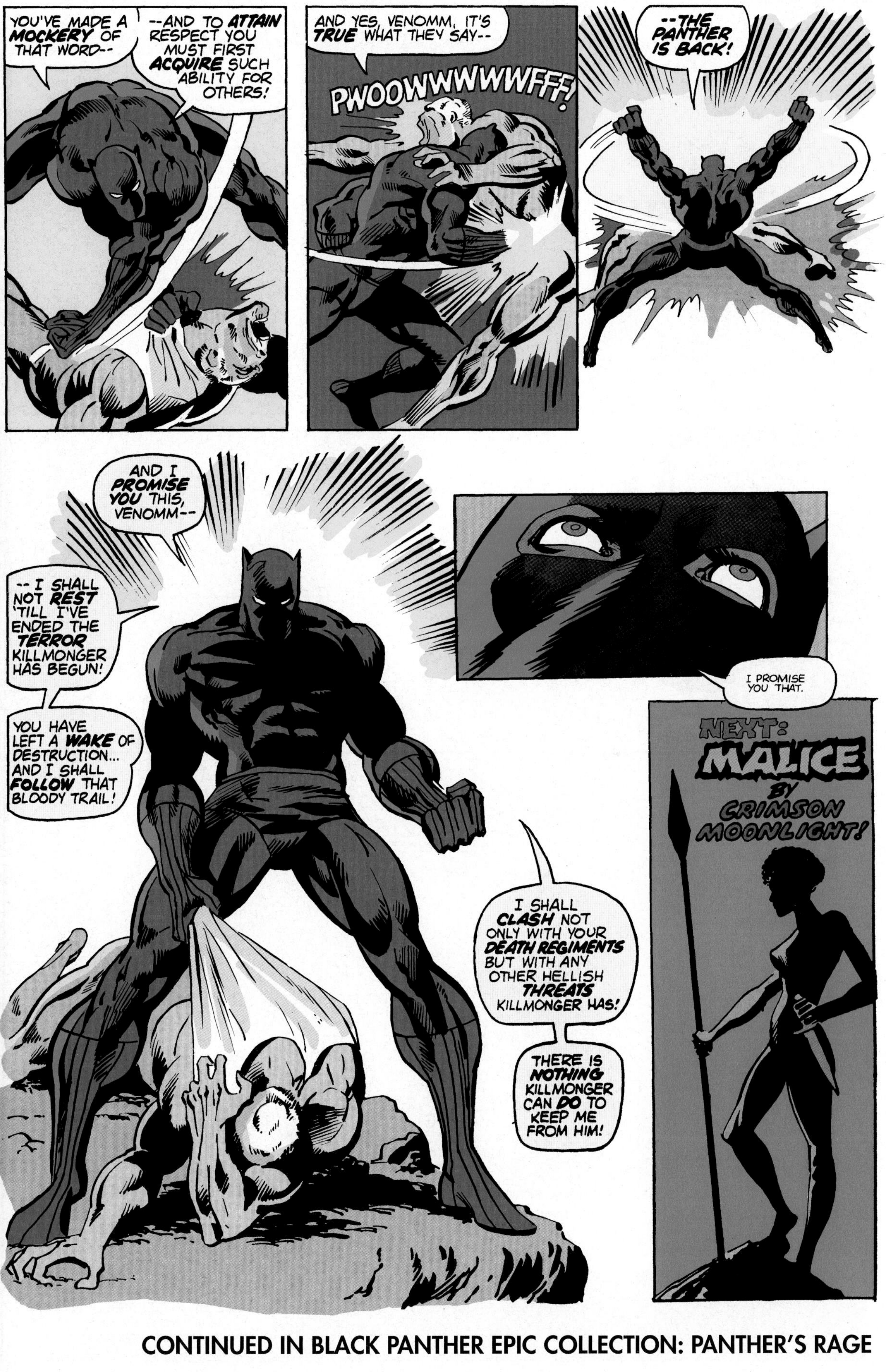
YOU'VE MADE A MOCKERY OF THAT WORD--
--AND TO ATTAIN RESPECT YOU MUST FIRST ACQUIRE SUCH ABILITY FOR OTHERS!
AND YES, VENOMM, IT'S TRUE WHAT THEY SAY--
PWOOWWWWWFFF!
--THE PANTHER IS BACK!
AND I PROMISE YOU THIS, VENOMM--
--I SHALL NOT REST 'TILL I'VE ENDED THE TERROR KILLMONGER HAS BEGUN!
YOU HAVE LEFT A WAKE OF DESTRUCTION... AND I SHALL FOLLOW THAT BLOODY TRAIL!
I SHALL CLASH NOT ONLY WITH YOUR DEATH REGIMENTS BUT WITH ANY OTHER HELLISH THREATS KILLMONGER HAS!
THERE IS NOTHING KILLMONGER CAN DO TO KEEP ME FROM HIM!
I PROMISE YOU THAT.
NEXT: MALICE BY CRIMSON MOONLIGHT!

CONTINUED IN BLACK PANTHER EPIC COLLECTION: PANTHER'S RAGE

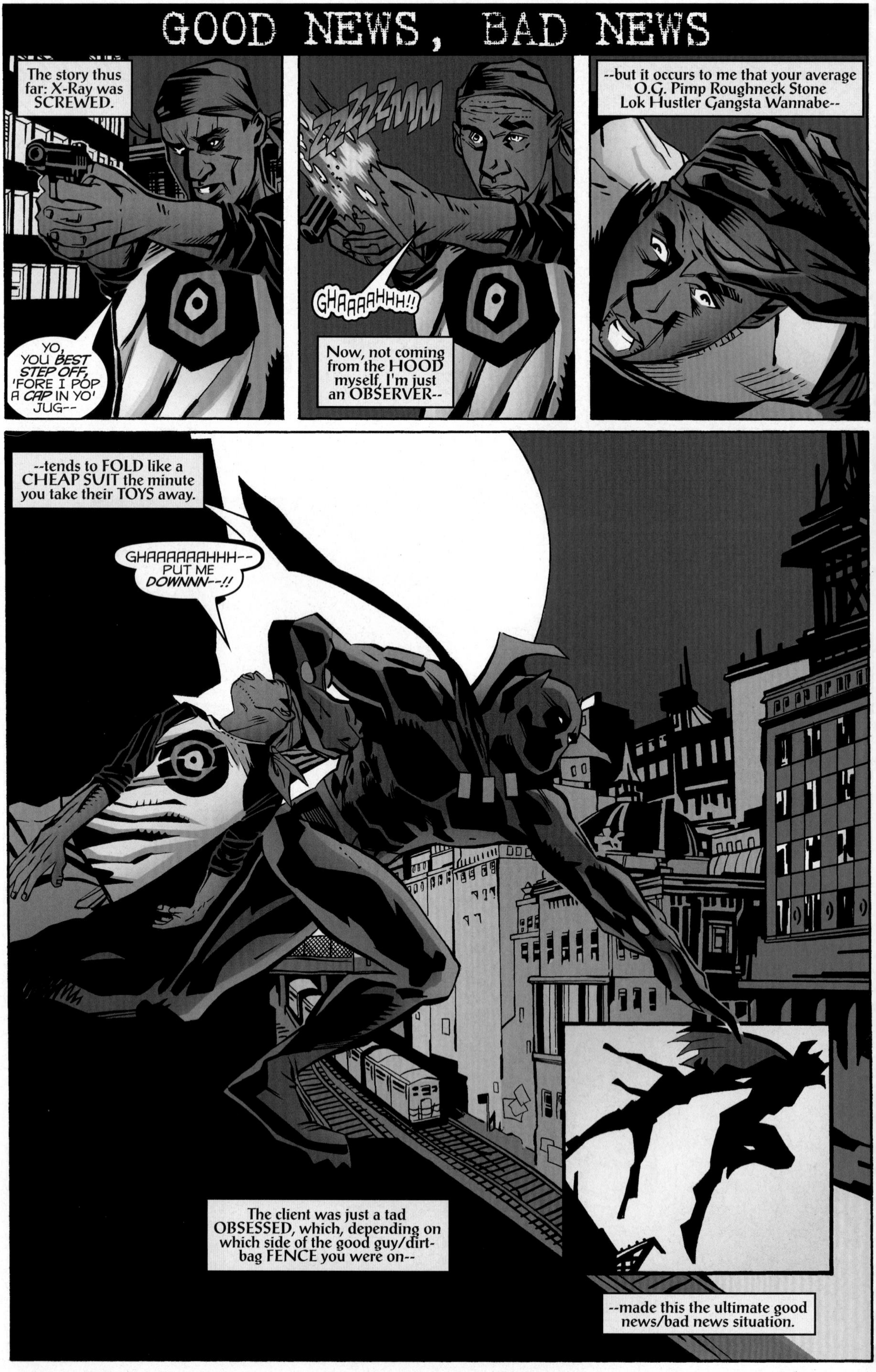

GOOD NEWS, BAD NEWS
The story thus far: X-Ray was SCREWED.
YO, YOU BEST STEP OFF, 'FORE I POP A CAP IN YO' JUG--
ZZZZZZMM
GHAAAAHHH!!
Now, not coming from the HOOD myself, I'm just an OBSERVER--
--but it occurs to me that your average O.G. Pimp Roughneck Stone Lok Hustler Gangsta Wannabe--
--tends to FOLD like a CHEAP SUIT the minute you take their TOYS away.
GHAAAAAAHHH-- PUT ME DOWNNN--!!
The client was just a tad OBSESSED, which, depending on which side of the good guy/dirt-bag FENCE you were on--
--made this the ultimate good news/bad news situation.

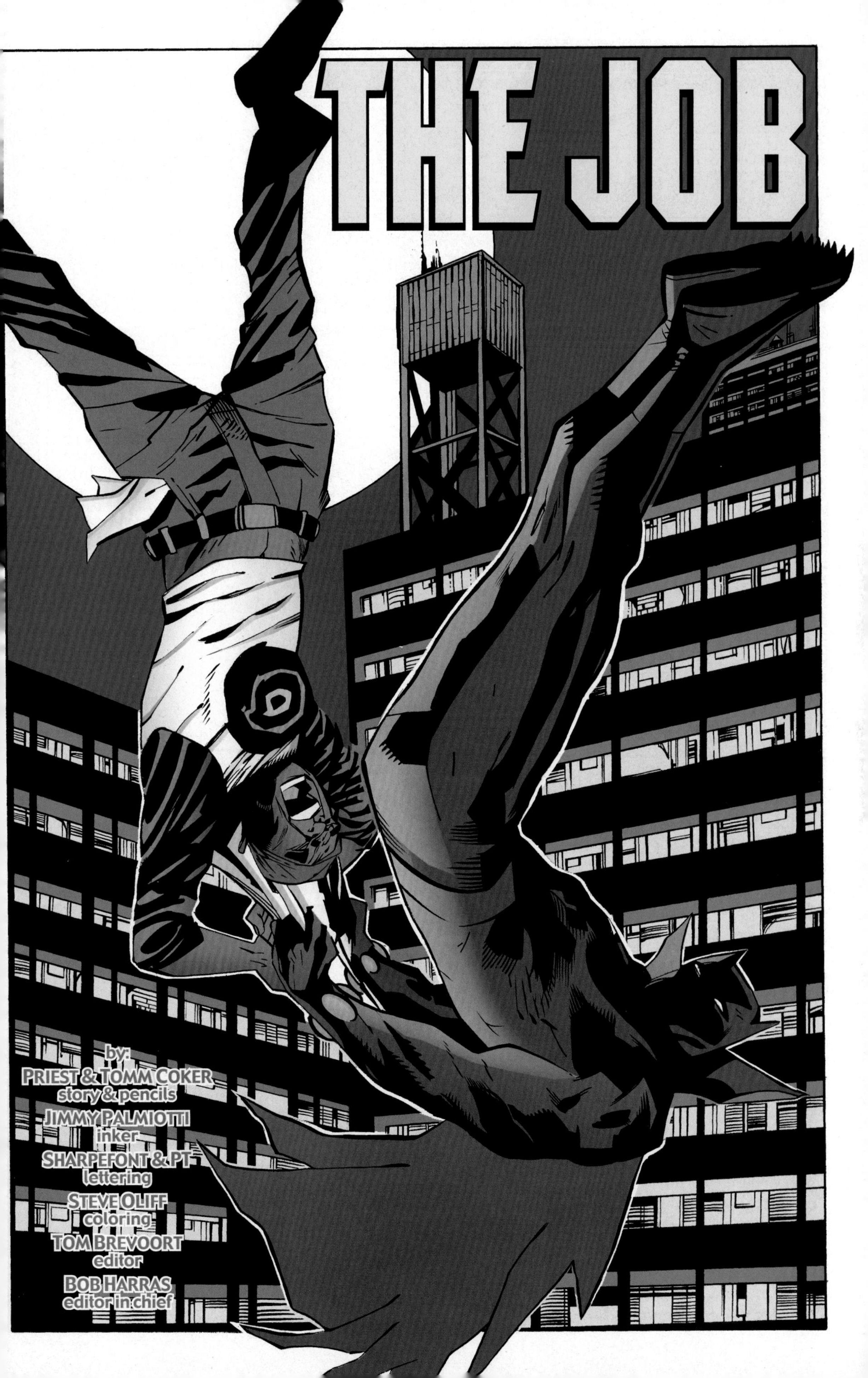
THE JOB
by:
PRIEST & TOMM COKER
story & pencils
JIMMY PALMIOTTI
inker
SHARPEFONT & PT
lettering
STEVE OLIFF
coloring
TOM BREVOORT
editor
BOB HARRAS
editor in chief

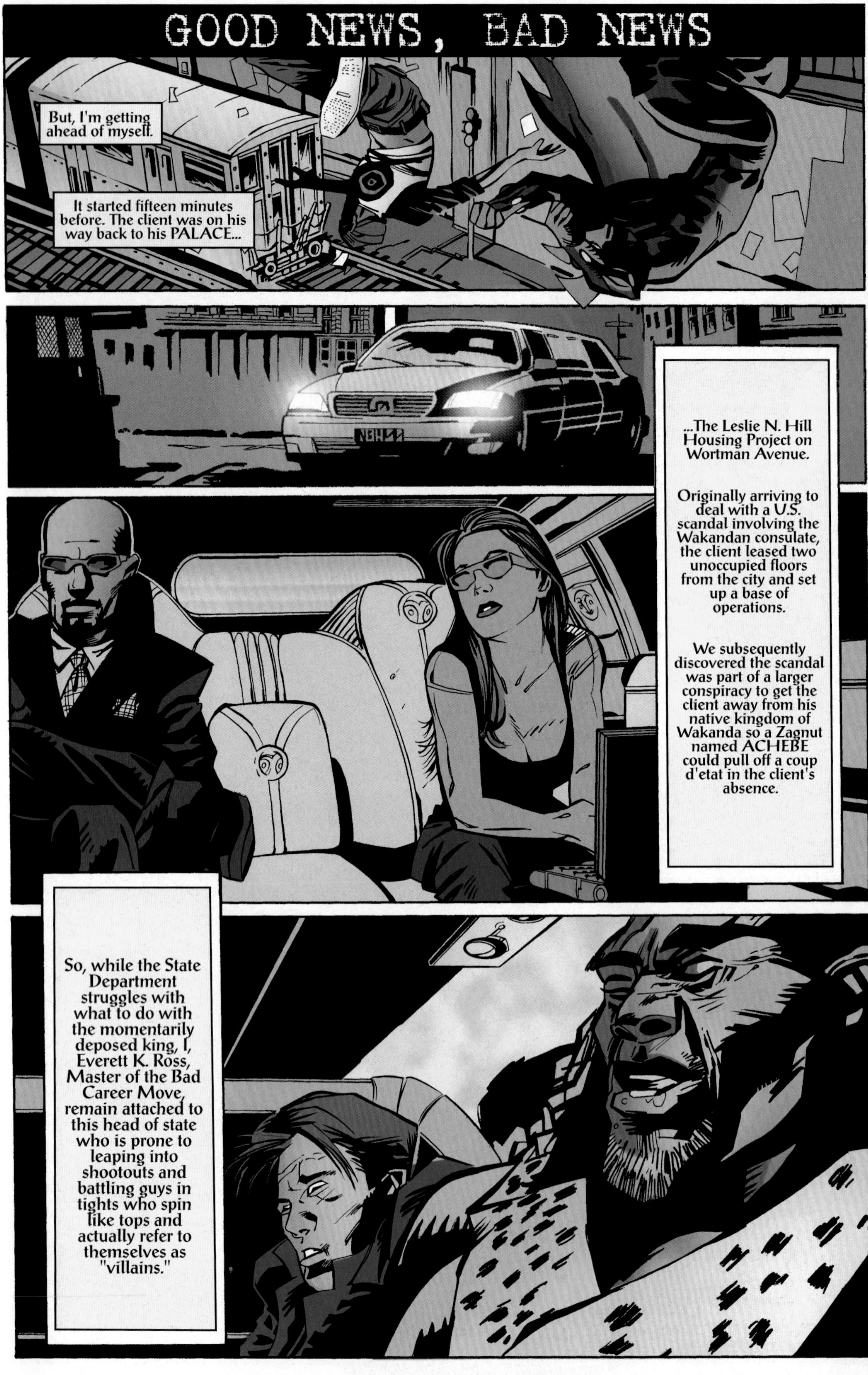
GOOD NEWS, BAD NEWS
But, I'm getting ahead of myself.
It started fifteen minutes before. The client was on his way back to his PALACE...
...The Leslie N. Hill Housing Project on Wortman Avenue.
Originally arriving to deal with a U.S. scandal involving the Wakandan consulate, the client leased two unoccupied floors from the city and set up a base of operations.
We subsequently discovered the scandal was part of a larger conspiracy to get the client away from his native kingdom of Wakanda so a Zagnut named ACHEBE could pull off a coup d'etat in the client's absence.
So, while the State Department struggles with what to do with the momentarily deposed king, I, Everett K. Ross, Master of the Bad Career Move, remain attached to this head of state who is prone to leaping into shootouts and battling guys in tights who spin like tops and actually refer to themselves as "villains."

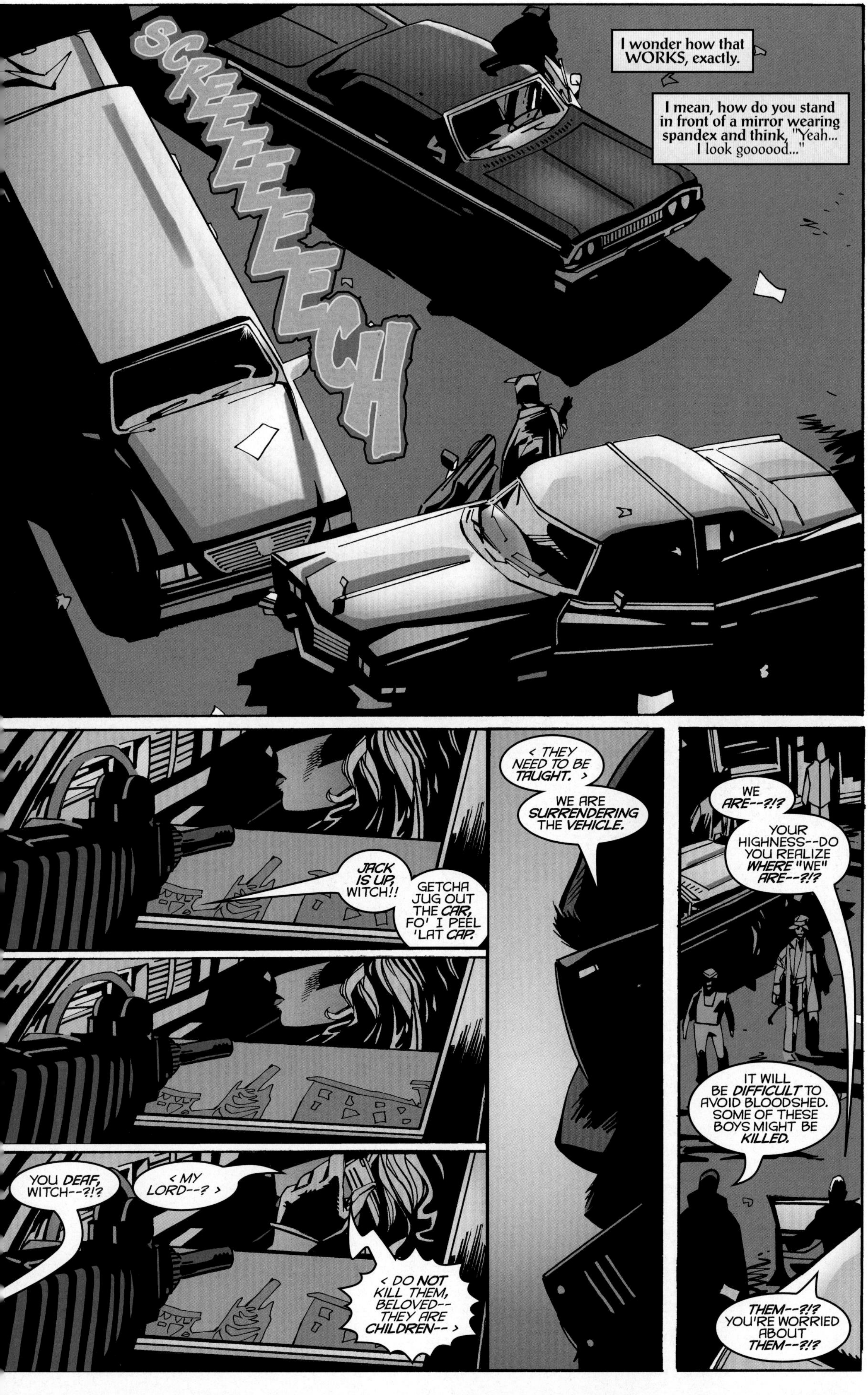
I wonder how that WORKS, exactly.
I mean, how do you stand in front of a mirror wearing spandex and think, "Yeah... I look goooood..."
SCREEEEEECH
JACK IS UP, WITCH!!
GETCHA JUG OUT THE CAR, FO' I PEEL 'LAT CAP.
YOU DEAF, WITCH--?!?
< MY LORD--? >
< DO NOT KILL THEM, BELOVED-- THEY ARE CHILDREN-- >
< THEY NEED TO BE TAUGHT. >
WE ARE SURRENDERING THE VEHICLE.
WE ARE--?!?
YOUR HIGHNESS--DO YOU REALIZE WHERE "WE" ARE--?!?
IT WILL BE DIFFICULT TO AVOID BLOODSHED. SOME OF THESE BOYS MIGHT BE KILLED.
THEM--?!? YOU'RE WORRIED ABOUT THEM--?!?

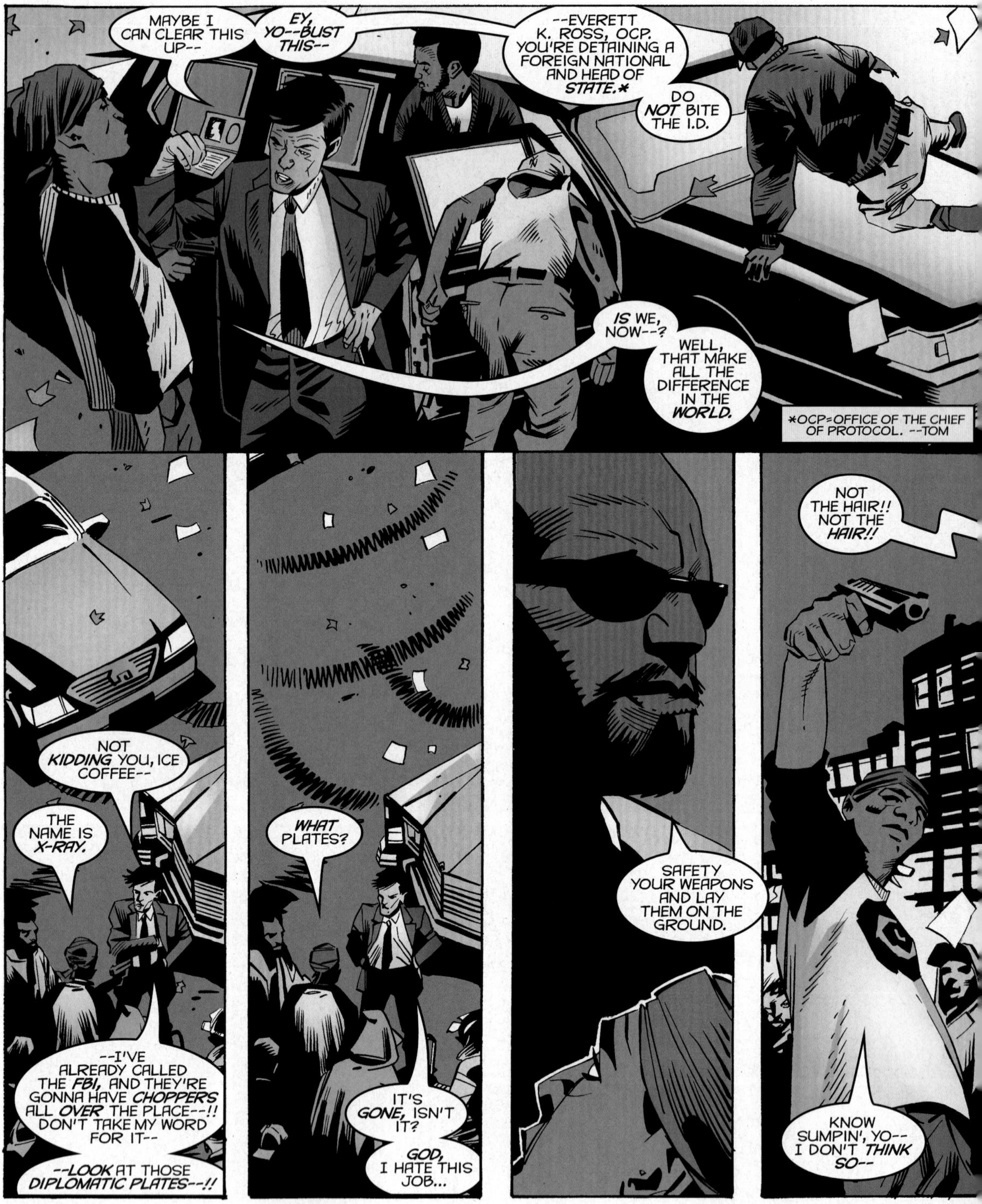
MAYBE I CAN CLEAR THIS UP--
EY, YO--BUST THIS--
--EVERETT K. ROSS, OCP. YOU'RE DETAINING A FOREIGN NATIONAL AND HEAD OF STATE.*
DO NOT BITE THE I.D.
IS WE, NOW--?
WELL, THAT MAKE ALL THE DIFFERENCE IN THE WORLD.
*OCP=OFFICE OF THE CHIEF OF PROTOCOL. --TOM
NOT KIDDING YOU, ICE COFFEE--
THE NAME IS X-RAY.
--I'VE ALREADY CALLED THE FBI, AND THEY'RE GONNA HAVE CHOPPERS ALL OVER THE PLACE--!! DON'T TAKE MY WORD FOR IT--
--LOOK AT THOSE DIPLOMATIC PLATES--!!
WHAT PLATES?
IT'S GONE, ISN'T IT?
GOD, I HATE THIS JOB...
SAFETY YOUR WEAPONS AND LAY THEM ON THE GROUND.
NOT THE HAIR!! NOT THE HAIR!!
KNOW SUMPIN', YO-- I DON'T THINK SO--

Suddenly, without making a sound, the biggest, brightest flashbulb I'd ever seen went off.

With my luck...I figured it was ALIENS...

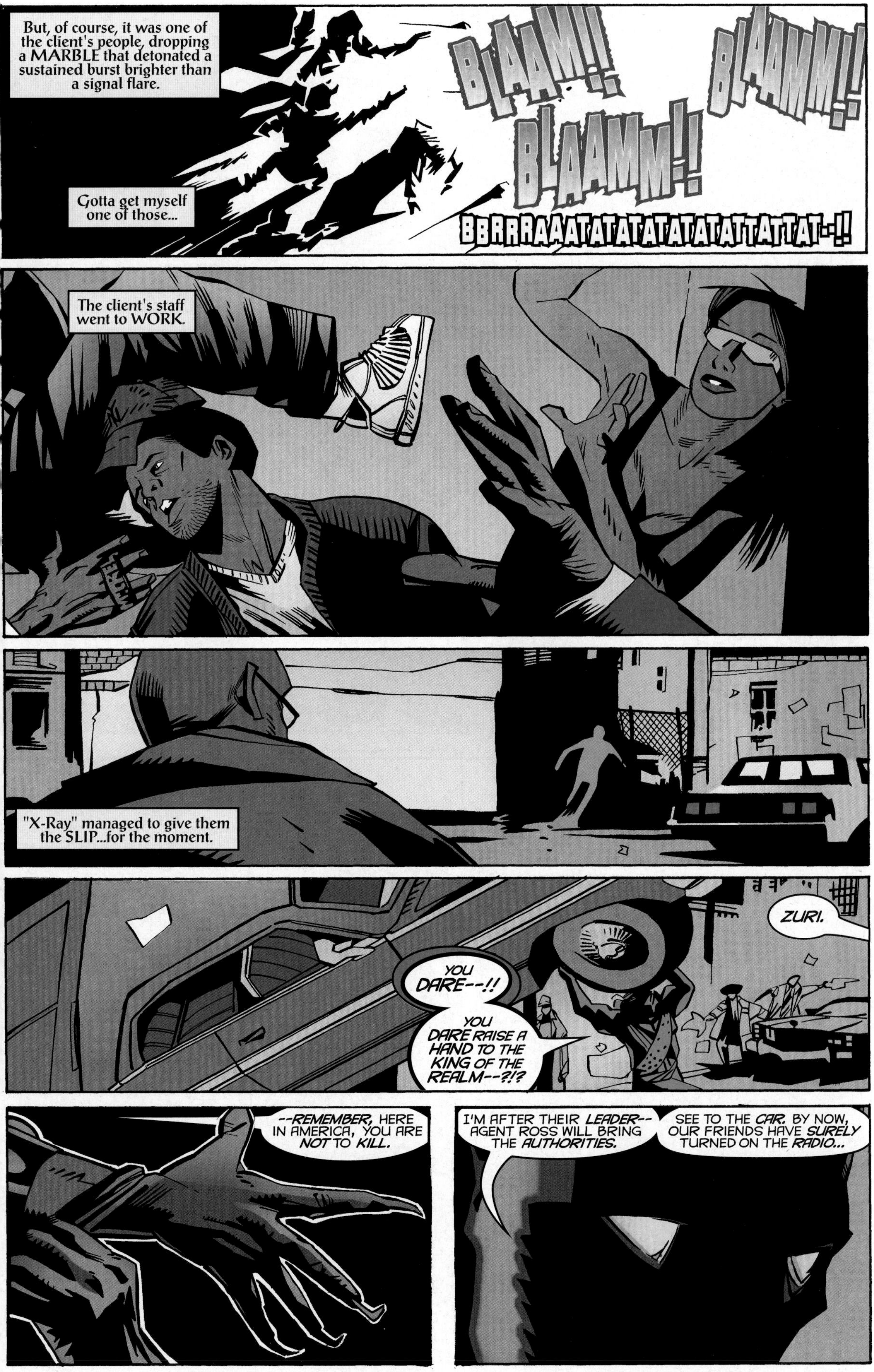
But, of course, it was one of the client's people, dropping a MARBLE that detonated a sustained burst brighter than a signal flare.
BLAAMM!!
BLAAMM!!
BLAAMM!!
Gotta get myself one of those...
BBRRRAAATATATATATATATTATTAT--!!
The client's staff went to WORK.
"X-Ray" managed to give them the SLIP...for the moment.
ZURI.
YOU DARE--!!
YOU DARE RAISE A HAND TO THE KING OF THE REALM--?!?
--REMEMBER, HERE IN AMERICA, YOU ARE NOT TO KILL.
I'M AFTER THEIR LEADER-- AGENT ROSS WILL BRING THE AUTHORITIES.
SEE TO THE CAR. BY NOW, OUR FRIENDS HAVE SURELY TURNED ON THE RADIO...

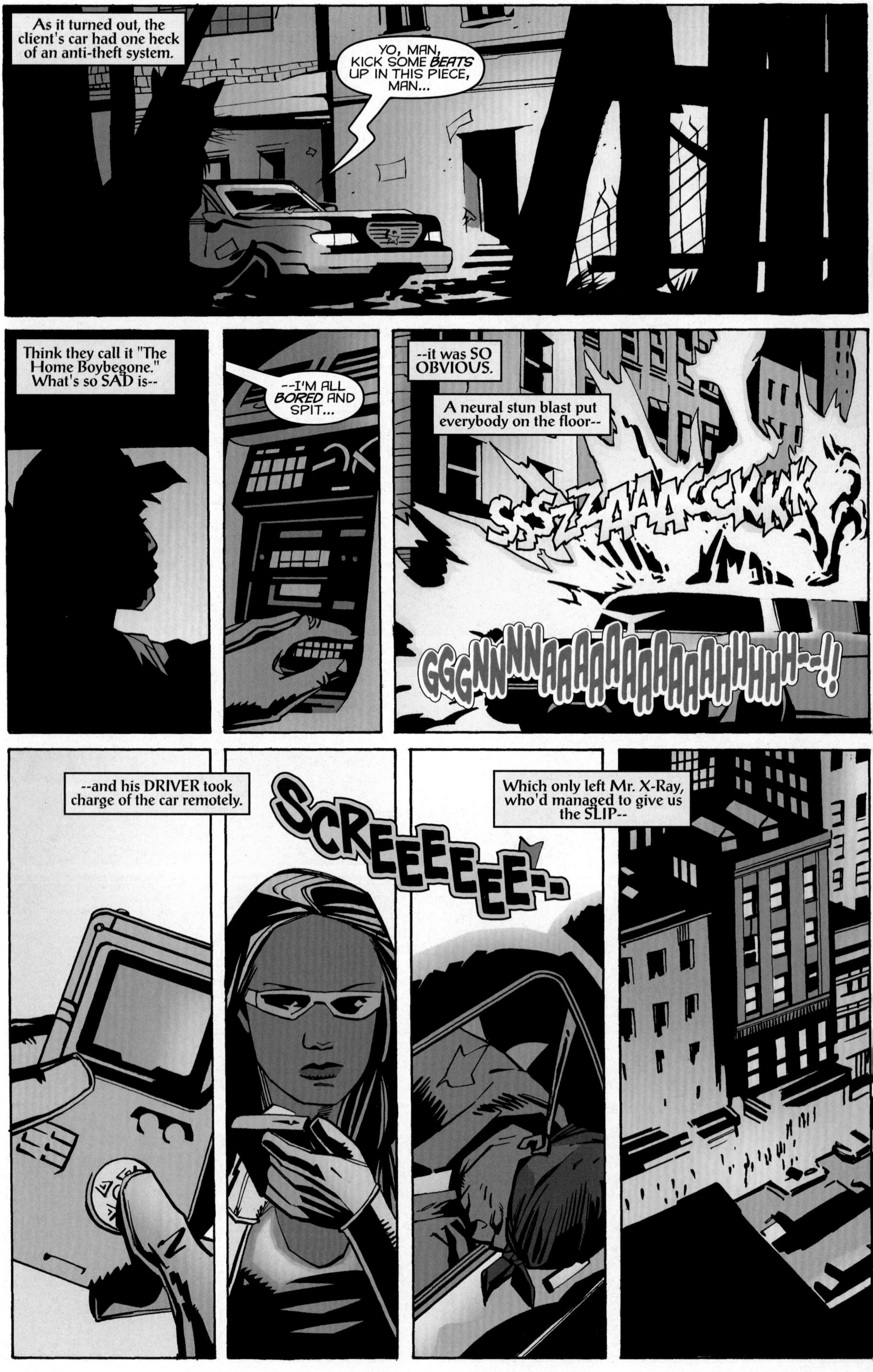

As it turned out, the client's car had one heck of an anti-theft system.
YO, MAN, KICK SOME BEATS UP IN THIS PIECE, MAN...
Think they call it "The Home Boybegone." What's so SAD is--
--I'M ALL BORED AND SPIT...
--it was SO OBVIOUS.
A neural stun blast put everybody on the floor--
SSSZZAAACKKK
GGGNNNNAAAAAAAAAAAHHHHH--!!
--and his DRIVER took charge of the car remotely.
SCREEEEEEE--
Which only left Mr. X-Ray, who'd managed to give us the SLIP--

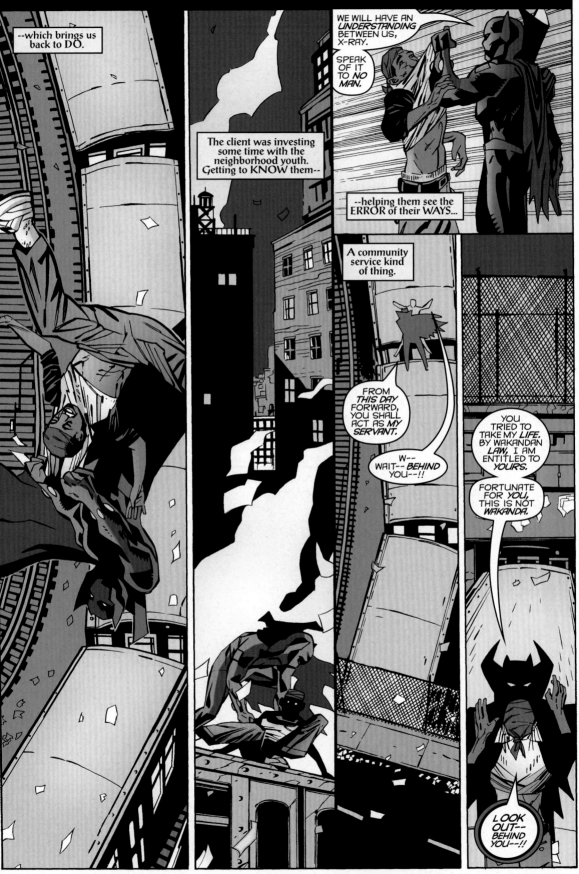

--which brings us back to DO.

The client was investing some time with the neighborhood youth. Getting to KNOW them--

WE WILL HAVE AN *UNDERSTANDING* BETWEEN US, X-RAY.

SPEAK OF IT TO *NO MAN.*

--helping them see the ERROR of their WAYS...

A community service kind of thing.

FROM *THIS DAY* FORWARD, YOU SHALL ACT AS *MY SERVANT.*

W-- WAIT-- *BEHIND* YOU--!!

YOU TRIED TO TAKE MY *LIFE.* BY WAKANDAN *LAW,* I AM ENTITLED TO *YOURS.*

FORTUNATE FOR *YOU,* THIS IS NOT *WAKANDA.*

LOOK OUT-- BEHIND YOU--!!

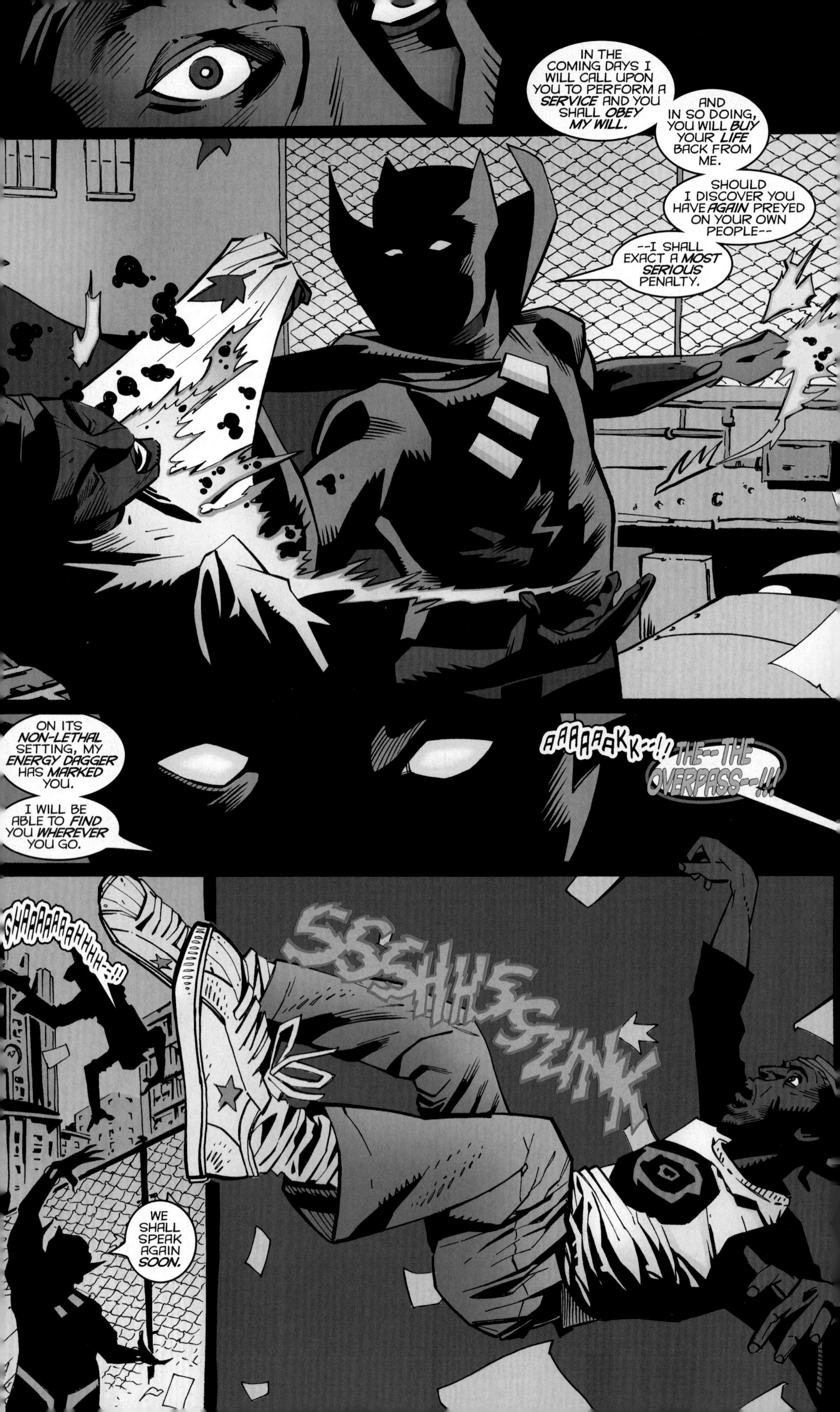

IN THE COMING DAYS I WILL CALL UPON YOU TO PERFORM A SERVICE AND YOU SHALL OBEY MY WILL.
AND IN SO DOING, YOU WILL BUY YOUR LIFE BACK FROM ME.
SHOULD I DISCOVER YOU HAVE AGAIN PREYED ON YOUR OWN PEOPLE--
--I SHALL EXACT A MOST SERIOUS PENALTY.
ON ITS NON-LETHAL SETTING, MY ENERGY DAGGER HAS MARKED YOU.
I WILL BE ABLE TO FIND YOU WHEREVER YOU GO.
AAAAAAAKK--!! THE-- THE OVERPASS--!!!
SSSHHSSZINK
SHAAAAAAAHHHH--!!
WE SHALL SPEAK AGAIN SOON.

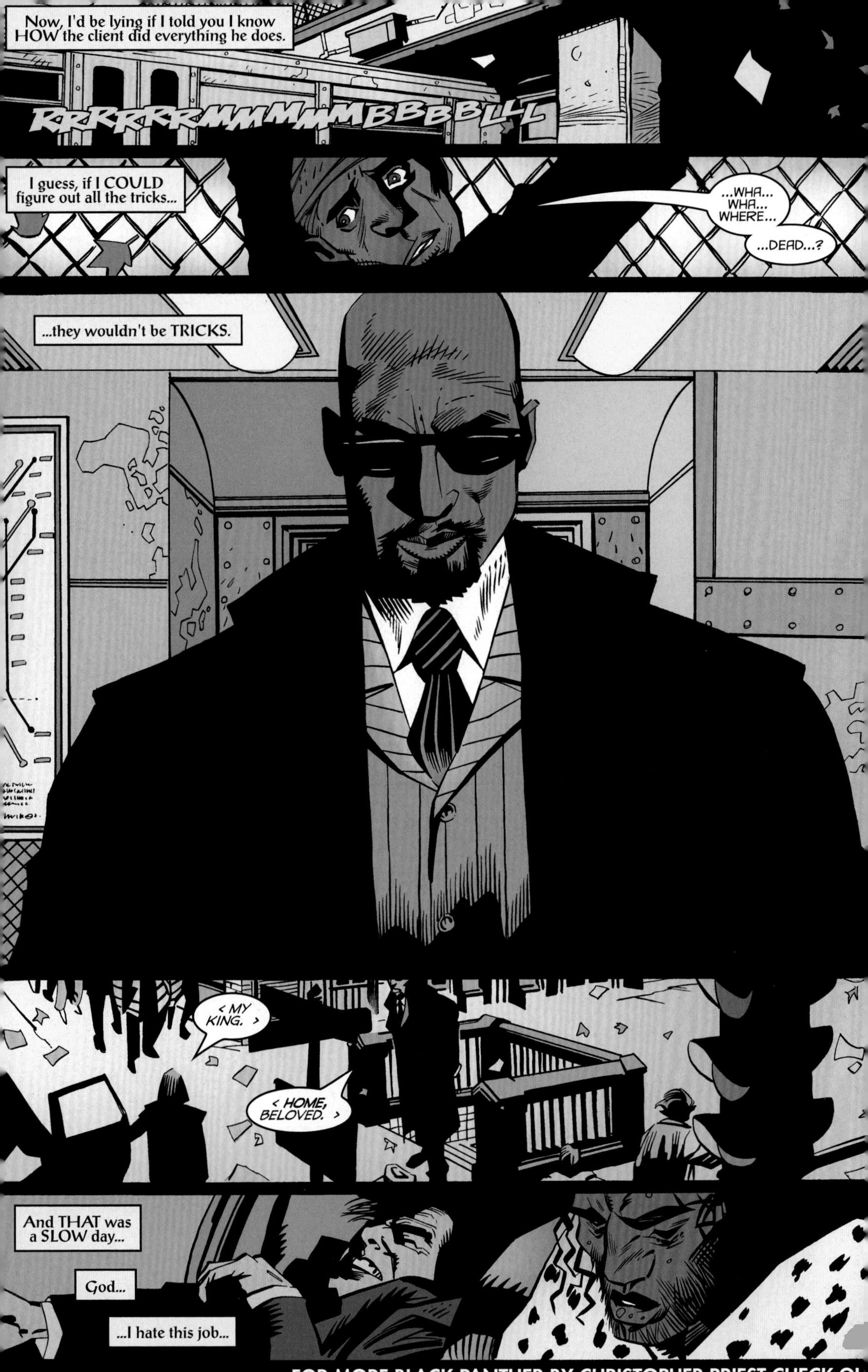

Now, I'd be lying if I told you I know HOW the client did everything he does.
RRRRRRMMMMMMBBBBLLL
I guess, if I COULD figure out all the tricks...
...WHA... WHA... WHERE...
...DEAD...?
...they wouldn't be TRICKS.
< MY KING. >
< HOME, BELOVED. >
And THAT was a SLOW day...
God...
...I hate this job...

HOLLYWOOD HEAVYWEIGHT REGINALD HUDLIN JOINS ARTIST JOHN ROMITA JR. TO RETELL THE BLACK PANTHER'S ORIGIN IN CINEMATIC SCOPE WITH SOCIAL SATIRE AND ALL-OUT ACTION. WHILE A TEAM OF SUPER-POWERED MERCENARIES PREPARES 'S ASSAULT ON WAKANDA, A CONTEST IS UNDER WAY IN THAT WARRIOR KINGDOM: WHO WILL BE THE NEXT BLACK PANTHER?

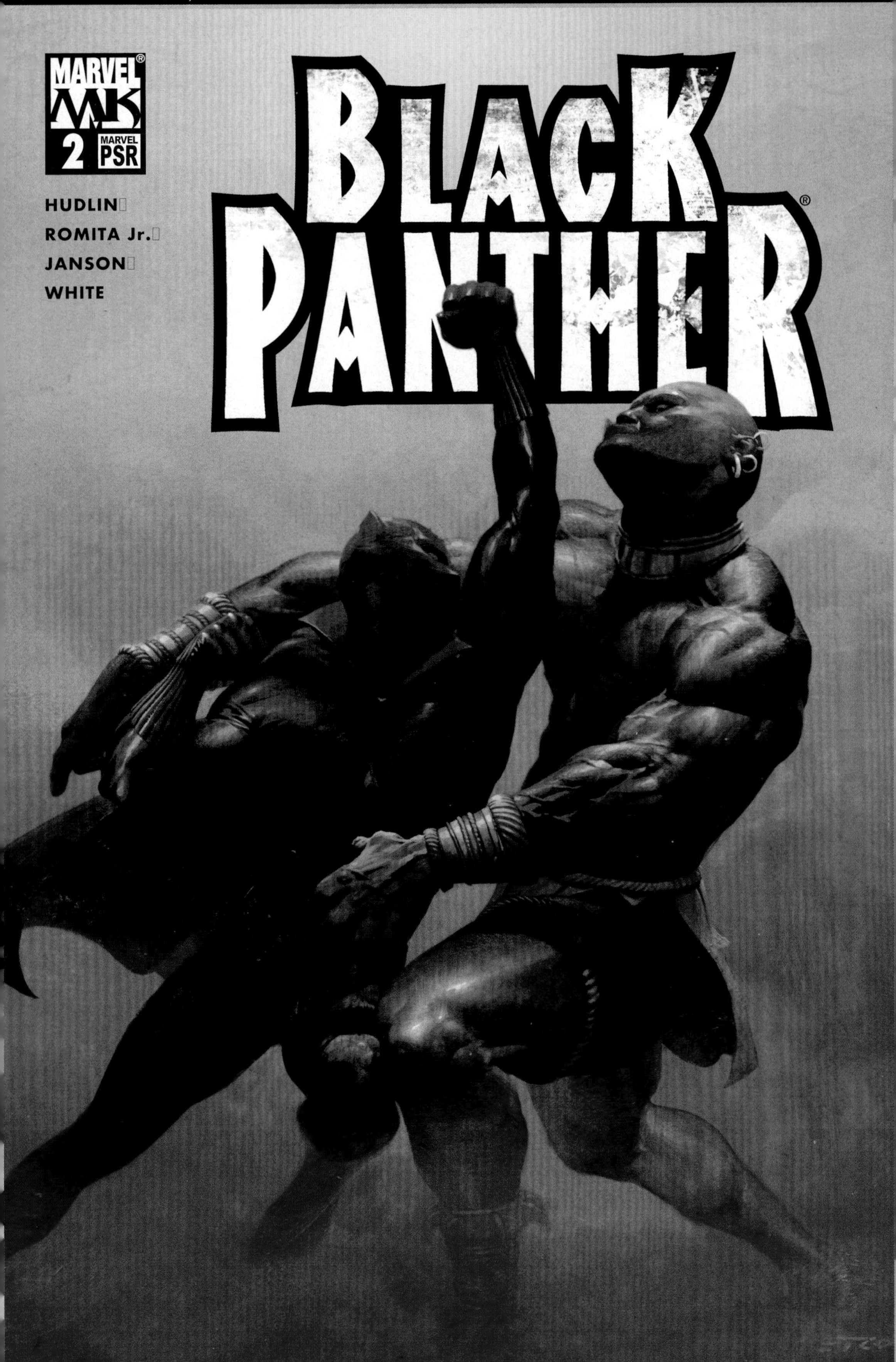
MARVEL MK
2 MARVEL PSR
HUDLIN
ROMITA Jr.
JANSON
WHITE
BLACK PANTHER®

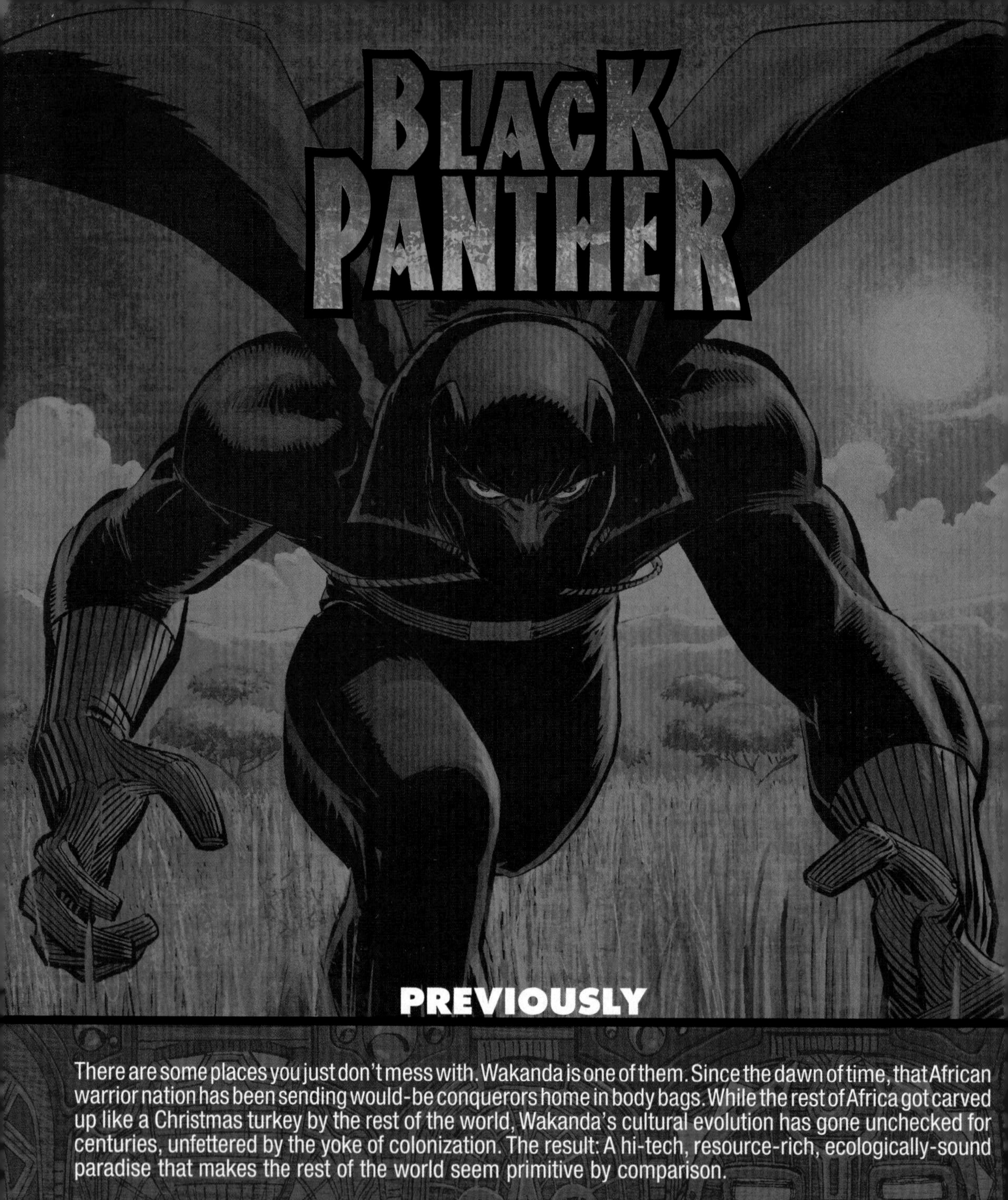
BLACK PANTHER

PREVIOUSLY

There are some places you just don't mess with. Wakanda is one of them. Since the dawn of time, that African warrior nation has been sending would-be conquerors home in body bags. While the rest of Africa got carved up like a Christmas turkey by the rest of the world, Wakanda's cultural evolution has gone unchecked for centuries, unfettered by the yoke of colonization. The result: A hi-tech, resource-rich, ecologically-sound paradise that makes the rest of the world seem primitive by comparison.

Ruling over all this is the Black Panther.

The Black Panther is more than just the embodiment of a warrior cult that's served as Wakanda's religious, political and military head since its inception. The Black Panther is the embodiment of the ideals of a people. Anyone who'd dare to make a move on Wakanda must go through him.

And that's exactly what someone intends to do. His name is Klaw, he's read the history books, and he knows exactly what he's getting himself into. Klaw is assembling a team to do what's never been done before.

To successfully invade Wakanda.

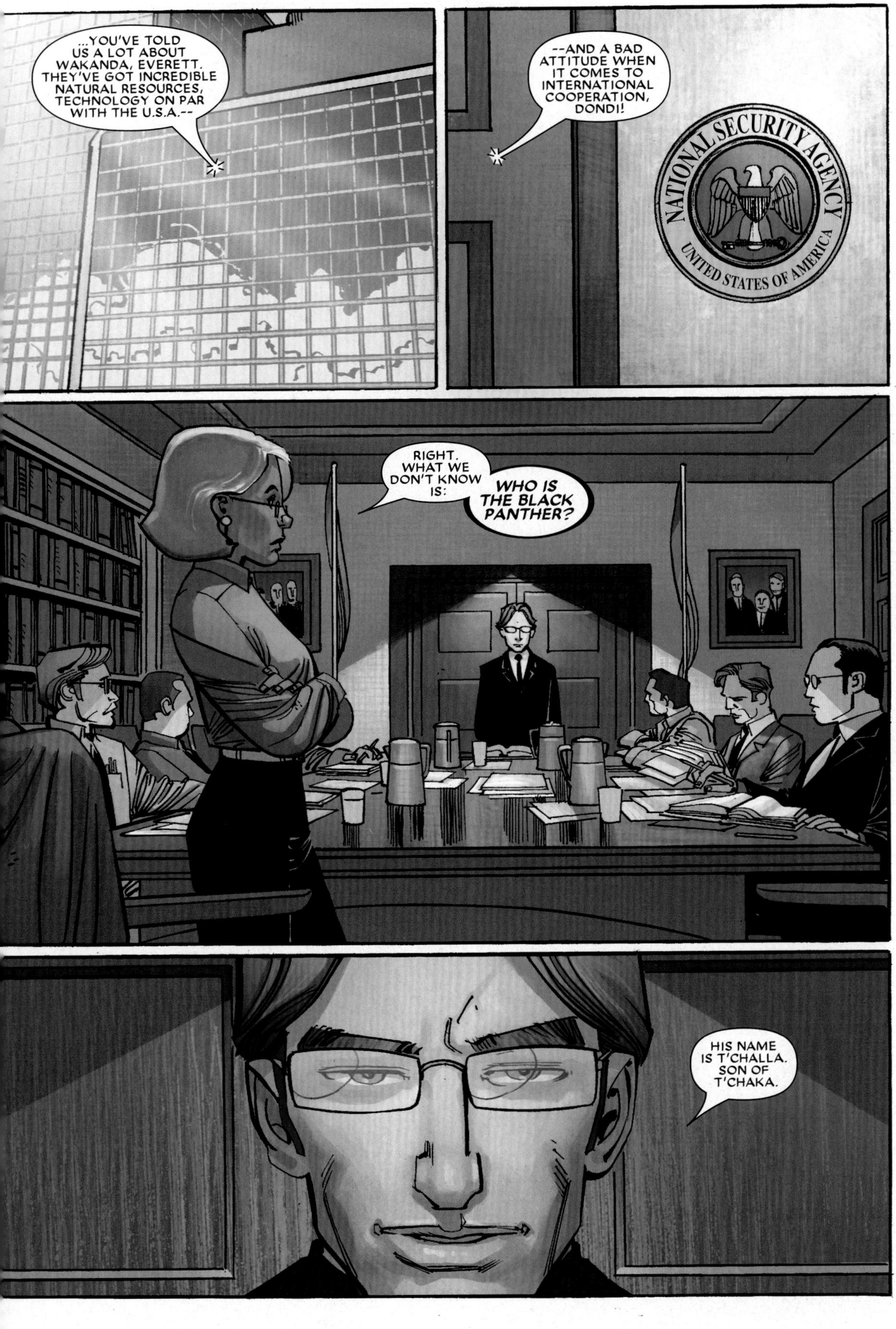
...YOU'VE TOLD US A LOT ABOUT WAKANDA, EVERETT. THEY'VE GOT INCREDIBLE NATURAL RESOURCES, TECHNOLOGY ON PAR WITH THE U.S.A.--
--AND A BAD ATTITUDE WHEN IT COMES TO INTERNATIONAL COOPERATION, DONDI!
NATIONAL SECURITY AGENCY
UNITED STATES OF AMERICA
RIGHT. WHAT WE DON'T KNOW IS: *WHO IS THE BLACK PANTHER?*
HIS NAME IS T'CHALLA. SON OF T'CHAKA.

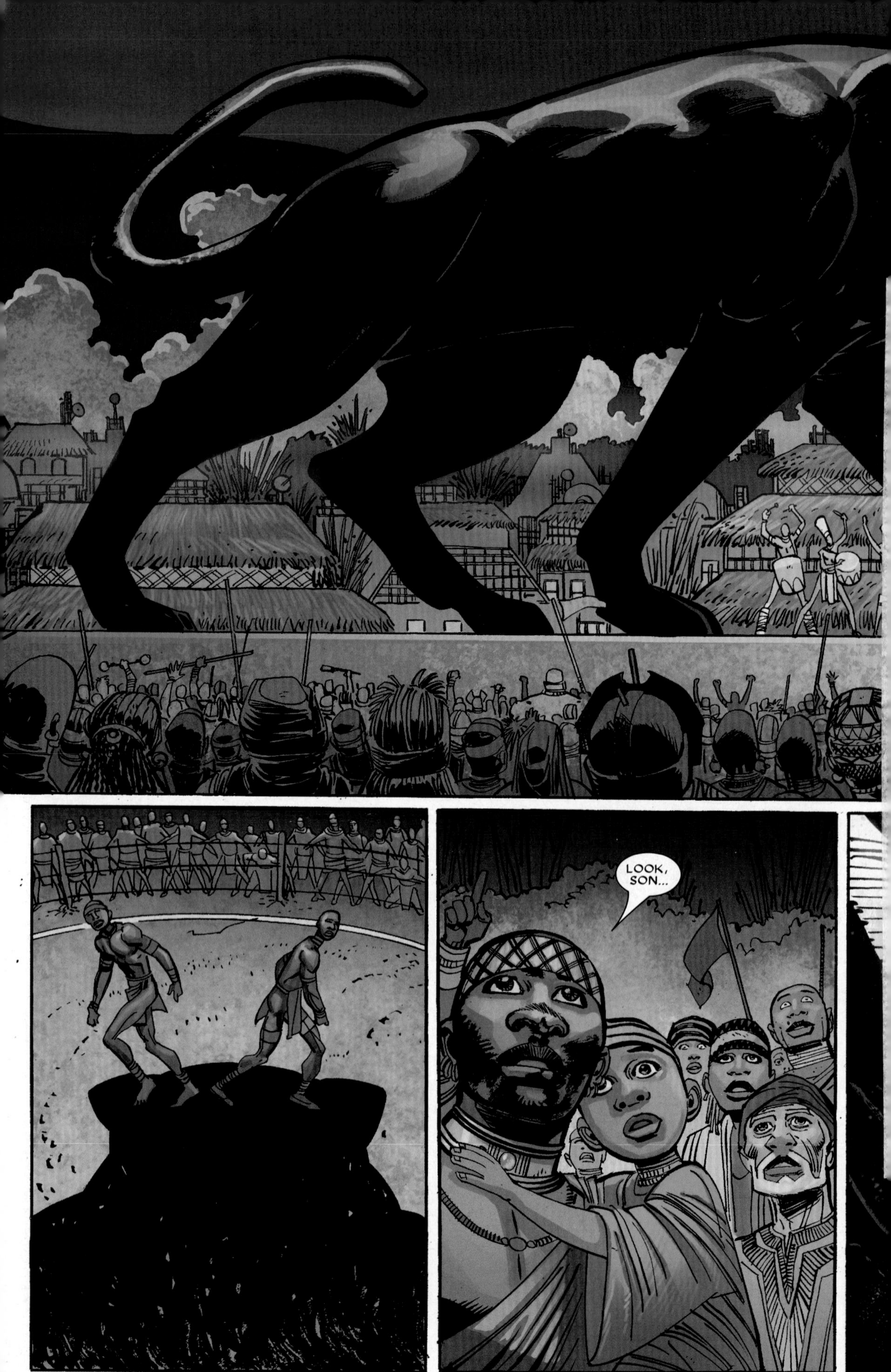
LOOK, SON...

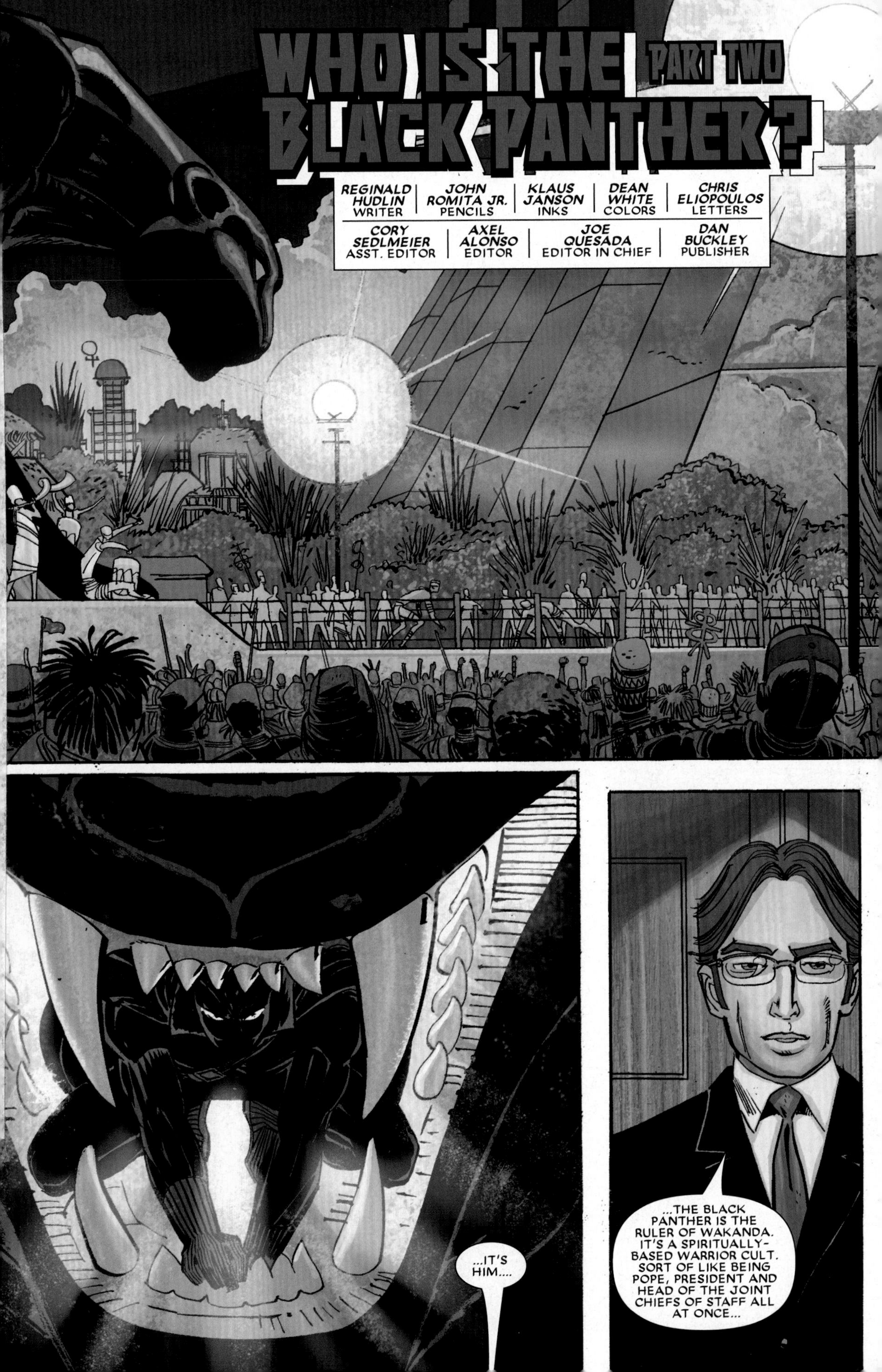

WHO IS THE BLACK PANTHER? PART TWO
REGINALD HUDLIN WRITER
JOHN ROMITA JR. PENCILS
KLAUS JANSON INKS
DEAN WHITE COLORS
CHRIS ELIOPOULOS LETTERS
CORY SEDLMEIER ASST. EDITOR
AXEL ALONSO EDITOR
JOE QUESADA EDITOR IN CHIEF
DAN BUCKLEY PUBLISHER
...IT'S HIM....
...THE BLACK PANTHER IS THE RULER OF WAKANDA. IT'S A SPIRITUALLY-BASED WARRIOR CULT. SORT OF LIKE BEING POPE, PRESIDENT AND HEAD OF THE JOINT CHIEFS OF STAFF ALL AT ONCE...

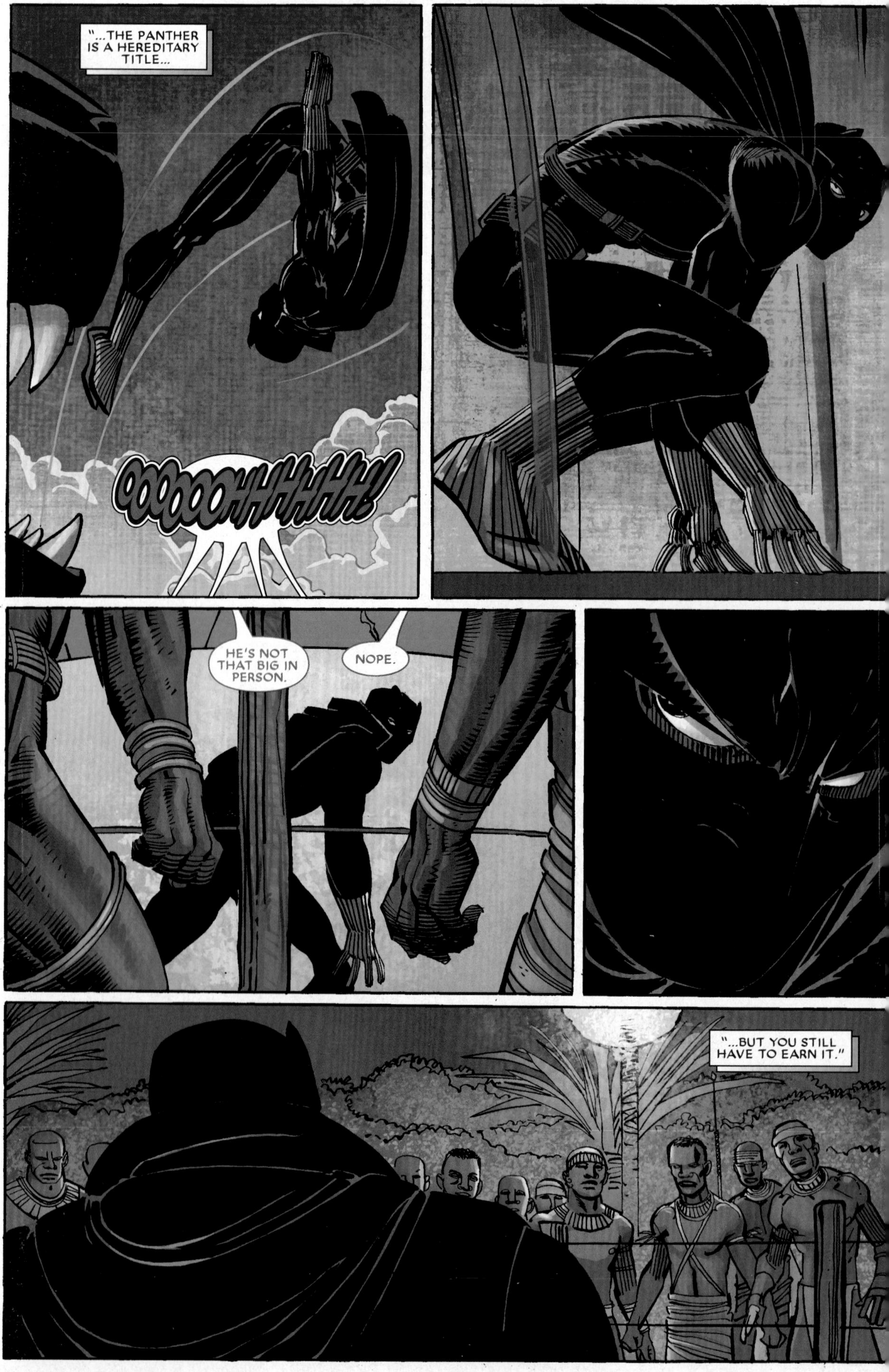
"...THE PANTHER IS A HEREDITARY TITLE...
OOOOOOOHHHHHHH!!
HE'S NOT THAT BIG IN PERSON.
NOPE.
"...BUT YOU STILL HAVE TO EARN IT."

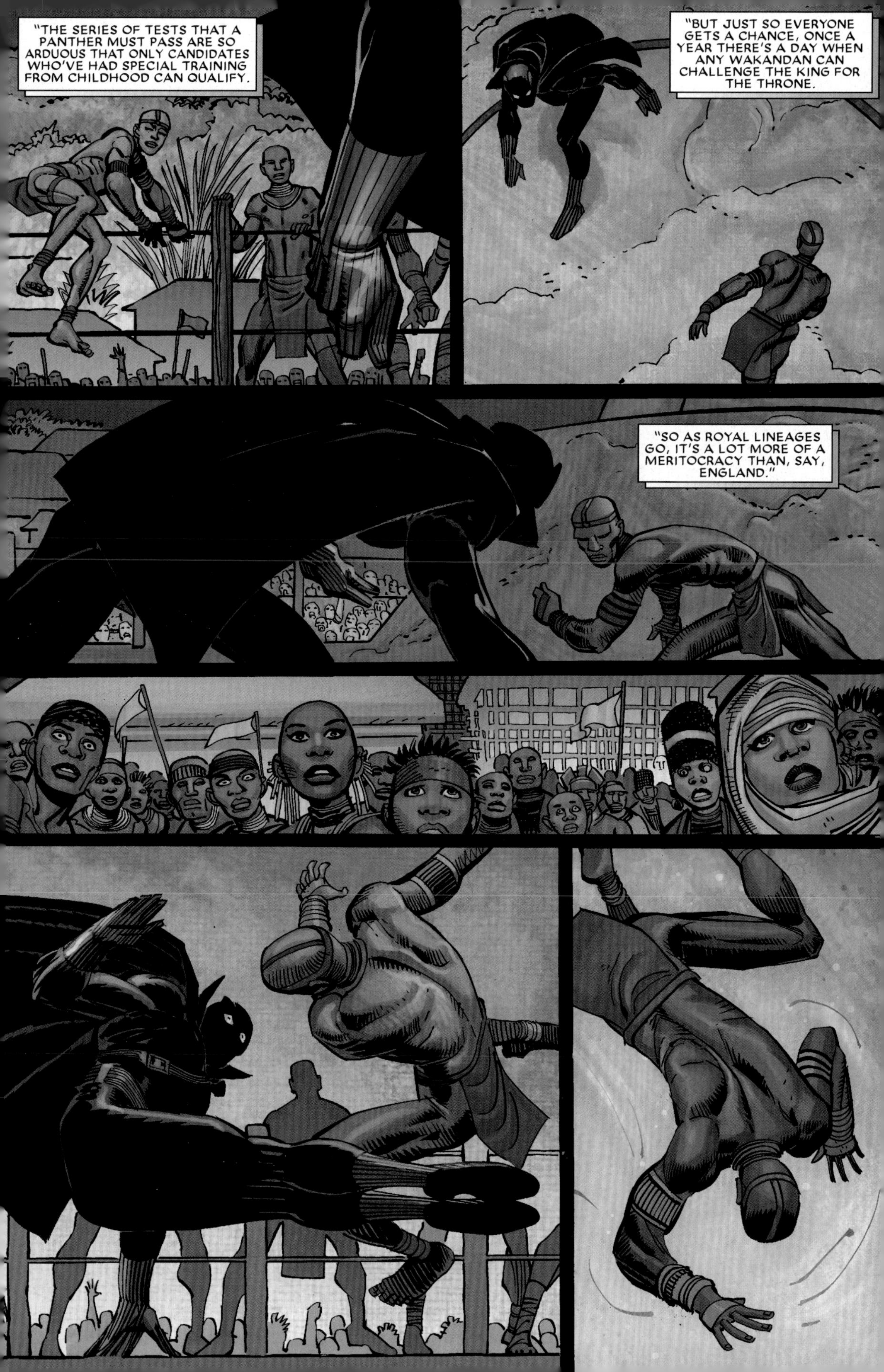
"THE SERIES OF TESTS THAT A PANTHER MUST PASS ARE SO ARDUOUS THAT ONLY CANDIDATES WHO'VE HAD SPECIAL TRAINING FROM CHILDHOOD CAN QUALIFY.
"BUT JUST SO EVERYONE GETS A CHANCE, ONCE A YEAR THERE'S A DAY WHEN ANY WAKANDAN CAN CHALLENGE THE KING FOR THE THRONE.
"SO AS ROYAL LINEAGES GO, IT'S A LOT MORE OF A MERITOCRACY THAN, SAY, ENGLAND."

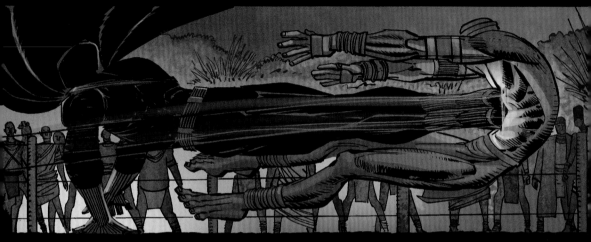

OW! WATCH WHERE YOU LAND!

OOOOOOOOOH...

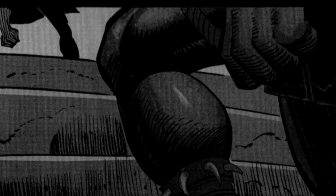

THAT'S A BIG ONE, K'TYAH.

TRULY, M'SHULA. WITH THOSE MUSCLES HE MUST BE A MINER.

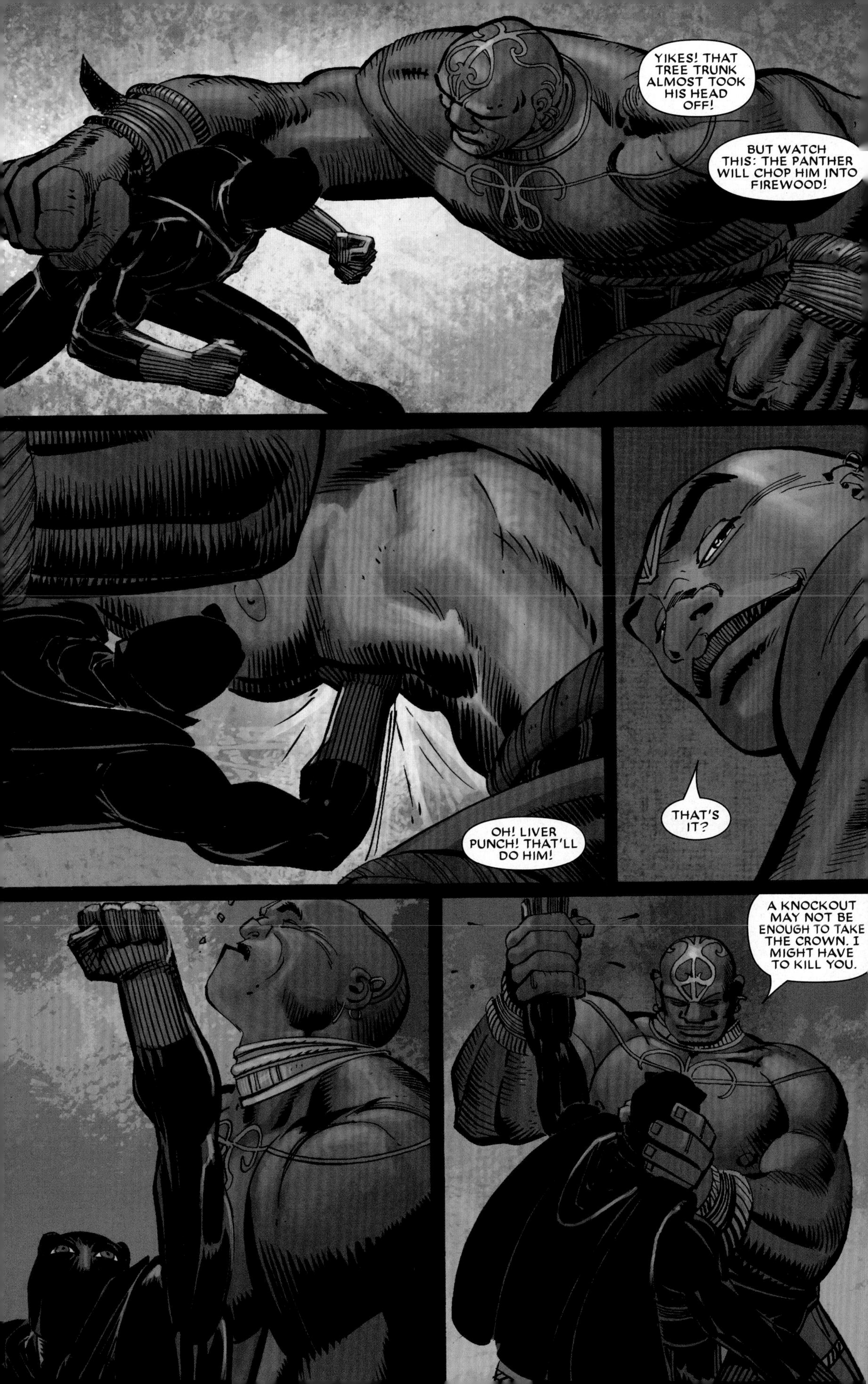
YIKES! THAT TREE TRUNK ALMOST TOOK HIS HEAD OFF!
BUT WATCH THIS: THE PANTHER WILL CHOP HIM INTO FIREWOOD!
OH! LIVER PUNCH! THAT'LL DO HIM!
THAT'S IT?
A KNOCKOUT MAY NOT BE ENOUGH TO TAKE THE CROWN. I MIGHT HAVE TO KILL YOU.

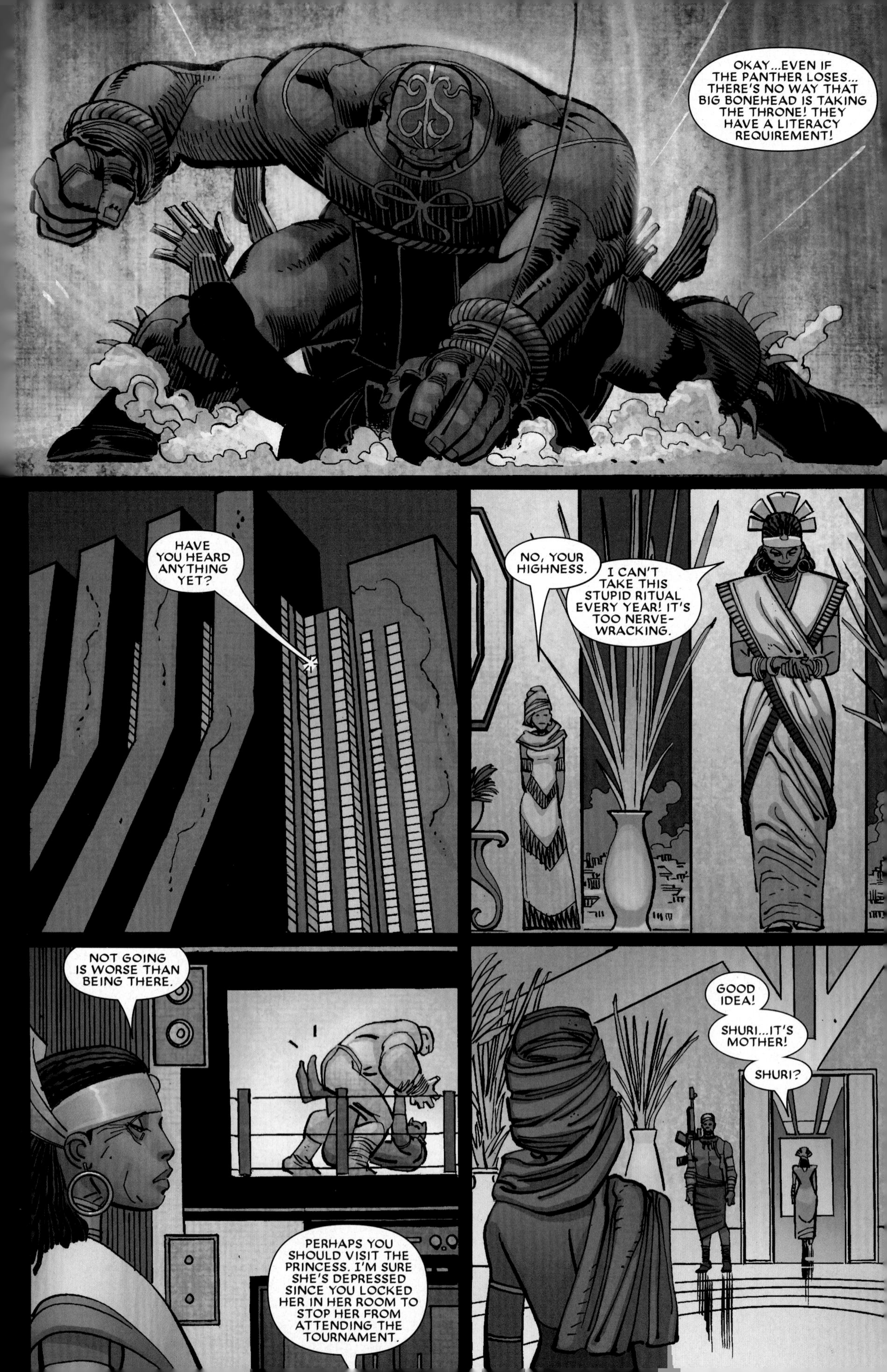
OKAY...EVEN IF THE PANTHER LOSES... THERE'S NO WAY THAT BIG BONEHEAD IS TAKING THE THRONE! THEY HAVE A LITERACY REQUIREMENT!
HAVE YOU HEARD ANYTHING YET?
NO, YOUR HIGHNESS.
I CAN'T TAKE THIS STUPID RITUAL EVERY YEAR! IT'S TOO NERVE-WRACKING.
NOT GOING IS WORSE THAN BEING THERE.
PERHAPS YOU SHOULD VISIT THE PRINCESS. I'M SURE SHE'S DEPRESSED SINCE YOU LOCKED HER IN HER ROOM TO STOP HER FROM ATTENDING THE TOURNAMENT.
GOOD IDEA!
SHURI...IT'S MOTHER!
SHURI?

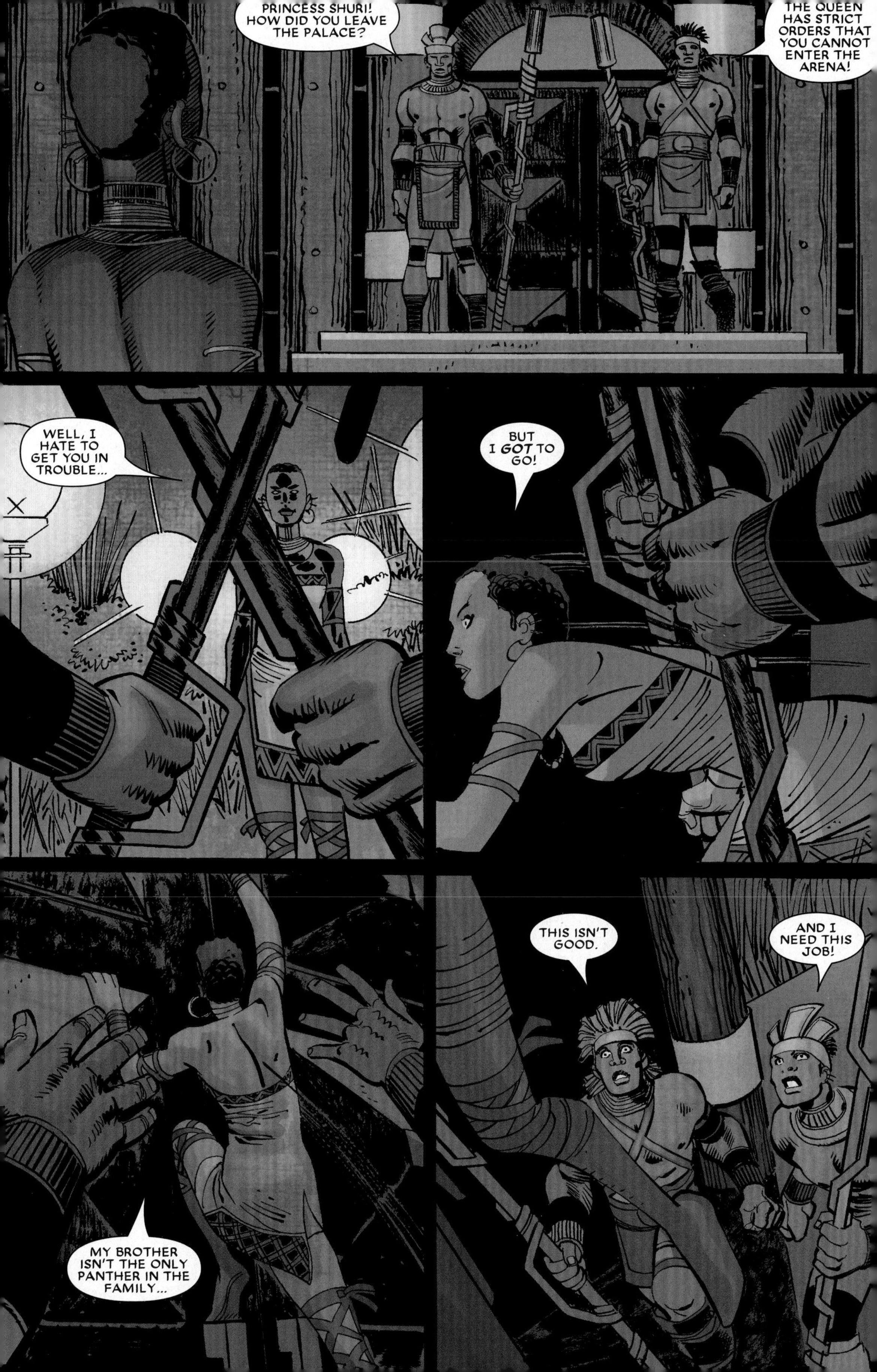
PRINCESS SHURI! HOW DID YOU LEAVE THE PALACE?
THE QUEEN HAS STRICT ORDERS THAT YOU CANNOT ENTER THE ARENA!
WELL, I HATE TO GET YOU IN TROUBLE...
BUT I GOT TO GO!
MY BROTHER ISN'T THE ONLY PANTHER IN THE FAMILY...
THIS ISN'T GOOD.
AND I NEED THIS JOB!

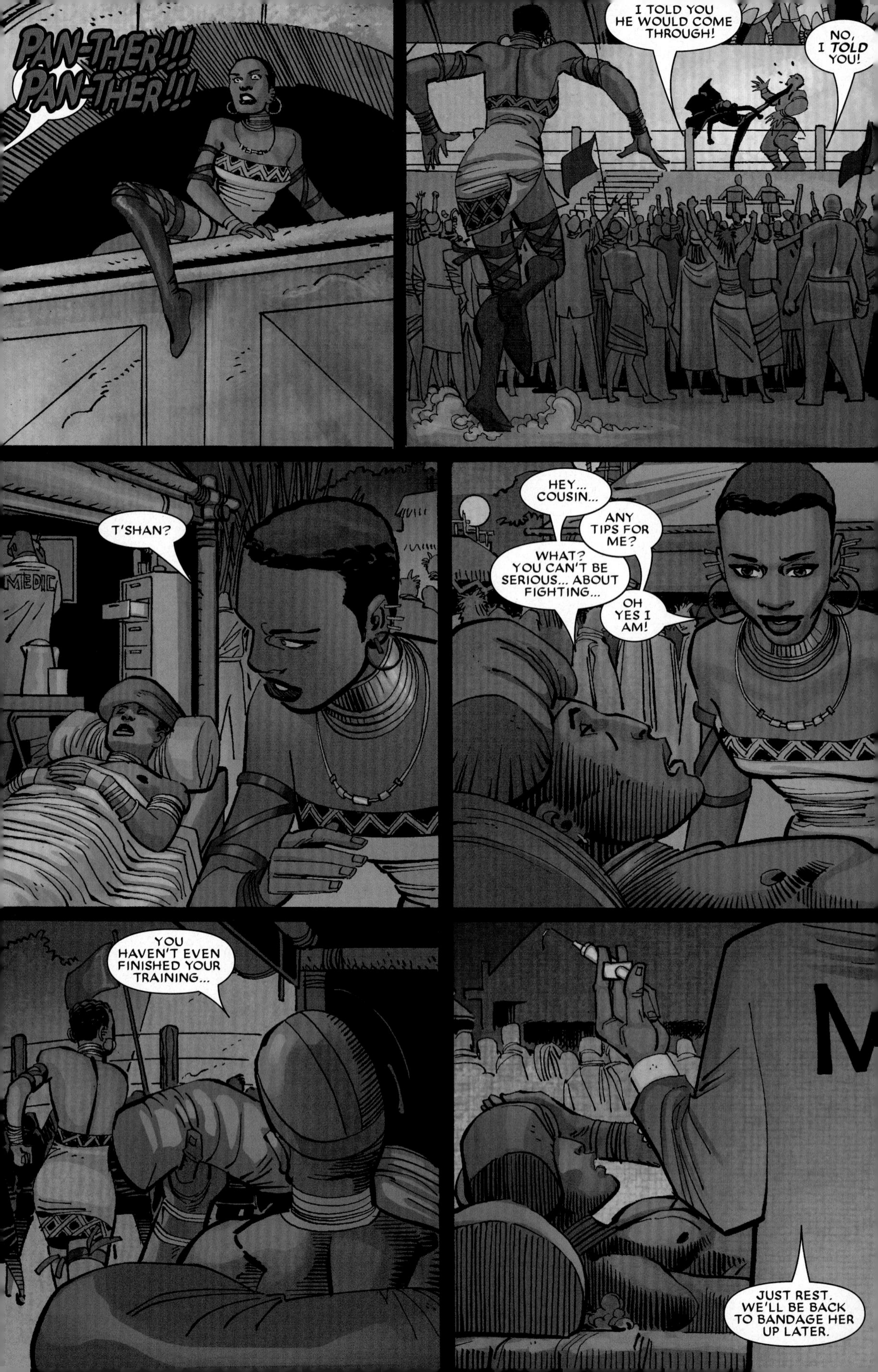
PAN-THER!!! PAN-THER!!!
I TOLD YOU HE WOULD COME THROUGH!
NO, I TOLD YOU!
MEDIC
T'SHAN?
HEY... COUSIN...
ANY TIPS FOR ME?
WHAT? YOU CAN'T BE SERIOUS... ABOUT FIGHTING...
OH YES I AM!
YOU HAVEN'T EVEN FINISHED YOUR TRAINING...
JUST REST. WE'LL BE BACK TO BANDAGE HER UP LATER.

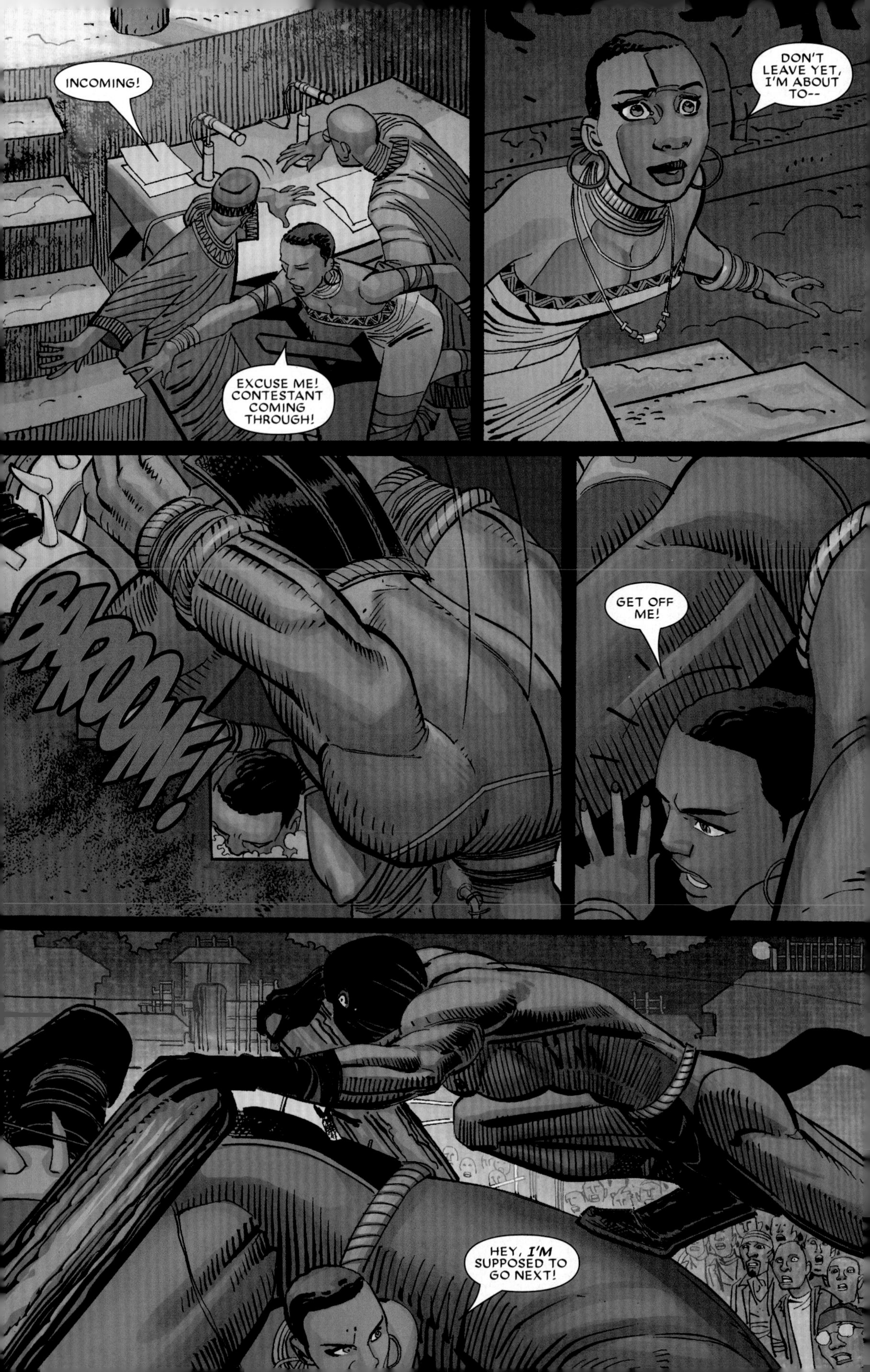
INCOMING!
EXCUSE ME! CONTESTANT COMING THROUGH!
DON'T LEAVE YET, I'M ABOUT TO--
BAROOM!
GET OFF ME!
HEY, *I'M* SUPPOSED TO GO NEXT!

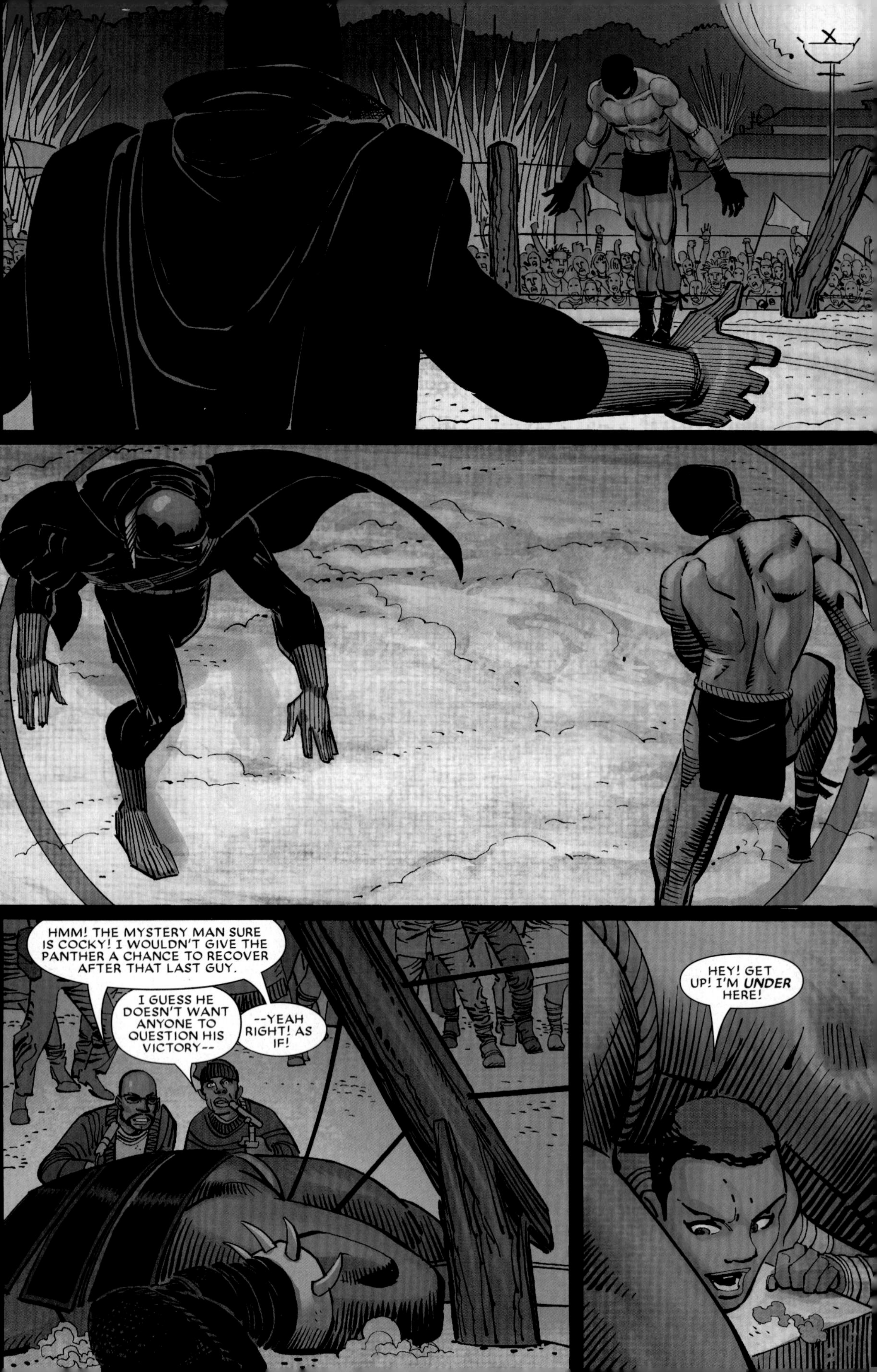
HMM! THE MYSTERY MAN SURE IS COCKY! I WOULDN'T GIVE THE PANTHER A CHANCE TO RECOVER AFTER THAT LAST GUY.
I GUESS HE DOESN'T WANT ANYONE TO QUESTION HIS VICTORY--
--YEAH RIGHT! AS IF!
HEY! GET UP! I'M *UNDER* HERE!

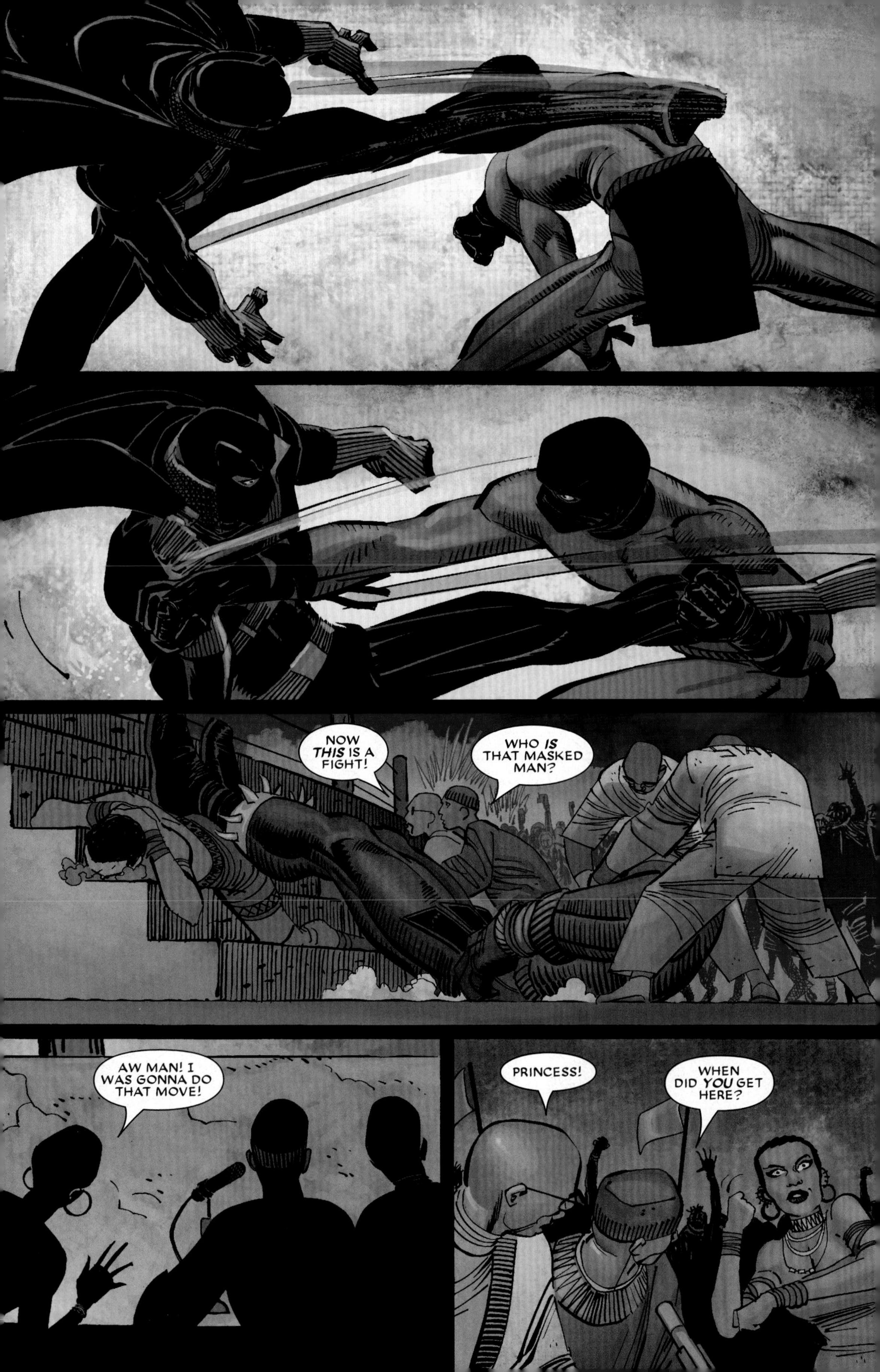
NOW THIS IS A FIGHT!
WHO IS THAT MASKED MAN?
AW MAN! I WAS GONNA DO THAT MOVE!
PRINCESS!
WHEN DID YOU GET HERE?

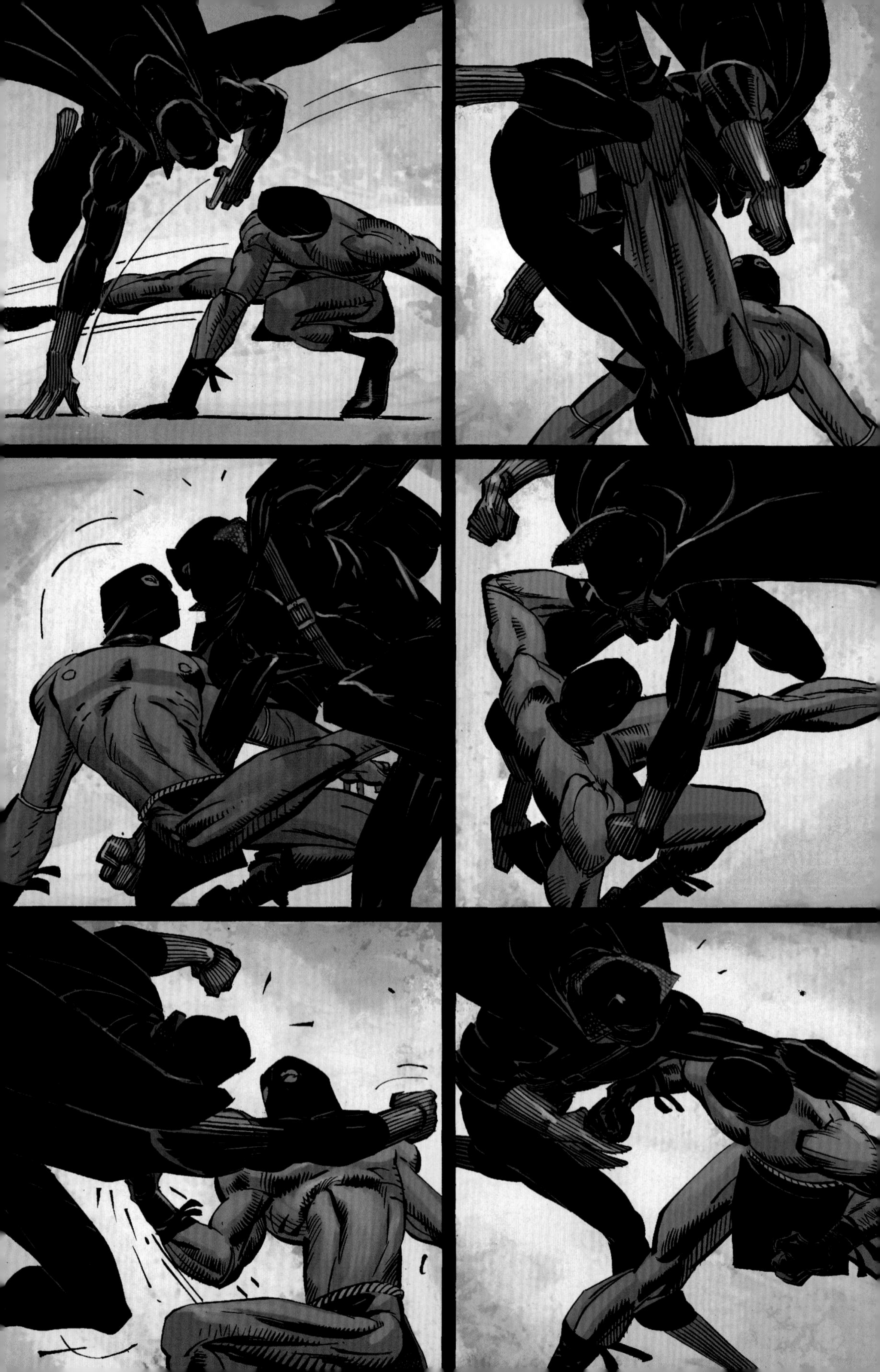

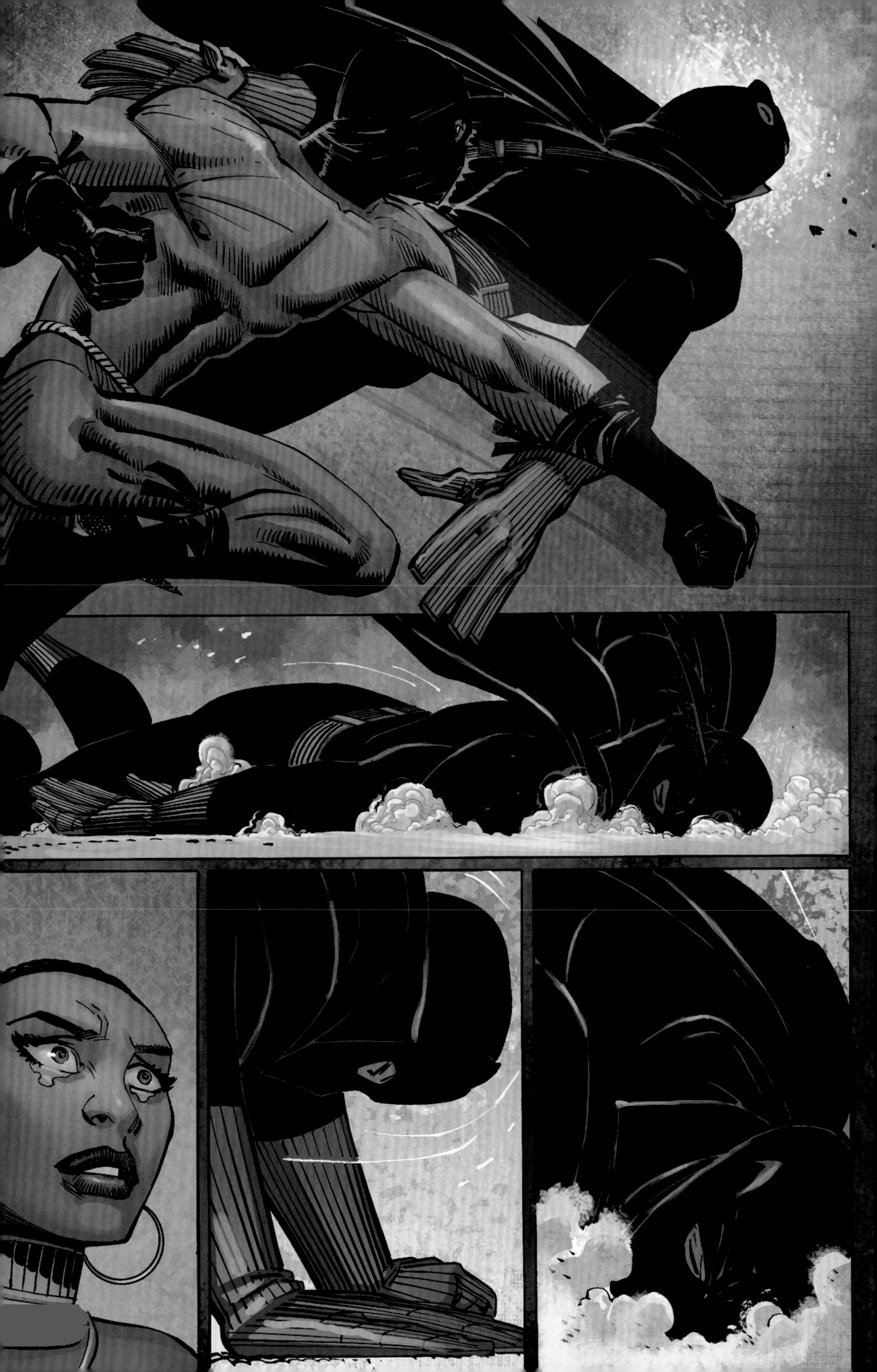

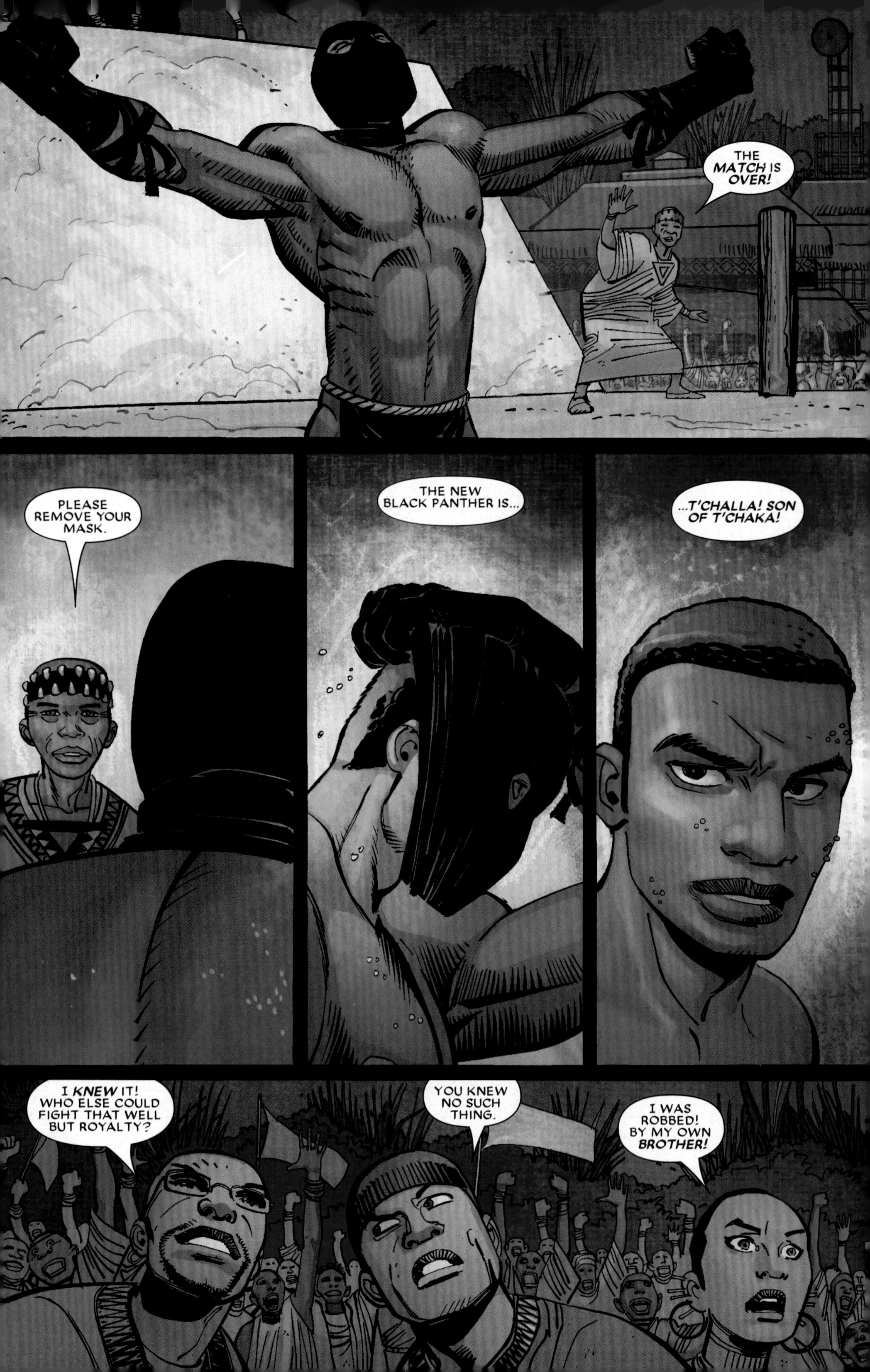
THE MATCH IS OVER!
PLEASE REMOVE YOUR MASK.
THE NEW BLACK PANTHER IS...
...T'CHALLA! SON OF T'CHAKA!
I KNEW IT! WHO ELSE COULD FIGHT THAT WELL BUT ROYALTY?
YOU KNEW NO SUCH THING.
I WAS ROBBED! BY MY OWN BROTHER!

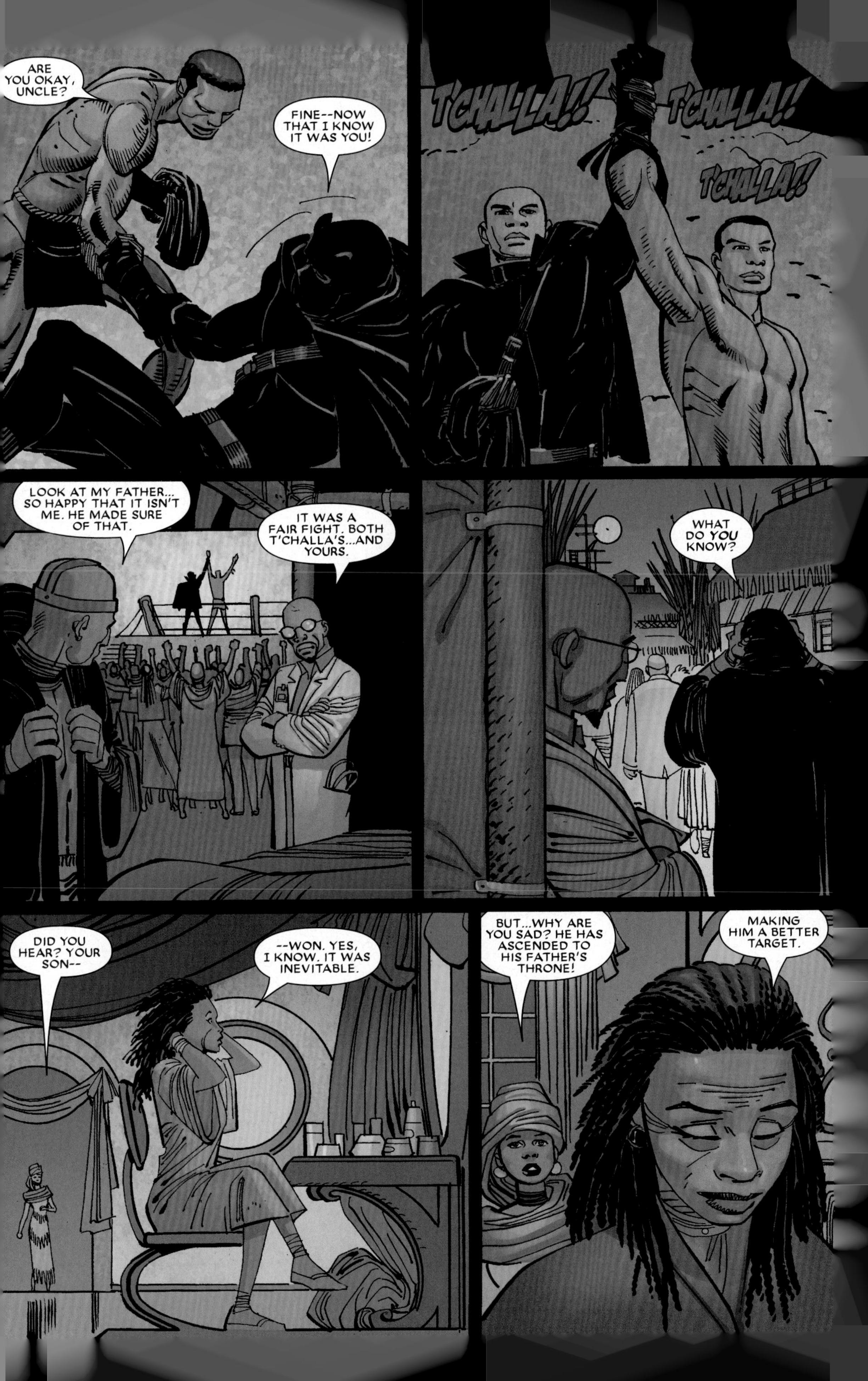
ARE YOU OKAY, UNCLE?
FINE--NOW THAT I KNOW IT WAS YOU!
T'CHAL-LA!!
T'CHAL-LA!!
T'CHAL-LA!!
LOOK AT MY FATHER... SO HAPPY THAT IT ISN'T ME. HE MADE SURE OF THAT.
IT WAS A FAIR FIGHT. BOTH T'CHALLA'S...AND YOURS.
WHAT DO *YOU* KNOW?
DID YOU HEAR? YOUR SON--
--WON. YES, I KNOW. IT WAS INEVITABLE.
BUT...WHY ARE YOU SAD? HE HAS ASCENDED TO HIS FATHER'S THRONE!
MAKING HIM A BETTER TARGET.

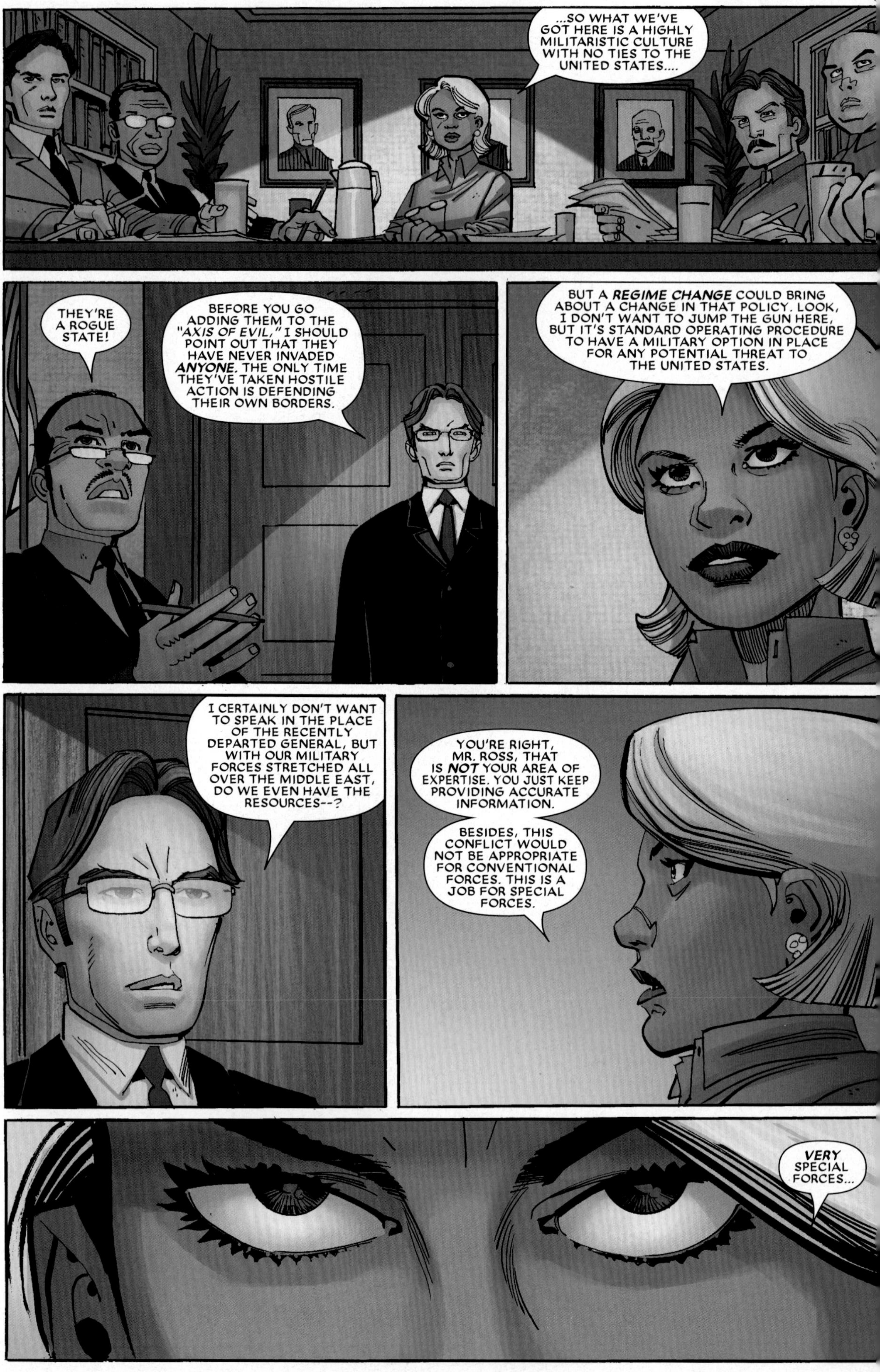
...SO WHAT WE'VE GOT HERE IS A HIGHLY MILITARISTIC CULTURE WITH NO TIES TO THE UNITED STATES....
THEY'RE A ROGUE STATE!
BEFORE YOU GO ADDING THEM TO THE "AXIS OF EVIL," I SHOULD POINT OUT THAT THEY HAVE NEVER INVADED ANYONE. THE ONLY TIME THEY'VE TAKEN HOSTILE ACTION IS DEFENDING THEIR OWN BORDERS.
BUT A REGIME CHANGE COULD BRING ABOUT A CHANGE IN THAT POLICY. LOOK, I DON'T WANT TO JUMP THE GUN HERE, BUT IT'S STANDARD OPERATING PROCEDURE TO HAVE A MILITARY OPTION IN PLACE FOR ANY POTENTIAL THREAT TO THE UNITED STATES.
I CERTAINLY DON'T WANT TO SPEAK IN THE PLACE OF THE RECENTLY DEPARTED GENERAL, BUT WITH OUR MILITARY FORCES STRETCHED ALL OVER THE MIDDLE EAST, DO WE EVEN HAVE THE RESOURCES--?
YOU'RE RIGHT, MR. ROSS, THAT IS NOT YOUR AREA OF EXPERTISE. YOU JUST KEEP PROVIDING ACCURATE INFORMATION.
BESIDES, THIS CONFLICT WOULD NOT BE APPROPRIATE FOR CONVENTIONAL FORCES. THIS IS A JOB FOR SPECIAL FORCES.
VERY SPECIAL FORCES...

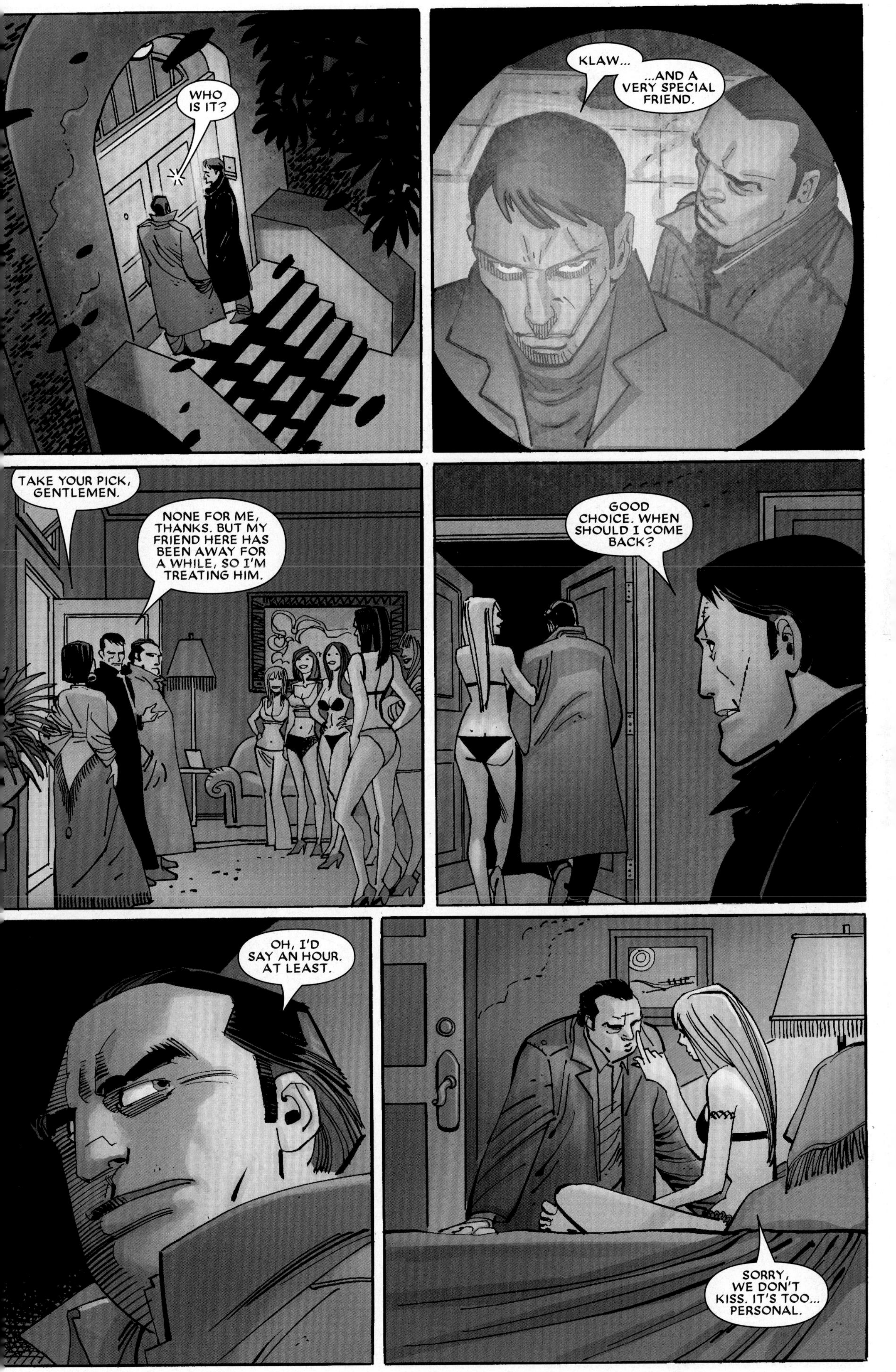
WHO IS IT?
KLAW...
...AND A VERY SPECIAL FRIEND.
TAKE YOUR PICK, GENTLEMEN.
NONE FOR ME, THANKS. BUT MY FRIEND HERE HAS BEEN AWAY FOR A WHILE, SO I'M TREATING HIM.
GOOD CHOICE. WHEN SHOULD I COME BACK?
OH, I'D SAY AN HOUR. AT LEAST.
SORRY, WE DON'T KISS. IT'S TOO... PERSONAL.

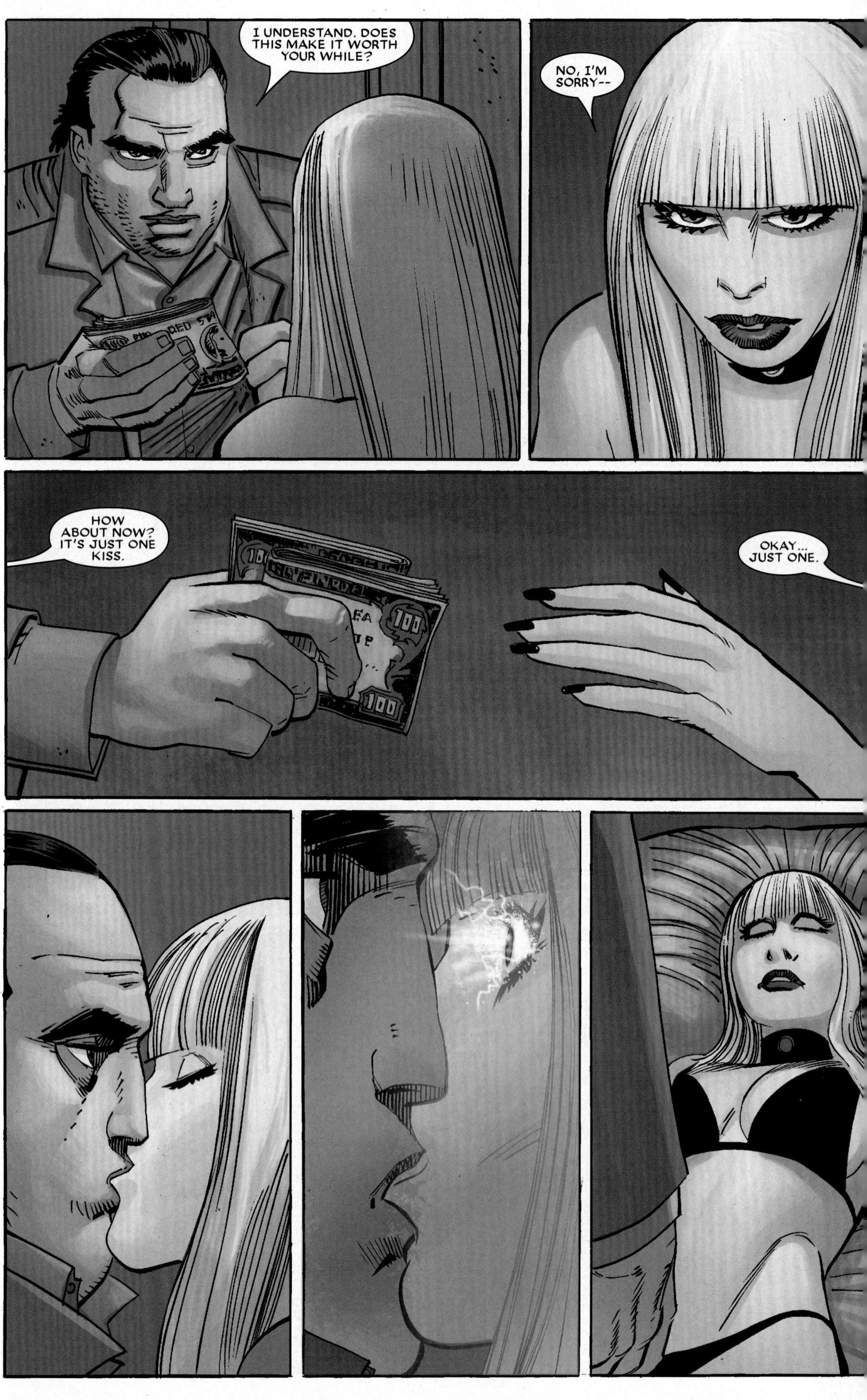
I UNDERSTAND. DOES THIS MAKE IT WORTH YOUR WHILE?
NO, I'M SORRY--
HOW ABOUT NOW? IT'S JUST ONE KISS.
OKAY... JUST ONE.

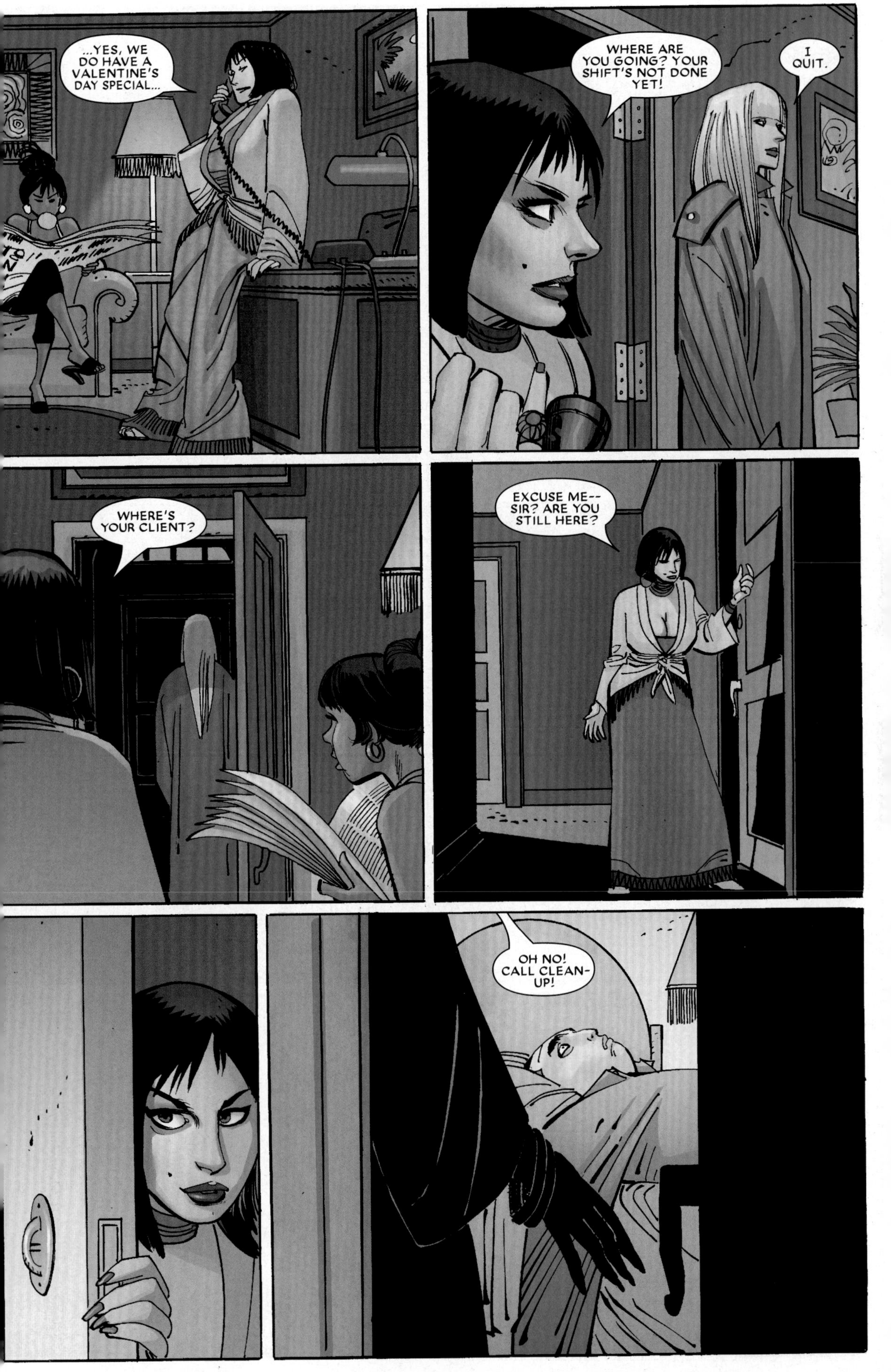
...YES, WE DO HAVE A VALENTINE'S DAY SPECIAL...
WHERE ARE YOU GOING? YOUR SHIFT'S NOT DONE YET!
I QUIT.
WHERE'S YOUR CLIENT?
EXCUSE ME-- SIR? ARE YOU STILL HERE?
OH NO! CALL CLEAN-UP!

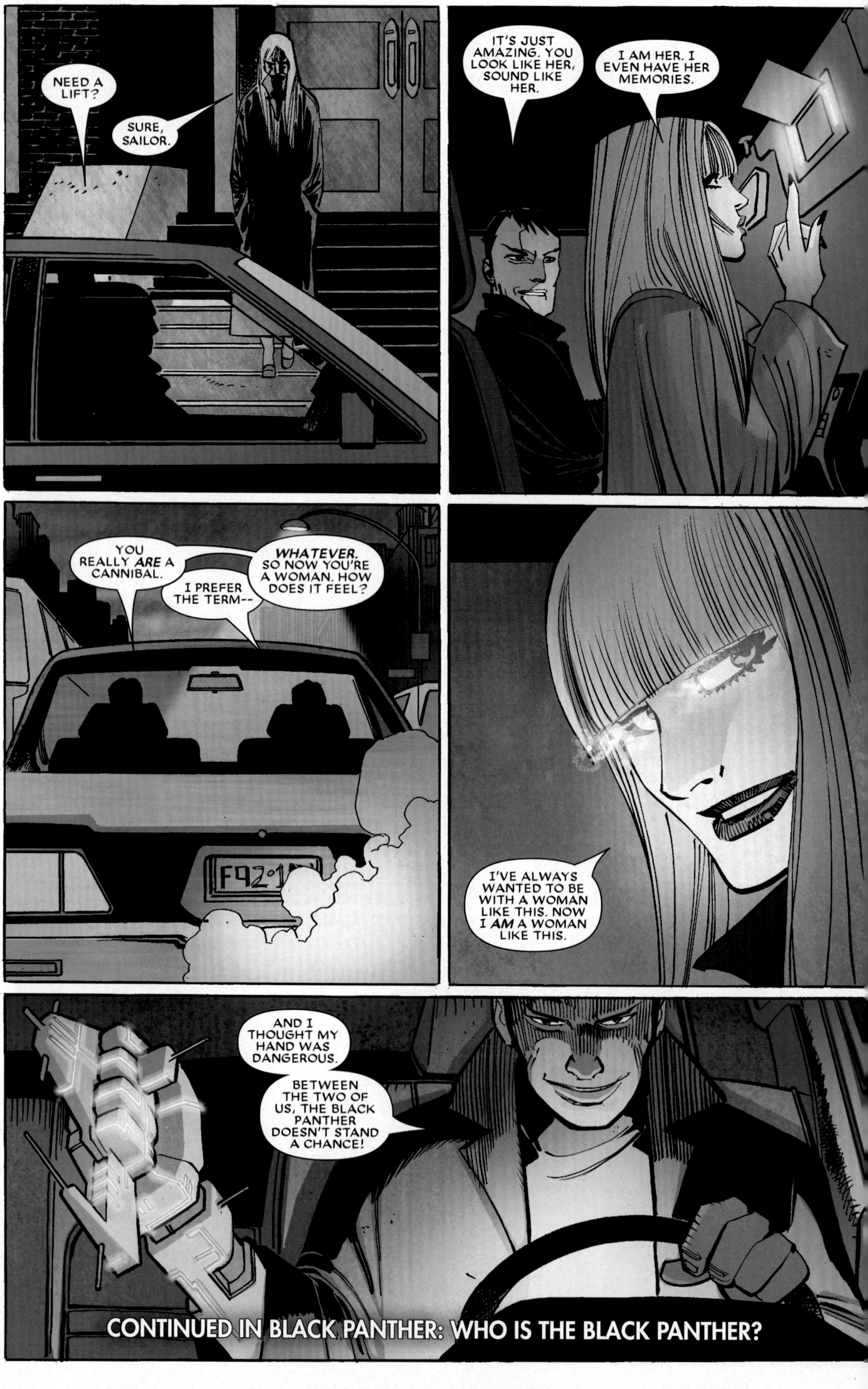

NEED A LIFT?
SURE, SAILOR.
IT'S JUST AMAZING. YOU LOOK LIKE HER, SOUND LIKE HER.
I AM HER. I EVEN HAVE HER MEMORIES.
YOU REALLY *ARE* A CANNIBAL.
I PREFER THE TERM--
WHATEVER. SO NOW YOU'RE A WOMAN. HOW DOES IT FEEL?
I'VE ALWAYS WANTED TO BE WITH A WOMAN LIKE THIS. NOW I *AM* A WOMAN LIKE THIS.
AND I THOUGHT MY HAND WAS DANGEROUS.
BETWEEN THE TWO OF US, THE BLACK PANTHER DOESN'T STAND A CHANCE!

CONTINUED IN BLACK PANTHER: WHO IS THE BLACK PANTHER?

A NEW ERA FOR THE BLACK PANTHER BEGINS, COURTESY OF BEST-SELLING AUTHOR TA-NEHISI COATES AND ARTIST BRIAN STELFREEZE. TESTED BY A SUPERHUMAN TERRORIST GROUP THAT HAS SPARKED A VIOLENT UPRISING AMONG THE CITIZENS OF WAKANDA, T'CHALLA KNOWS THE COUNTRY MUST CHANGE TO SURVIVE — BUT WILL HE SURVIVE THE CHANGE?

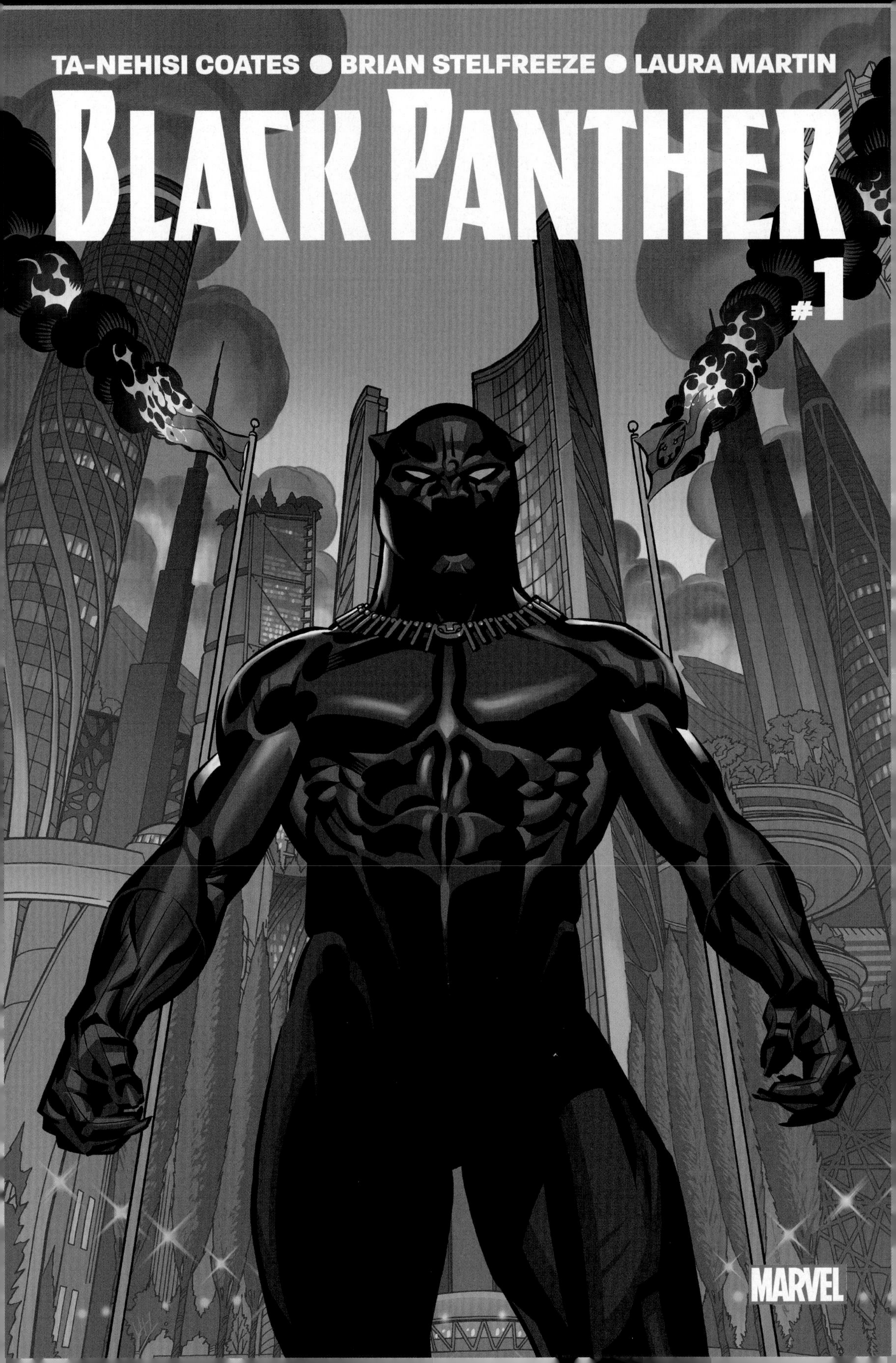
TA-NEHISI COATES ● BRIAN STELFREEZE ● LAURA MARTIN
BLACK PANTHER
#1
MARVEL

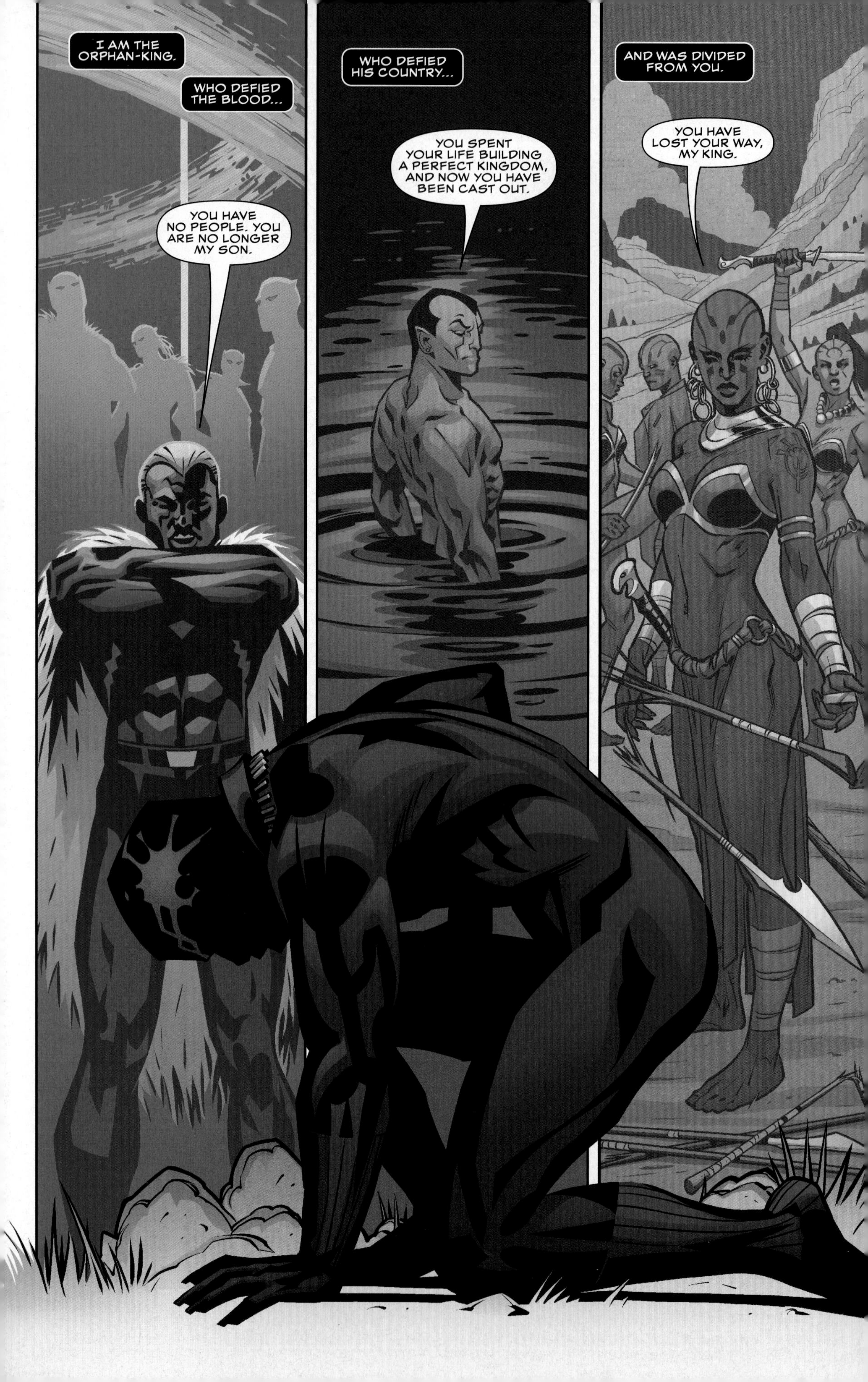
I AM THE ORPHAN-KING.
WHO DEFIED THE BLOOD...
YOU HAVE NO PEOPLE. YOU ARE NO LONGER MY SON.
WHO DEFIED HIS COUNTRY...
YOU SPENT YOUR LIFE BUILDING A PERFECT KINGDOM, AND NOW YOU HAVE BEEN CAST OUT.
AND WAS DIVIDED FROM YOU.
YOU HAVE LOST YOUR WAY, MY KING.

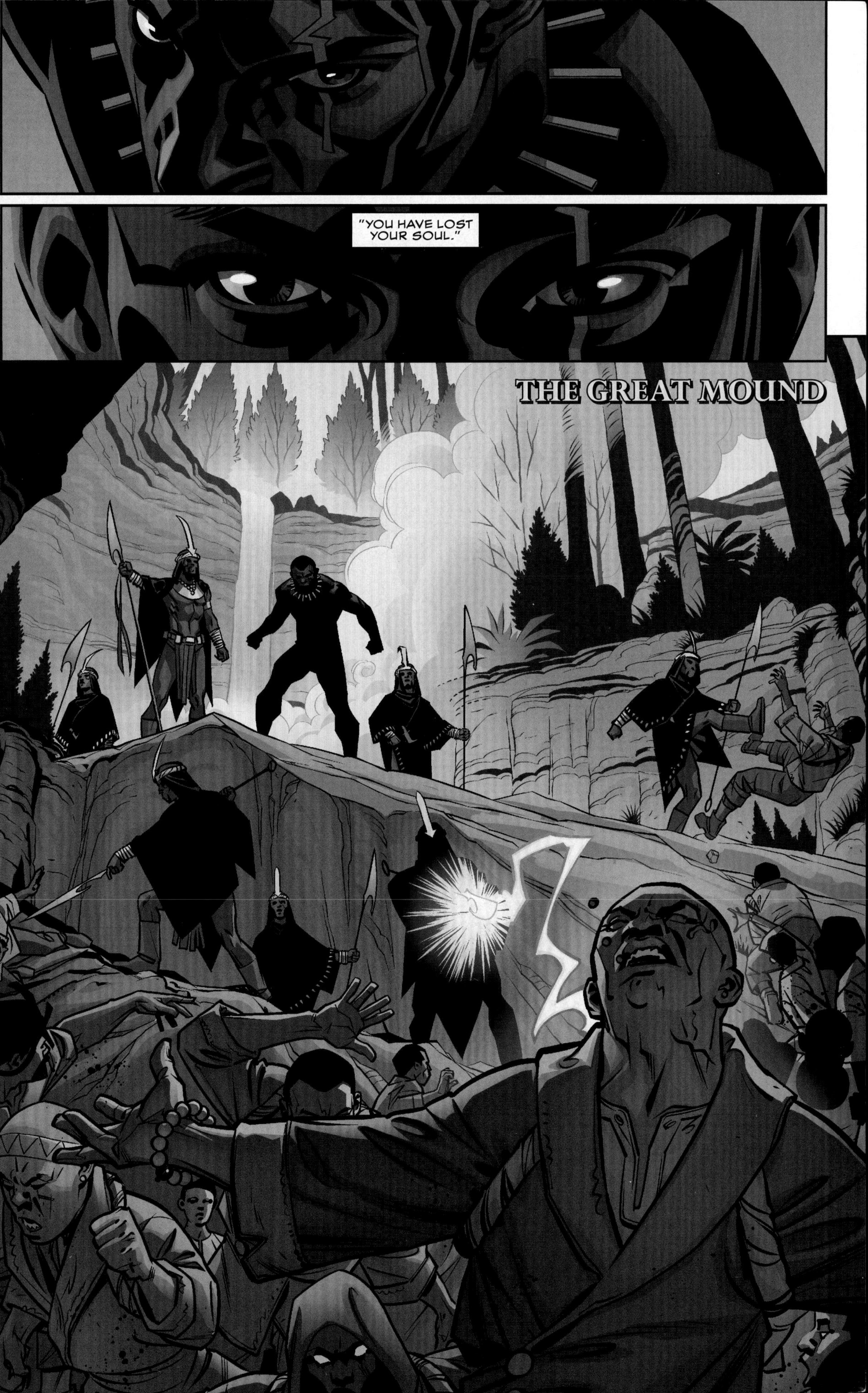
"YOU HAVE LOST YOUR SOUL."
THE GREAT MOUND

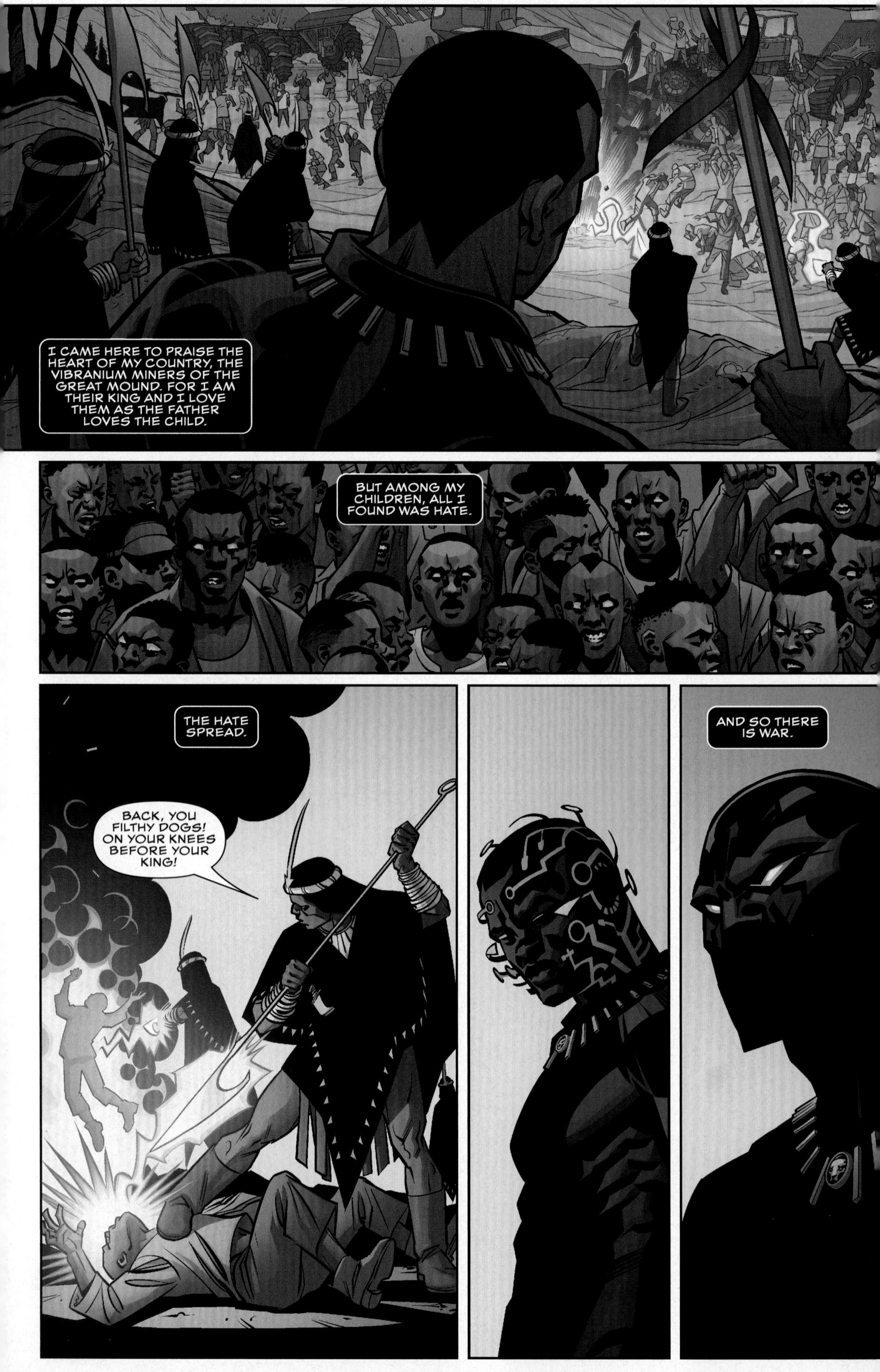
I CAME HERE TO PRAISE THE HEART OF MY COUNTRY, THE VIBRANIUM MINERS OF THE GREAT MOUND. FOR I AM THEIR KING AND I LOVE THEM AS THE FATHER LOVES THE CHILD.
BUT AMONG MY CHILDREN, ALL I FOUND WAS HATE.
THE HATE SPREAD.
BACK, YOU FILTHY DOGS! ON YOUR KNEES BEFORE YOUR KING!
AND SO THERE IS WAR.

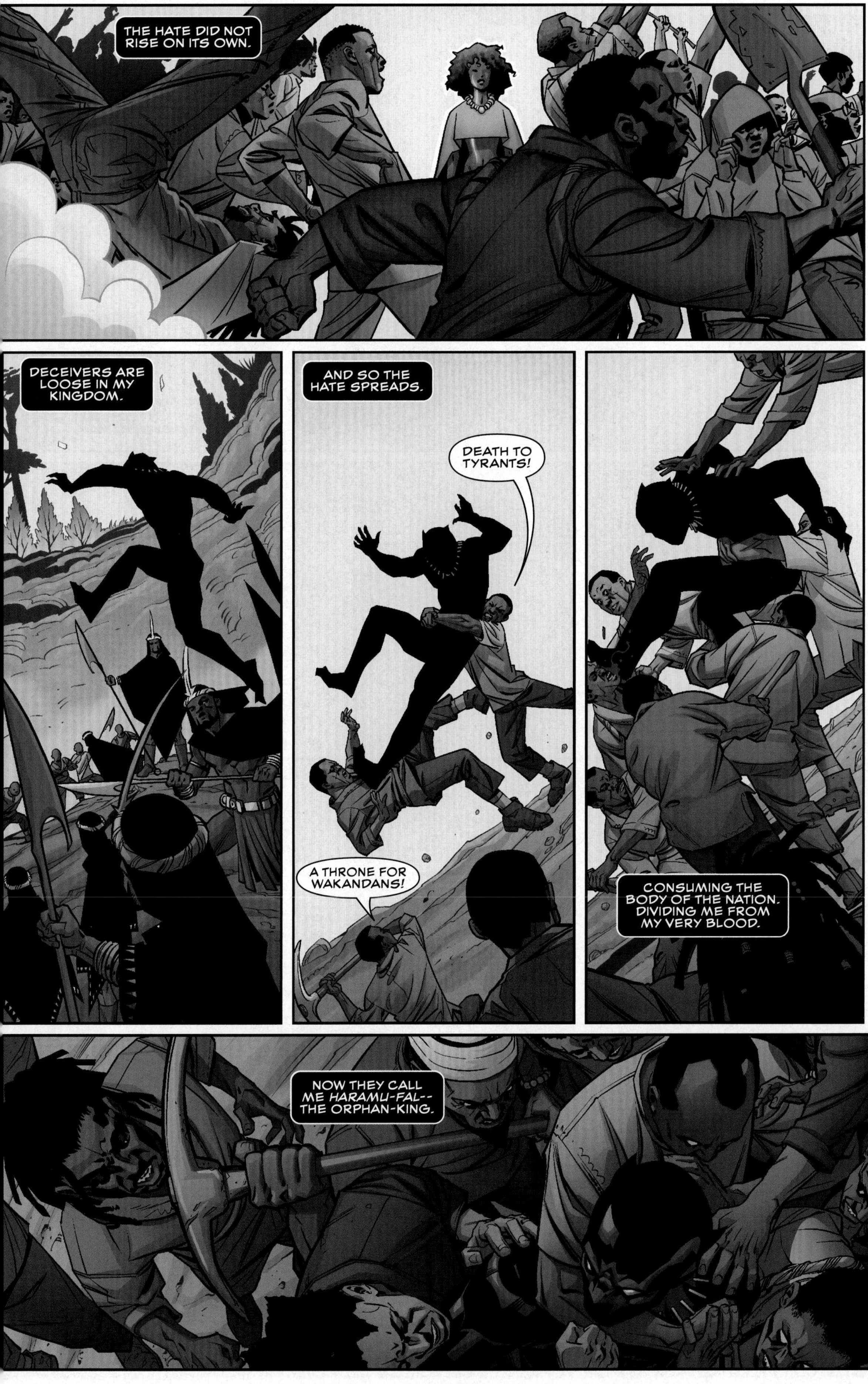
THE HATE DID NOT RISE ON ITS OWN.
DECEIVERS ARE LOOSE IN MY KINGDOM.
AND SO THE HATE SPREADS.
DEATH TO TYRANTS!
A THRONE FOR WAKANDANS!
CONSUMING THE BODY OF THE NATION. DIVIDING ME FROM MY VERY BLOOD.
NOW THEY CALL ME HARAMU-FAL-- THE ORPHAN-KING.

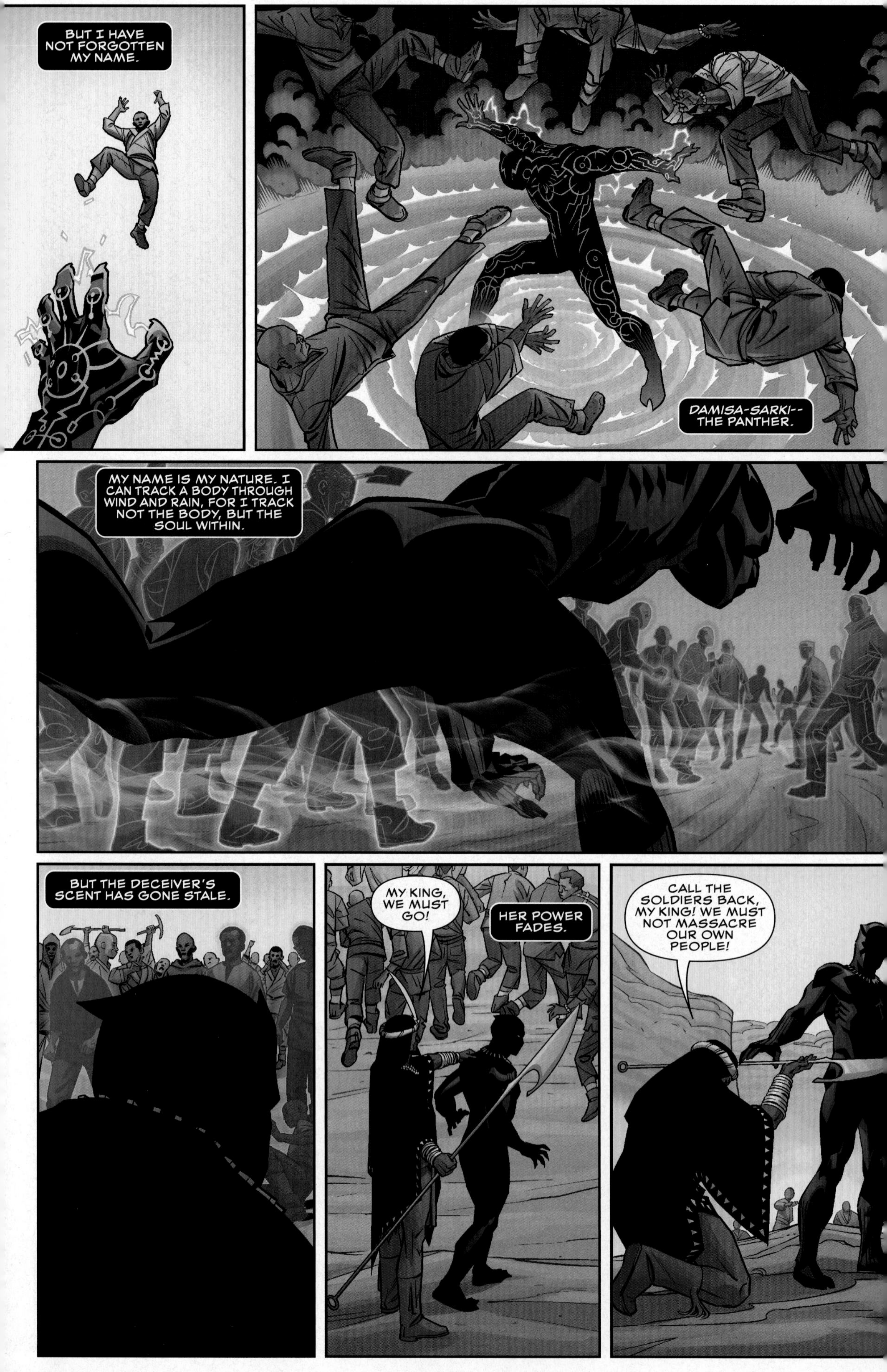
BUT I HAVE NOT FORGOTTEN MY NAME.
DAMISA-SARKI-- THE PANTHER.
MY NAME IS MY NATURE. I CAN TRACK A BODY THROUGH WIND AND RAIN, FOR I TRACK NOT THE BODY, BUT THE SOUL WITHIN.
BUT THE DECEIVER'S SCENT HAS GONE STALE.
MY KING, WE MUST GO!
HER POWER FADES.
CALL THE SOLDIERS BACK, MY KING! WE MUST NOT MASSACRE OUR OWN PEOPLE!

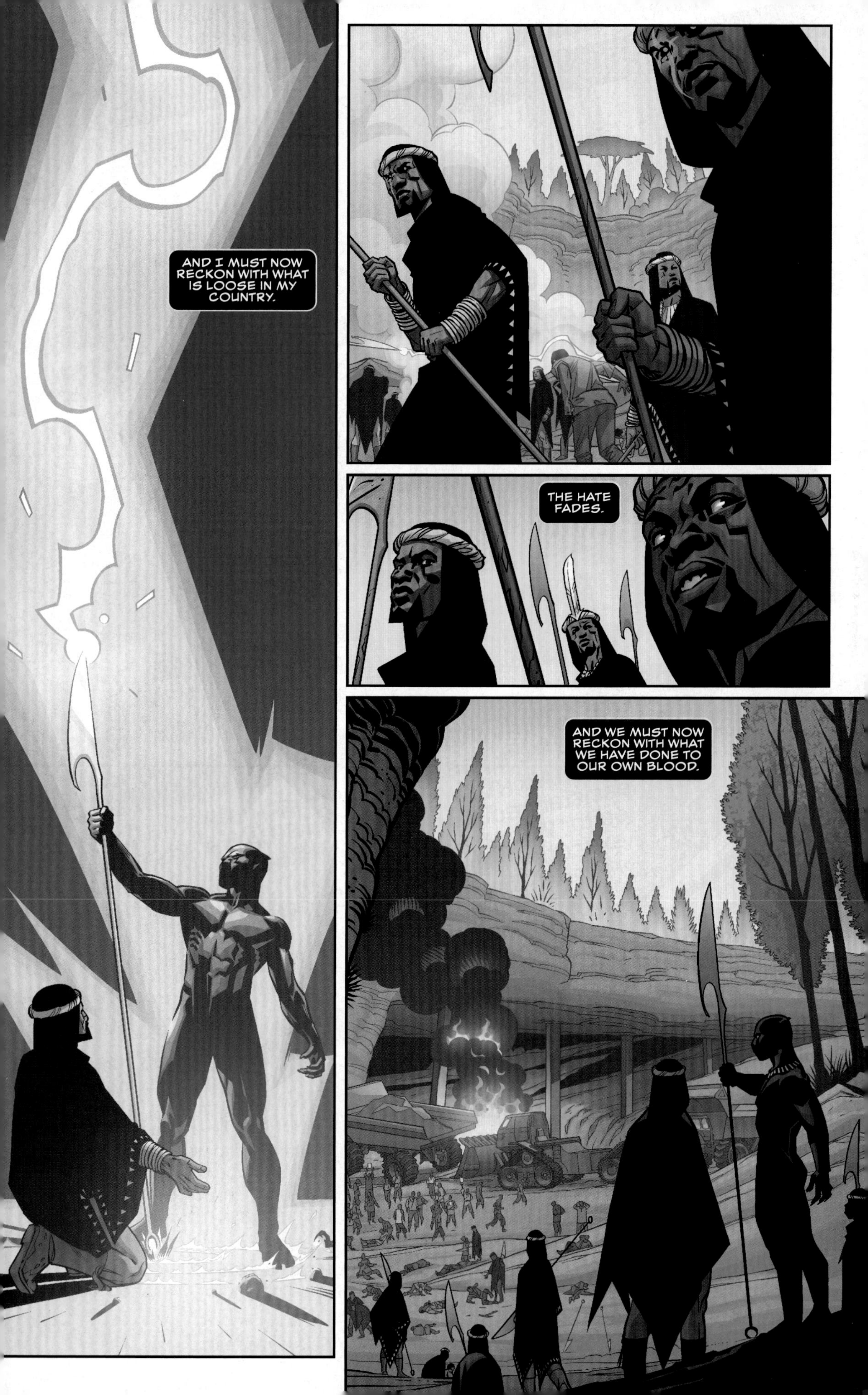
AND I MUST NOW RECKON WITH WHAT IS LOOSE IN MY COUNTRY.
THE HATE FADES.
AND WE MUST NOW RECKON WITH WHAT WE HAVE DONE TO OUR OWN BLOOD.

writer **TA-NEHISI COATES**

artist **BRIAN STELFREEZE**

color artist **LAURA MARTIN**

A NATIO
UNDER OUR

letterer **VC's JOE SABINO** design **MANNY MEDEROS**
logo **RIAN HUGHES** cover by **BRIAN STELFREEZE**
assistant editor **CHRIS ROBINSON**
editor **WIL MOSS**
executive editor **TOM BREVOORT**
editor in chief **AXEL ALONSO**
chief creative officer **JOE QUESADA**
president **DAN BUCKLEY**
executive producer **ALAN FINE**

Black Panther is
the ancestral ceremonial
title of **T'CHALLA**, the king of
Wakanda. T'Challa splits his time between
protecting his kingdom, with the aid of his elite female royal
guard, the **DORA MILAJE**, and helping protect the entire world, as a
member of super hero teams such as the Avengers and the Ultimates.

The African nation **WAKANDA** is the most technologically advanced society on the
globe. It sits upon a large deposit of an extremely rare natural resource called vibranium.
Wakanda long boasted of having never been conquered. But recent events — a biblical flood
that killed thousands, a coup orchestrated by Doctor Doom, an invasion by the
villain Thanos — have humbled the kingdom.

T'Challa recently spent some time away from the throne. His sister **SHURI** had been ruling
as both queen and Black Panther in his absence, but she died defending Wakanda against
Thanos' army.

Now T'Challa is king once more, but the people of Wakanda are restless...

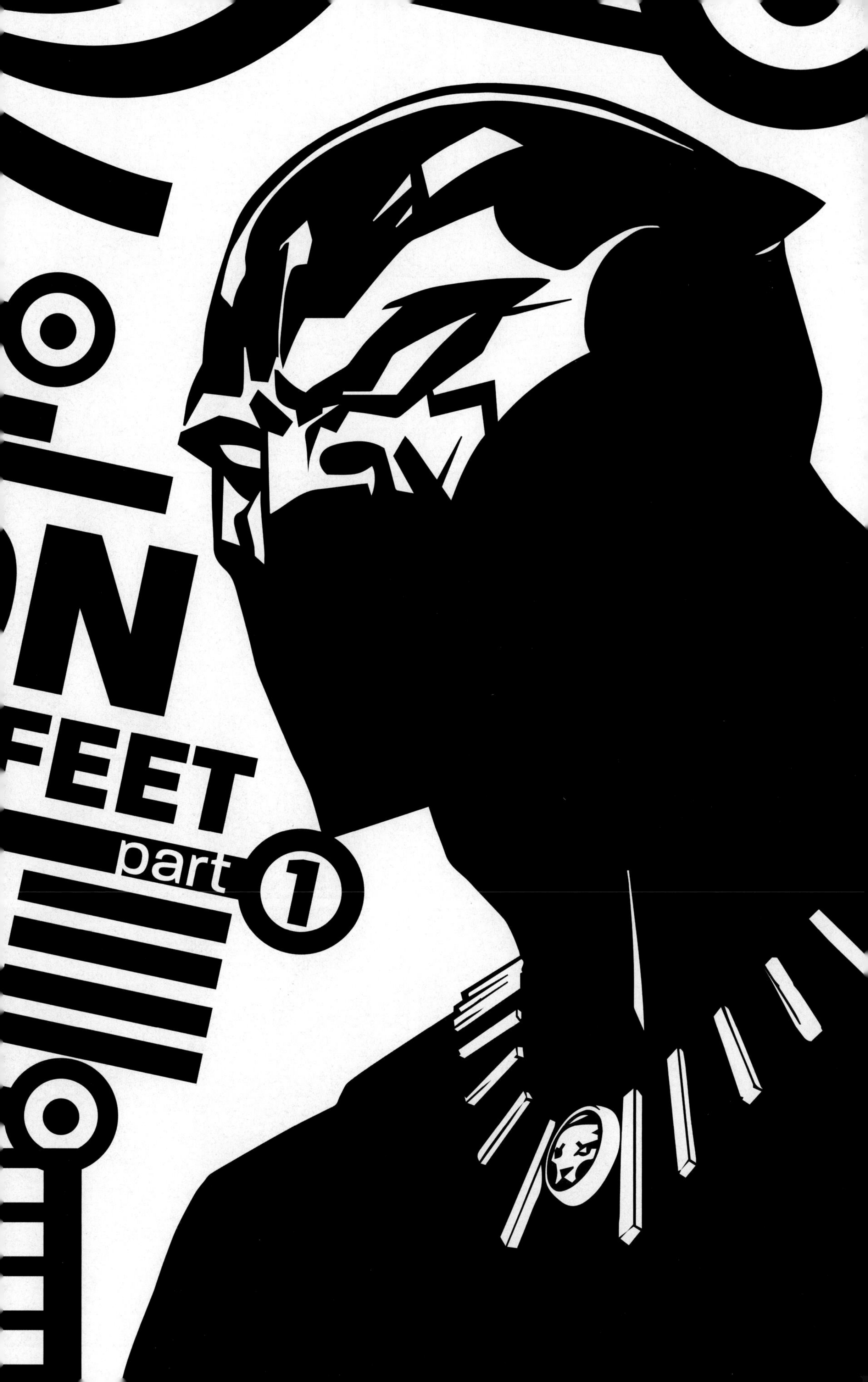

N
FEET
part 1

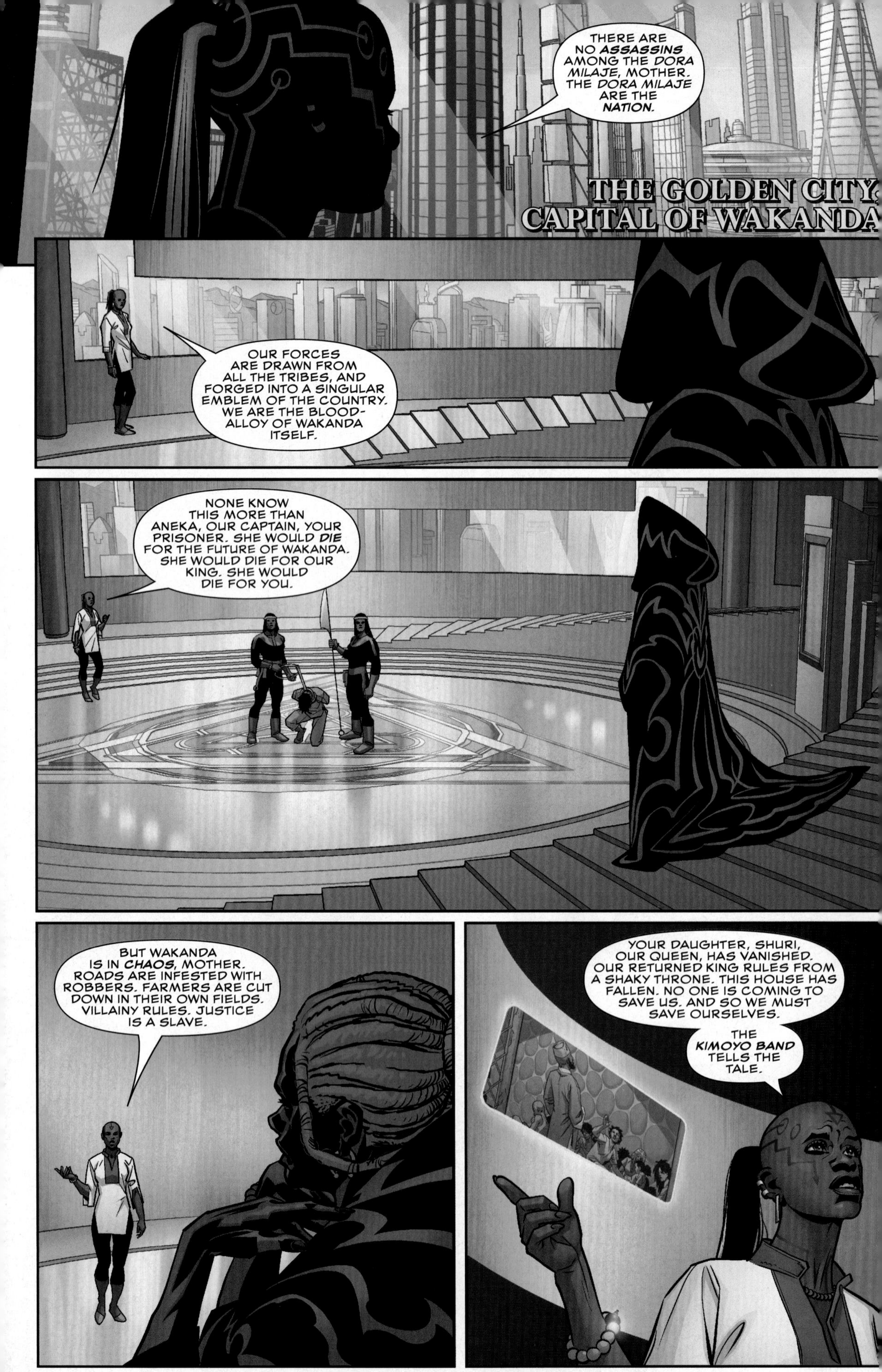
THERE ARE NO ASSASSINS AMONG THE DORA MILAJE, MOTHER. THE DORA MILAJE ARE THE NATION.
THE GOLDEN CITY, CAPITAL OF WAKANDA
OUR FORCES ARE DRAWN FROM ALL THE TRIBES, AND FORGED INTO A SINGULAR EMBLEM OF THE COUNTRY. WE ARE THE BLOOD-ALLOY OF WAKANDA ITSELF.
NONE KNOW THIS MORE THAN ANEKA, OUR CAPTAIN, YOUR PRISONER. SHE WOULD DIE FOR THE FUTURE OF WAKANDA. SHE WOULD DIE FOR OUR KING. SHE WOULD DIE FOR YOU.
BUT WAKANDA IS IN CHAOS, MOTHER. ROADS ARE INFESTED WITH ROBBERS. FARMERS ARE CUT DOWN IN THEIR OWN FIELDS. VILLAINY RULES. JUSTICE IS A SLAVE.
YOUR DAUGHTER, SHURI, OUR QUEEN, HAS VANISHED. OUR RETURNED KING RULES FROM A SHAKY THRONE. THIS HOUSE HAS FALLEN. NO ONE IS COMING TO SAVE US. AND SO WE MUST SAVE OURSELVES.
THE KIMOYO BAND TELLS THE TALE.

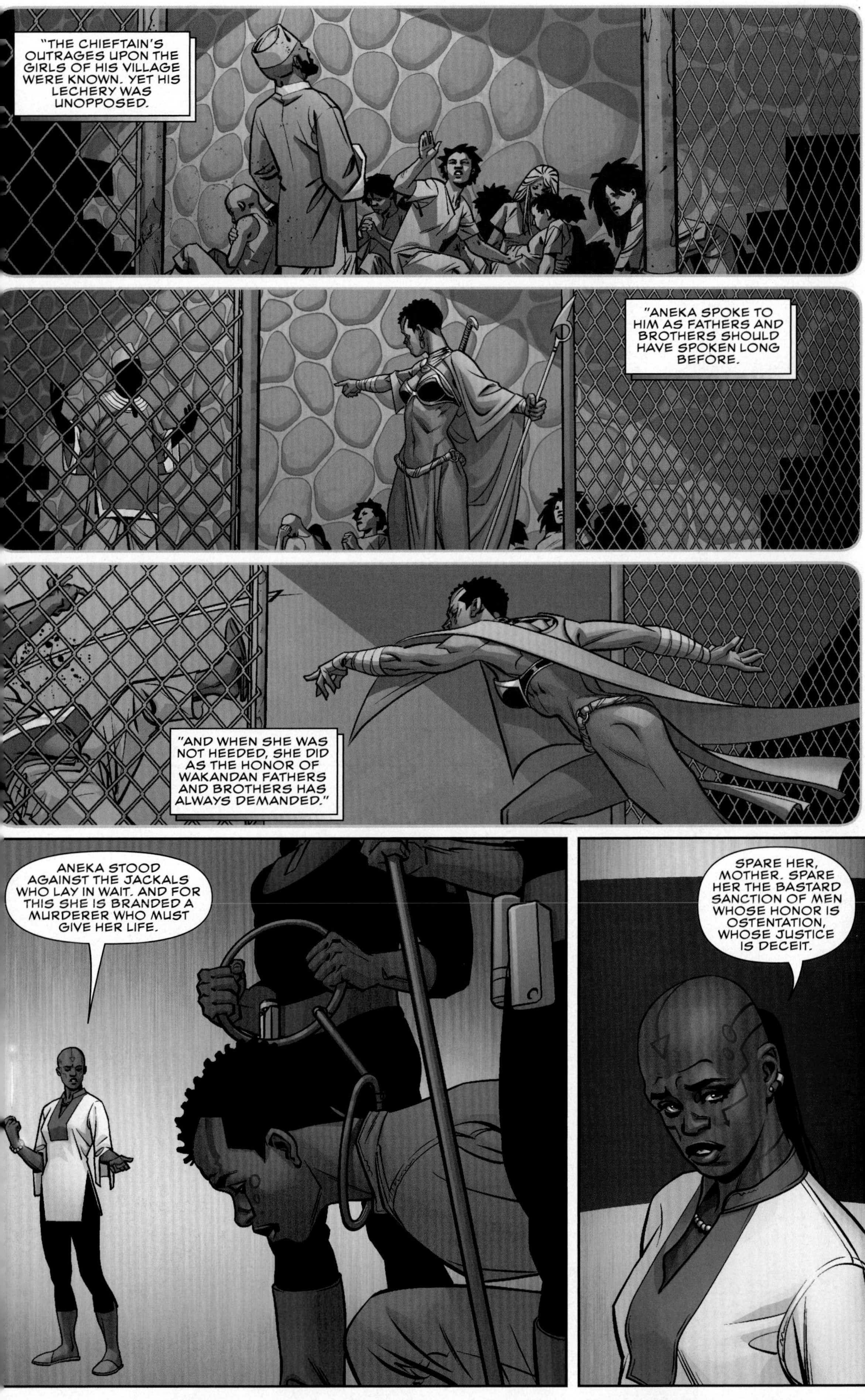
"THE CHIEFTAIN'S OUTRAGES UPON THE GIRLS OF HIS VILLAGE WERE KNOWN. YET HIS LECHERY WAS UNOPPOSED.
"ANEKA SPOKE TO HIM AS FATHERS AND BROTHERS SHOULD HAVE SPOKEN LONG BEFORE.
"AND WHEN SHE WAS NOT HEEDED, SHE DID AS THE HONOR OF WAKANDAN FATHERS AND BROTHERS HAS ALWAYS DEMANDED."
ANEKA STOOD AGAINST THE JACKALS WHO LAY IN WAIT. AND FOR THIS SHE IS BRANDED A MURDERER WHO MUST GIVE HER LIFE.
SPARE HER, MOTHER. SPARE HER THE BASTARD SANCTION OF MEN WHOSE HONOR IS OSTENTATION, WHOSE JUSTICE IS DECEIT.

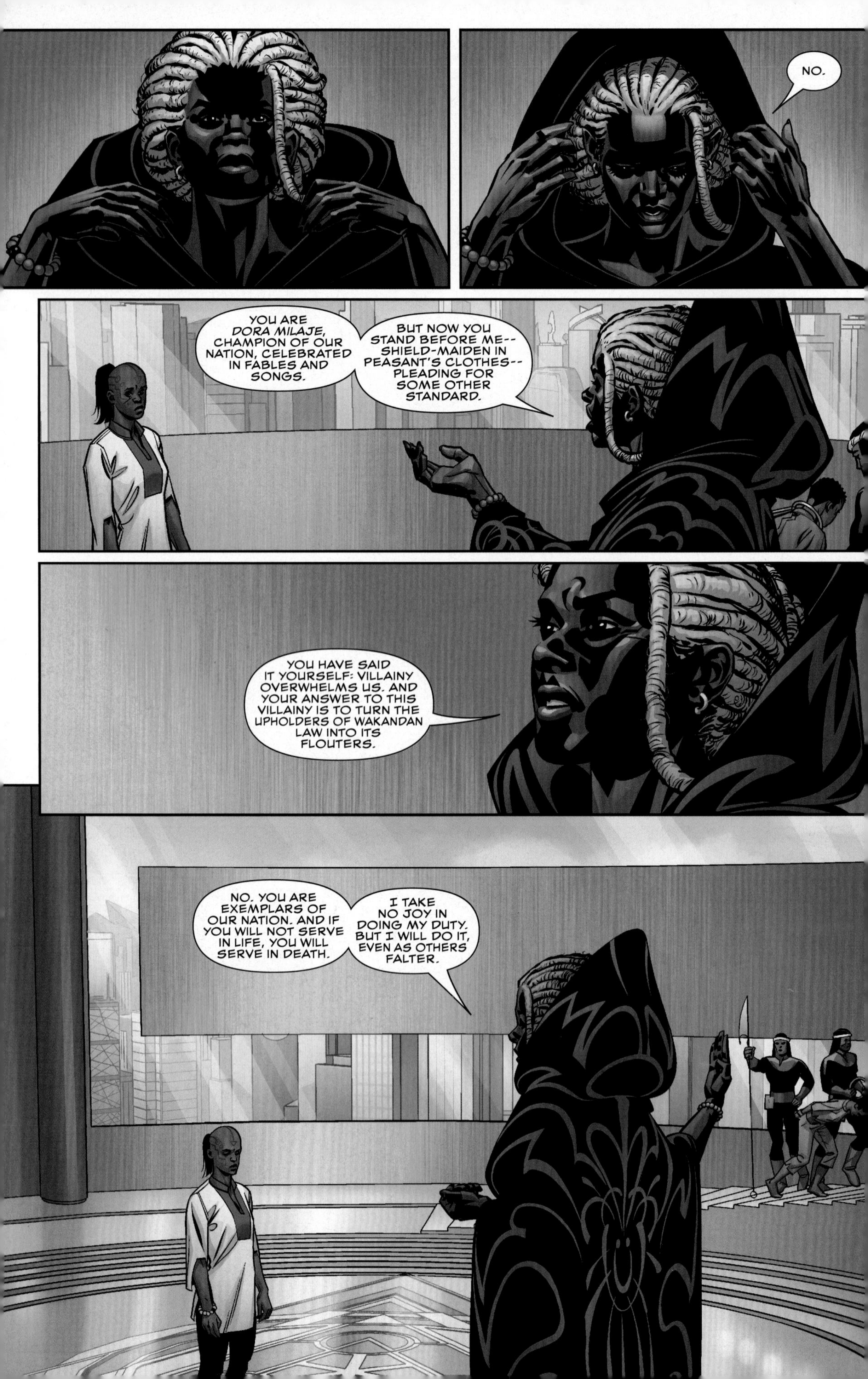
NO.
YOU ARE *DORA MILAJE*, CHAMPION OF OUR NATION, CELEBRATED IN FABLES AND SONGS.
BUT NOW YOU STAND BEFORE ME--SHIELD-MAIDEN IN PEASANT'S CLOTHES--PLEADING FOR SOME OTHER STANDARD.
YOU HAVE SAID IT YOURSELF: VILLAINY OVERWHELMS US. AND YOUR ANSWER TO THIS VILLAINY IS TO TURN THE UPHOLDERS OF WAKANDAN LAW INTO ITS FLOUTERS.
NO. YOU ARE EXEMPLARS OF OUR NATION. AND IF YOU WILL NOT SERVE IN LIFE, YOU WILL SERVE IN DEATH.
I TAKE NO JOY IN DOING MY DUTY. BUT I WILL DO IT, EVEN AS OTHERS FALTER.

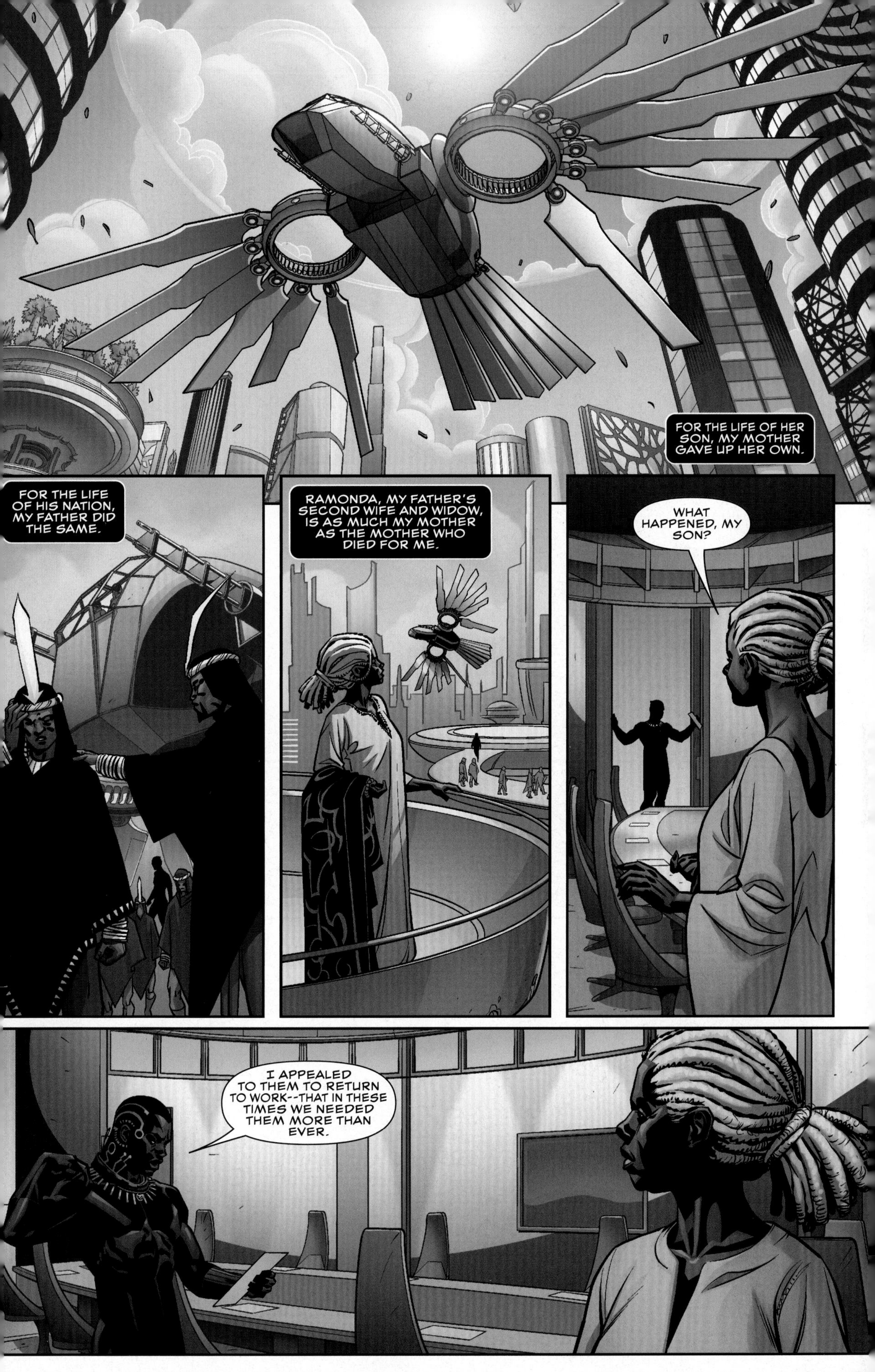
FOR THE LIFE OF HER SON, MY MOTHER GAVE UP HER OWN.
FOR THE LIFE OF HIS NATION, MY FATHER DID THE SAME.
RAMONDA, MY FATHER'S SECOND WIFE AND WIDOW, IS AS MUCH MY MOTHER AS THE MOTHER WHO DIED FOR ME.
WHAT HAPPENED, MY SON?
I APPEALED TO THEM TO RETURN TO WORK--THAT IN THESE TIMES WE NEEDED THEM MORE THAN EVER.

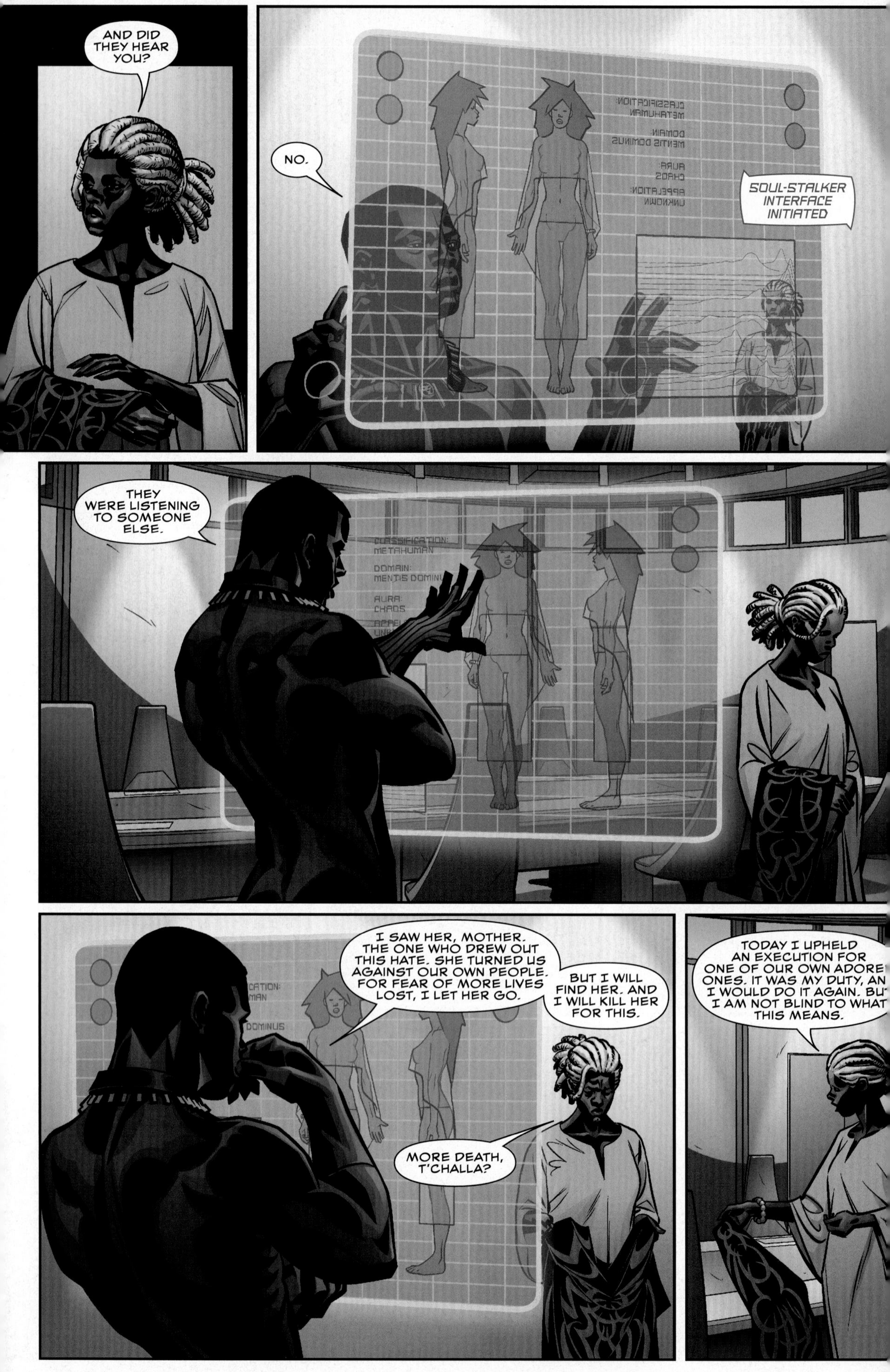
AND DID THEY HEAR YOU?
NO.
CLASSIFICATION: METAHUMAN
DOMAIN: MENTIS DOMINUS
AURA: CHAOS
APPELLATION: UNKNOWN
SOUL-STALKER INTERFACE INITIATED
THEY WERE LISTENING TO SOMEONE ELSE.
I SAW HER, MOTHER. THE ONE WHO DREW OUT THIS HATE. SHE TURNED US AGAINST OUR OWN PEOPLE. FOR FEAR OF MORE LIVES LOST, I LET HER GO.
BUT I WILL FIND HER. AND I WILL KILL HER FOR THIS.
MORE DEATH, T'CHALLA?
TODAY I UPHELD AN EXECUTION FOR ONE OF OUR OWN ADORE ONES. IT WAS MY DUTY, AN I WOULD DO IT AGAIN. BU I AM NOT BLIND TO WHAT THIS MEANS.

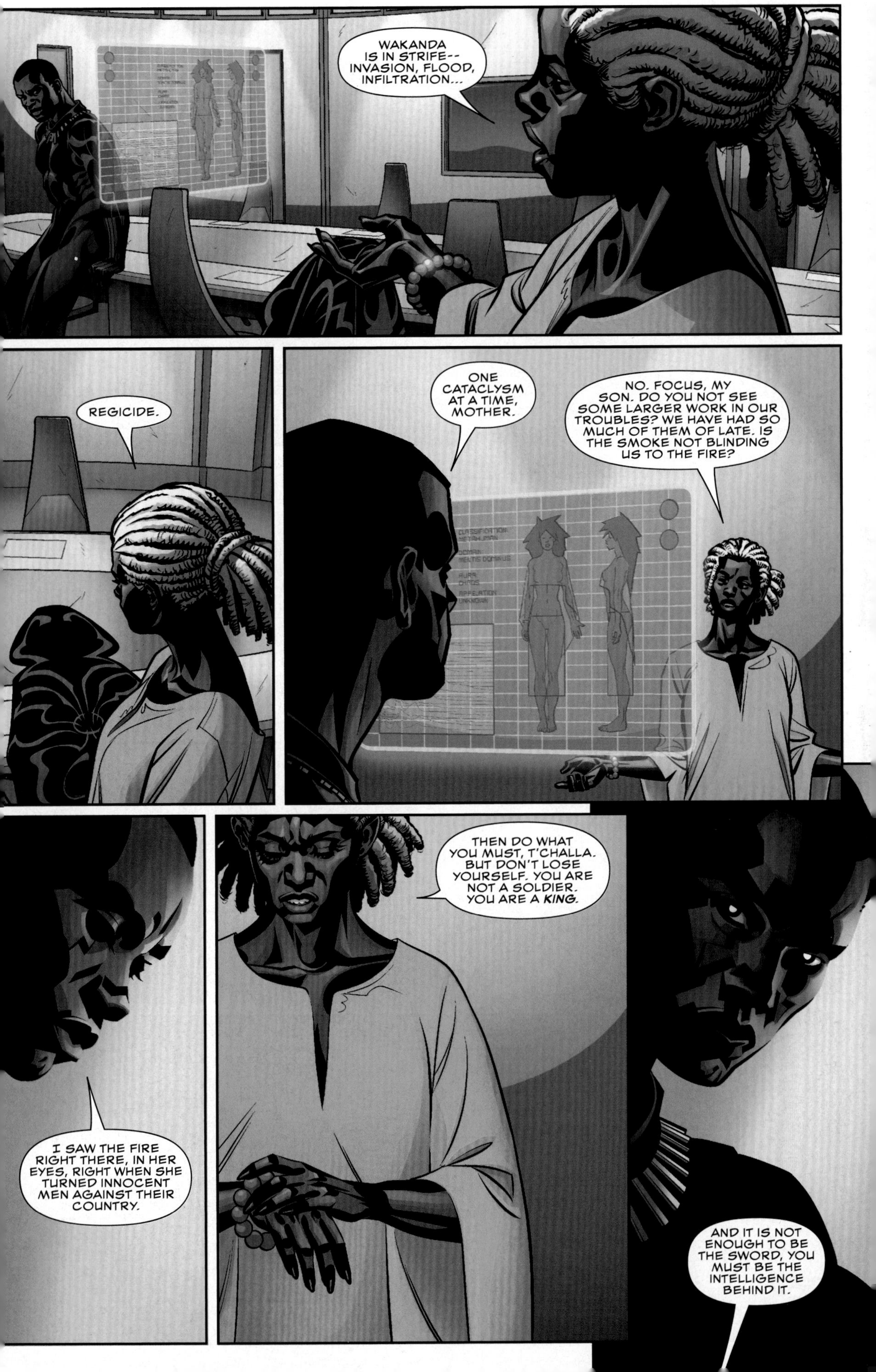
WAKANDA IS IN STRIFE-- INVASION, FLOOD, INFILTRATION...
REGICIDE.
ONE CATACLYSM AT A TIME, MOTHER.
NO. FOCUS, MY SON. DO YOU NOT SEE SOME LARGER WORK IN OUR TROUBLES? WE HAVE HAD SO MUCH OF THEM OF LATE. IS THE SMOKE NOT BLINDING US TO THE FIRE?
I SAW THE FIRE RIGHT THERE, IN HER EYES, RIGHT WHEN SHE TURNED INNOCENT MEN AGAINST THEIR COUNTRY.
THEN DO WHAT YOU MUST, T'CHALLA. BUT DON'T LOSE YOURSELF. YOU ARE NOT A SOLDIER. YOU ARE A *KING*.
AND IT IS NOT ENOUGH TO BE THE SWORD, YOU MUST BE THE INTELLIGENCE BEHIND IT.

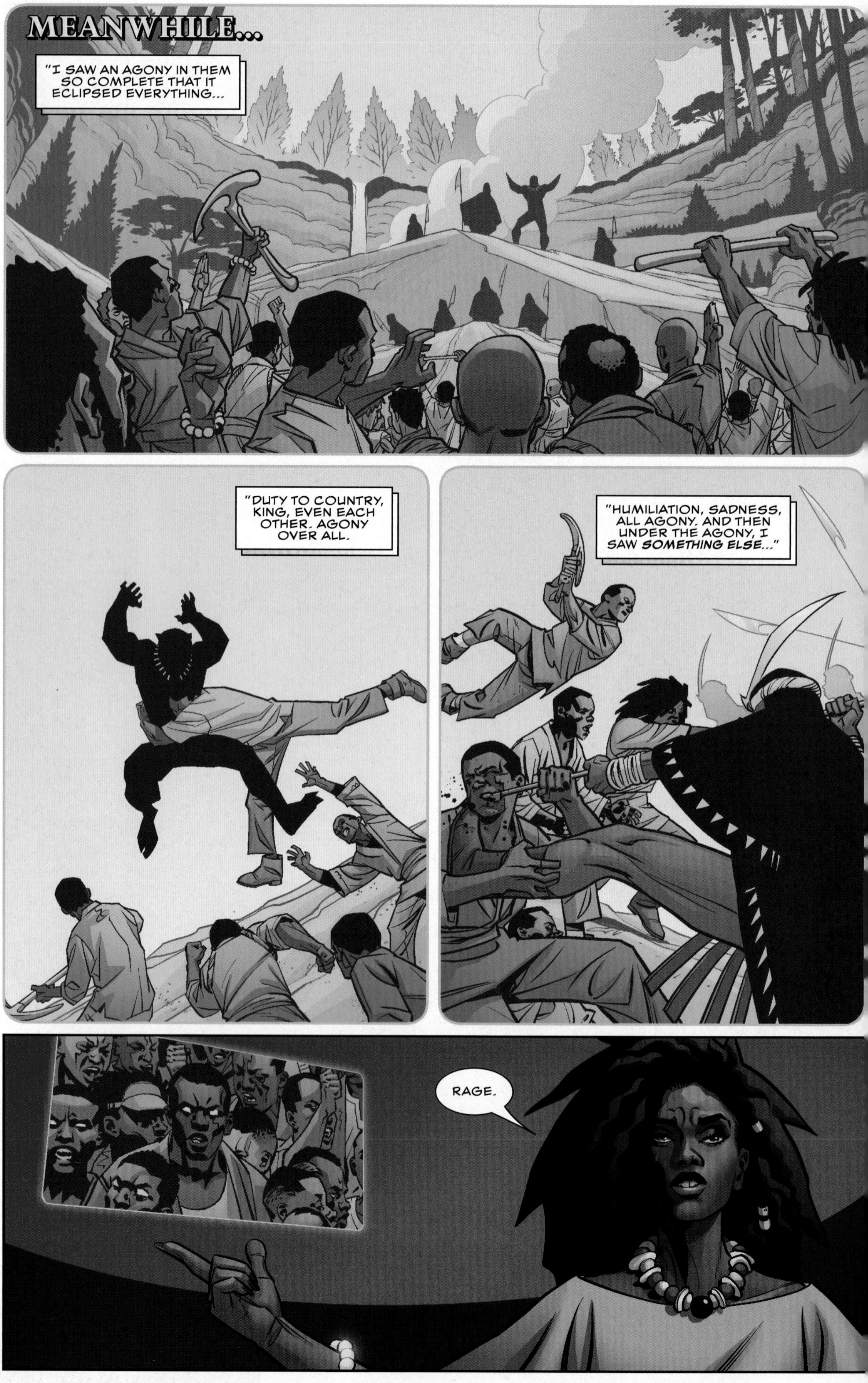
MEANWHILE...
"I SAW AN AGONY IN THEM SO COMPLETE THAT IT ECLIPSED EVERYTHING...
"DUTY TO COUNTRY, KING, EVEN EACH OTHER. AGONY OVER ALL.
"HUMILIATION, SADNESS, ALL AGONY. AND THEN UNDER THE AGONY, I SAW SOMETHING ELSE..."
RAGE.

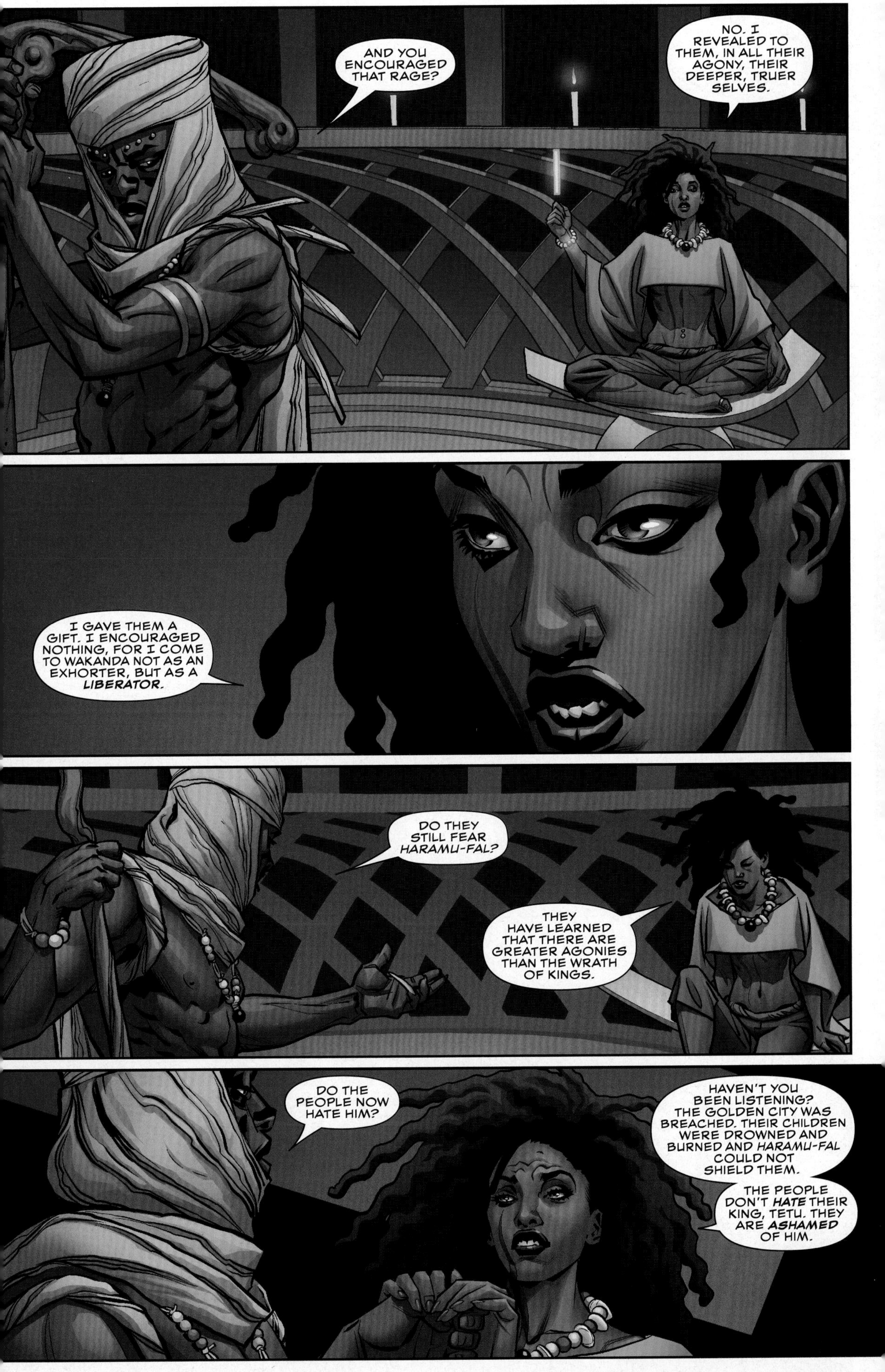
AND YOU ENCOURAGED THAT RAGE?
NO. I REVEALED TO THEM, IN ALL THEIR AGONY, THEIR DEEPER, TRUER SELVES.
I GAVE THEM A GIFT. I ENCOURAGED NOTHING, FOR I COME TO WAKANDA NOT AS AN EXHORTER, BUT AS A *LIBERATOR*.
DO THEY STILL FEAR *HARAMU-FAL*?
THEY HAVE LEARNED THAT THERE ARE GREATER AGONIES THAN THE WRATH OF KINGS.
DO THE PEOPLE NOW HATE HIM?
HAVEN'T YOU BEEN LISTENING? THE GOLDEN CITY WAS BREACHED. THEIR CHILDREN WERE DROWNED AND BURNED AND *HARAMU-FAL* COULD NOT SHIELD THEM.
THE PEOPLE DON'T *HATE* THEIR KING, TETU. THEY ARE *ASHAMED* OF HIM.

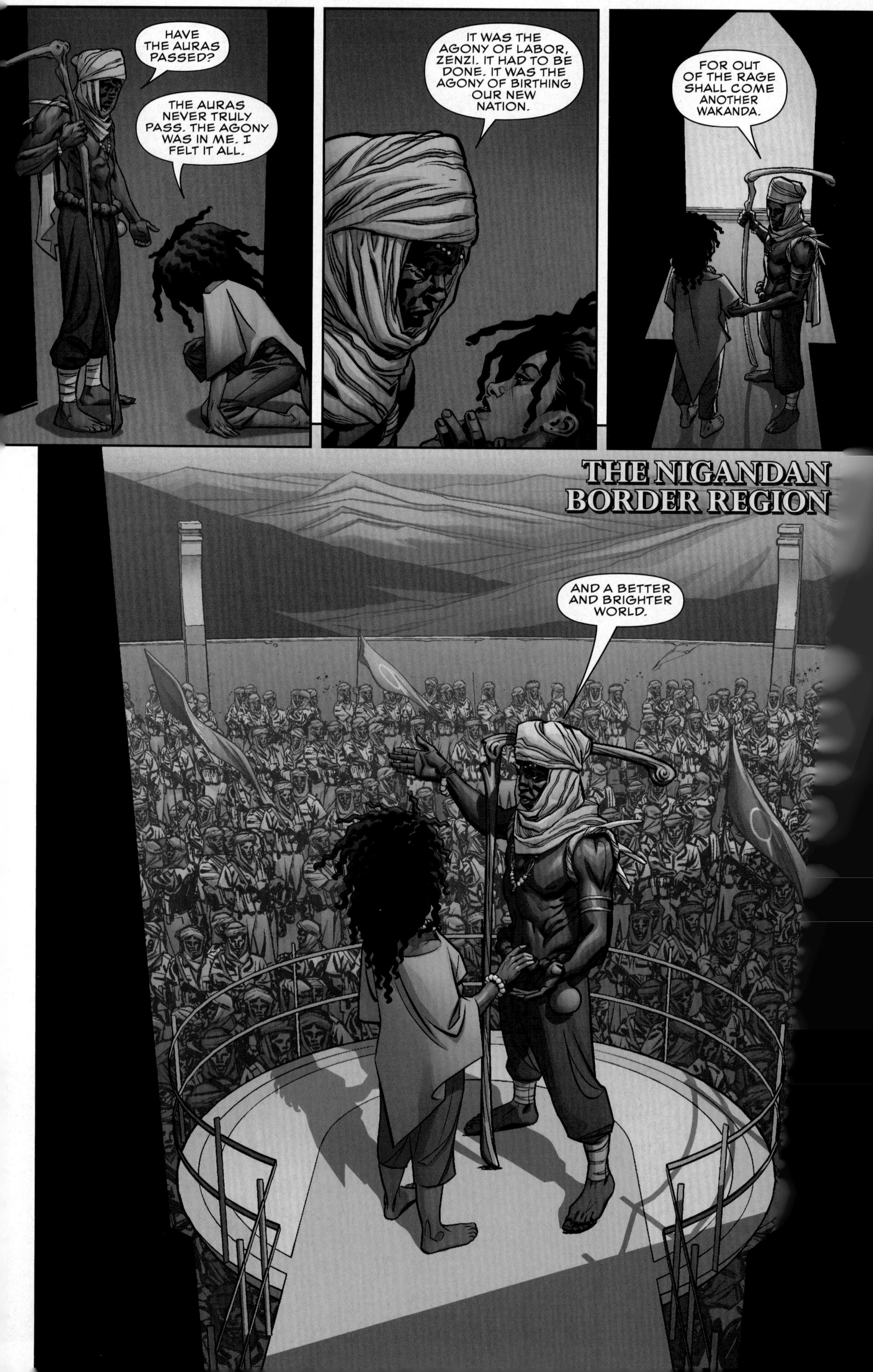
HAVE THE AURAS PASSED?
THE AURAS NEVER TRULY PASS. THE AGONY WAS IN ME. I FELT IT ALL.
IT WAS THE AGONY OF LABOR, ZENZI. IT HAD TO BE DONE. IT WAS THE AGONY OF BIRTHING OUR NEW NATION.
FOR OUT OF THE RAGE SHALL COME ANOTHER WAKANDA.
THE NIGANDAN BORDER REGION
AND A BETTER AND BRIGHTER WORLD.

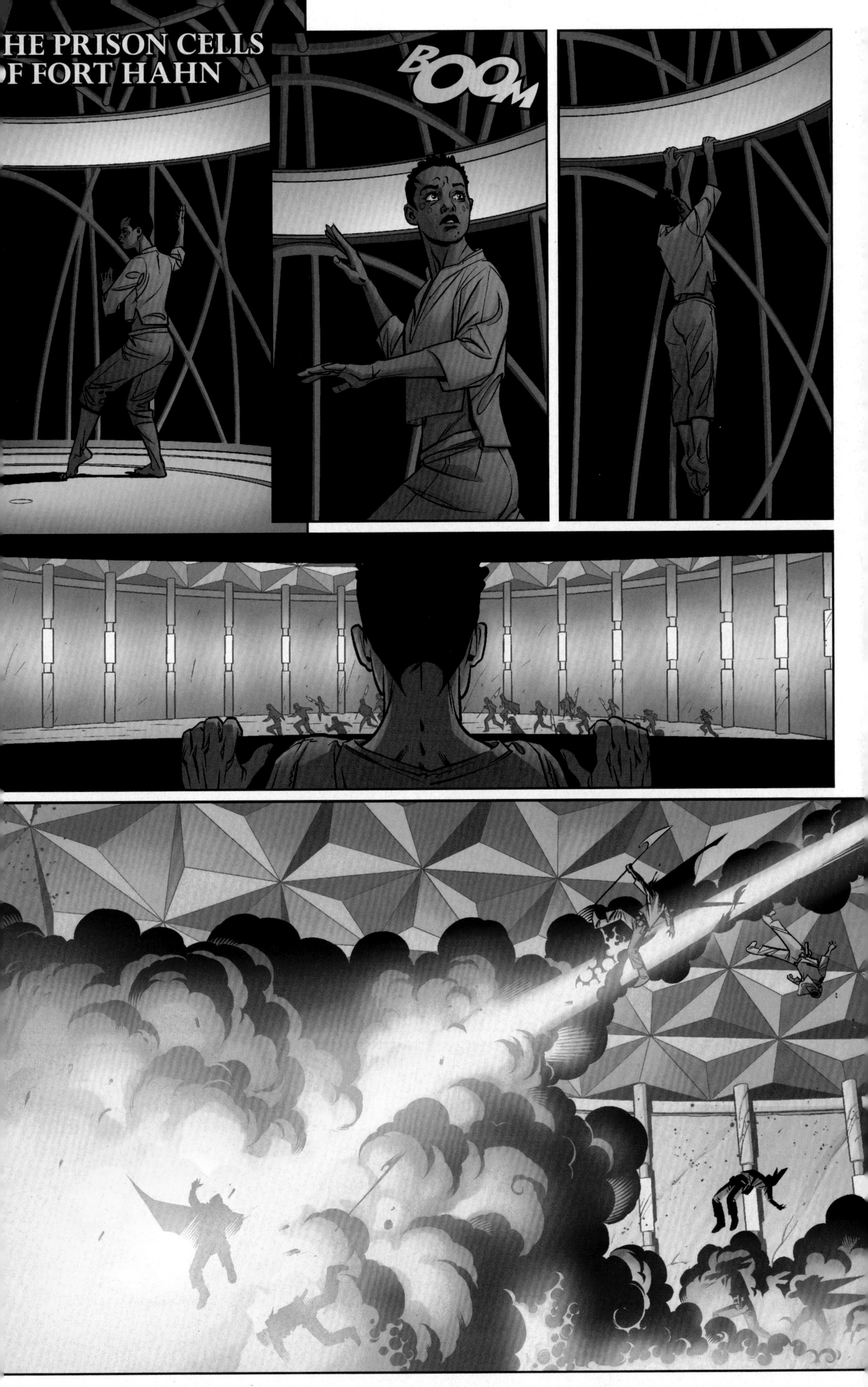
HE PRISON CELLS
OF FORT HAHN
BOOM

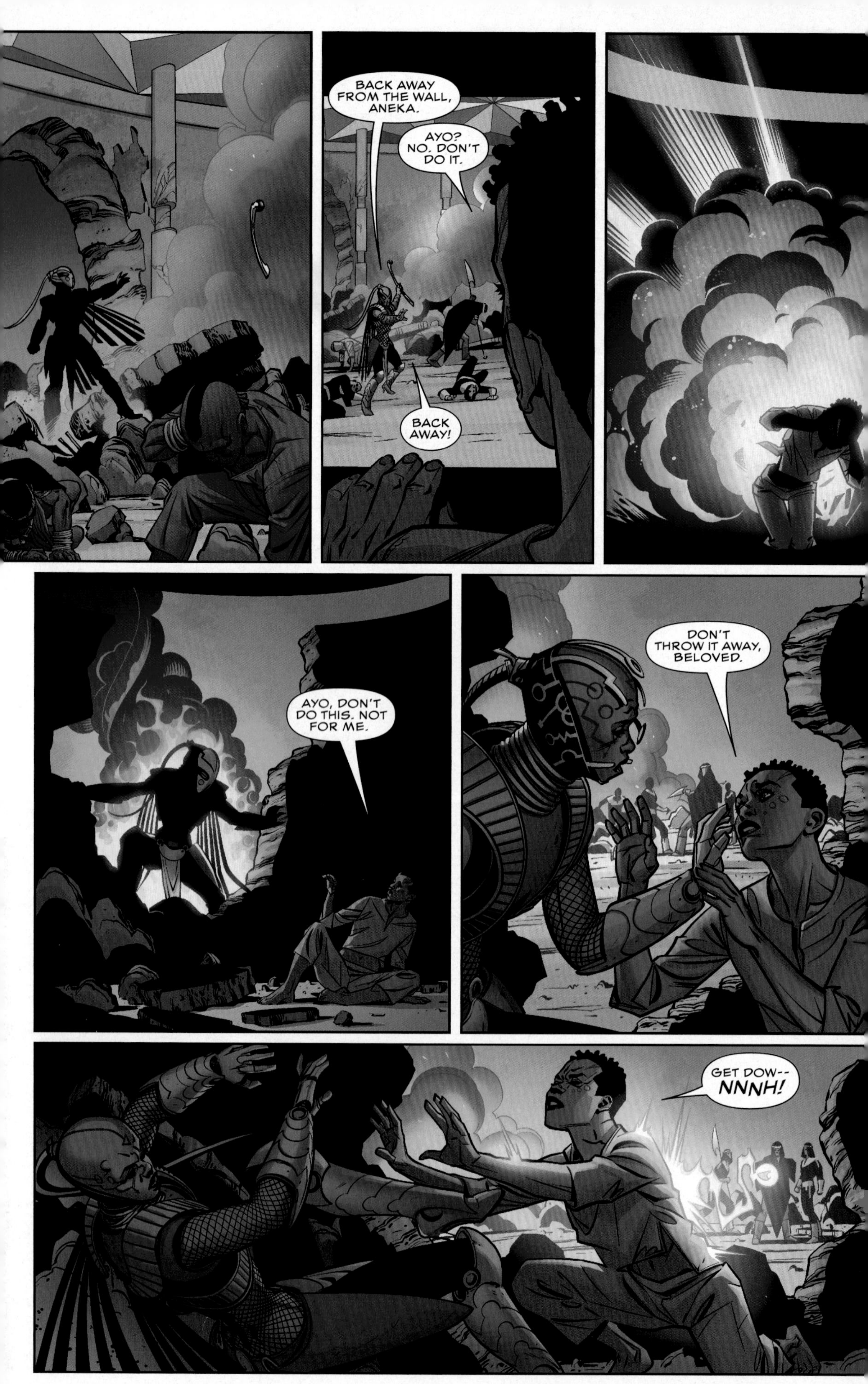
BACK AWAY FROM THE WALL, ANEKA.
AYO? NO. DON'T DO IT.
BACK AWAY!
AYO, DON'T DO THIS. NOT FOR ME.
DON'T THROW IT AWAY, BELOVED.
GET DOW-- NNNH!

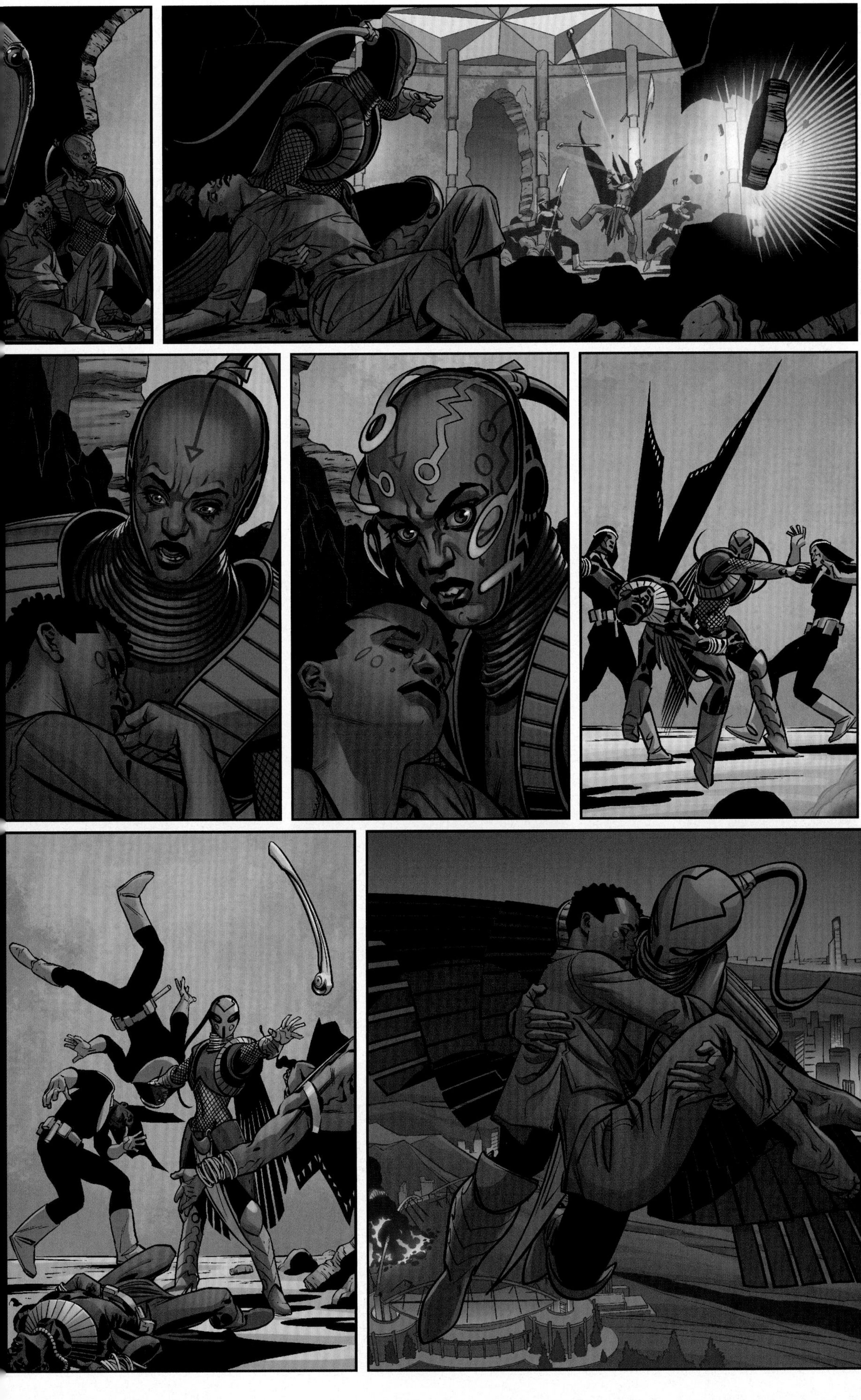

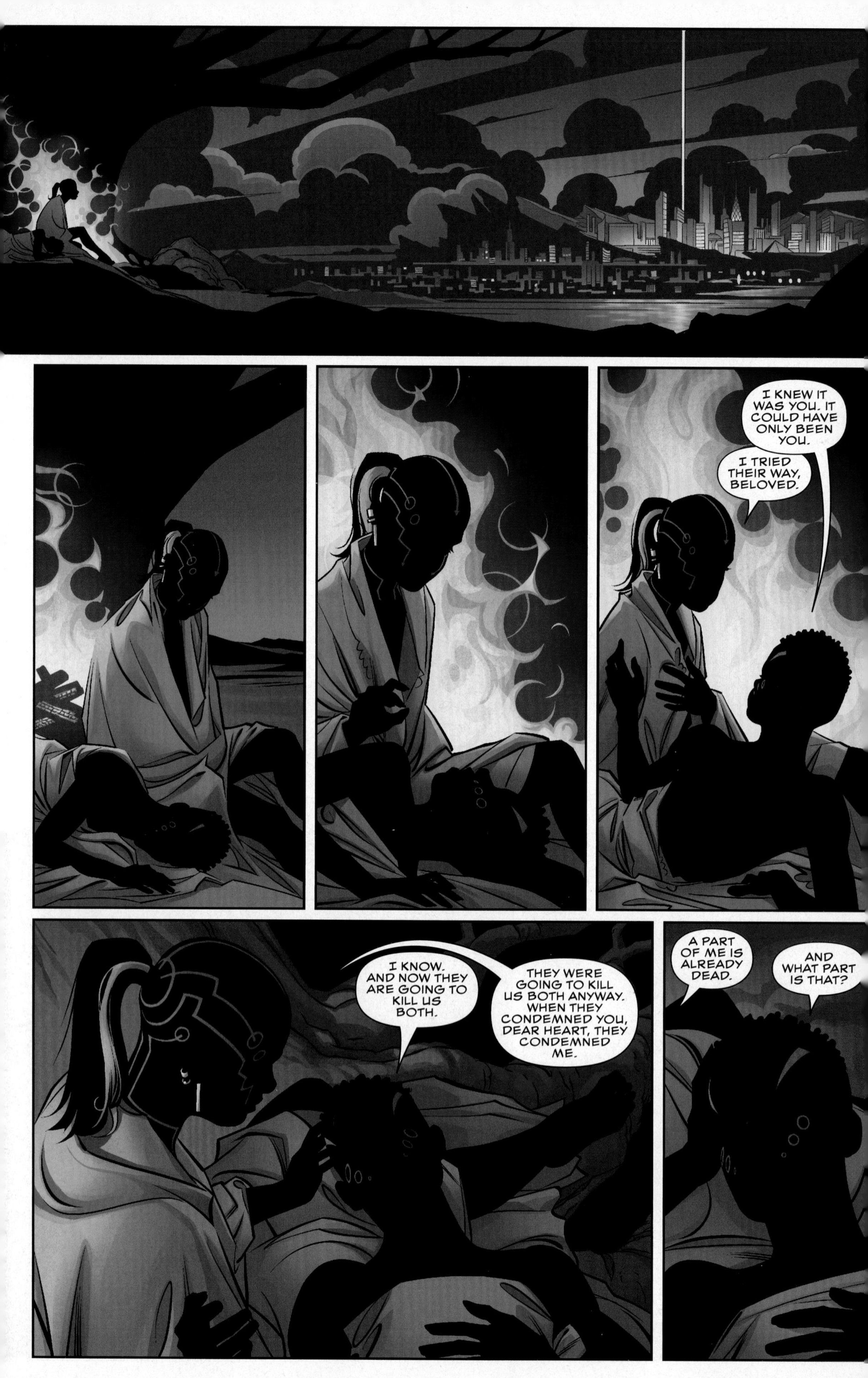
I KNEW IT WAS YOU. IT COULD HAVE ONLY BEEN YOU.
I TRIED THEIR WAY, BELOVED.
I KNOW. AND NOW THEY ARE GOING TO KILL US BOTH.
THEY WERE GOING TO KILL US BOTH ANYWAY. WHEN THEY CONDEMNED YOU, DEAR HEART, THEY CONDEMNED ME.
A PART OF ME IS ALREADY DEAD.
AND WHAT PART IS THAT?

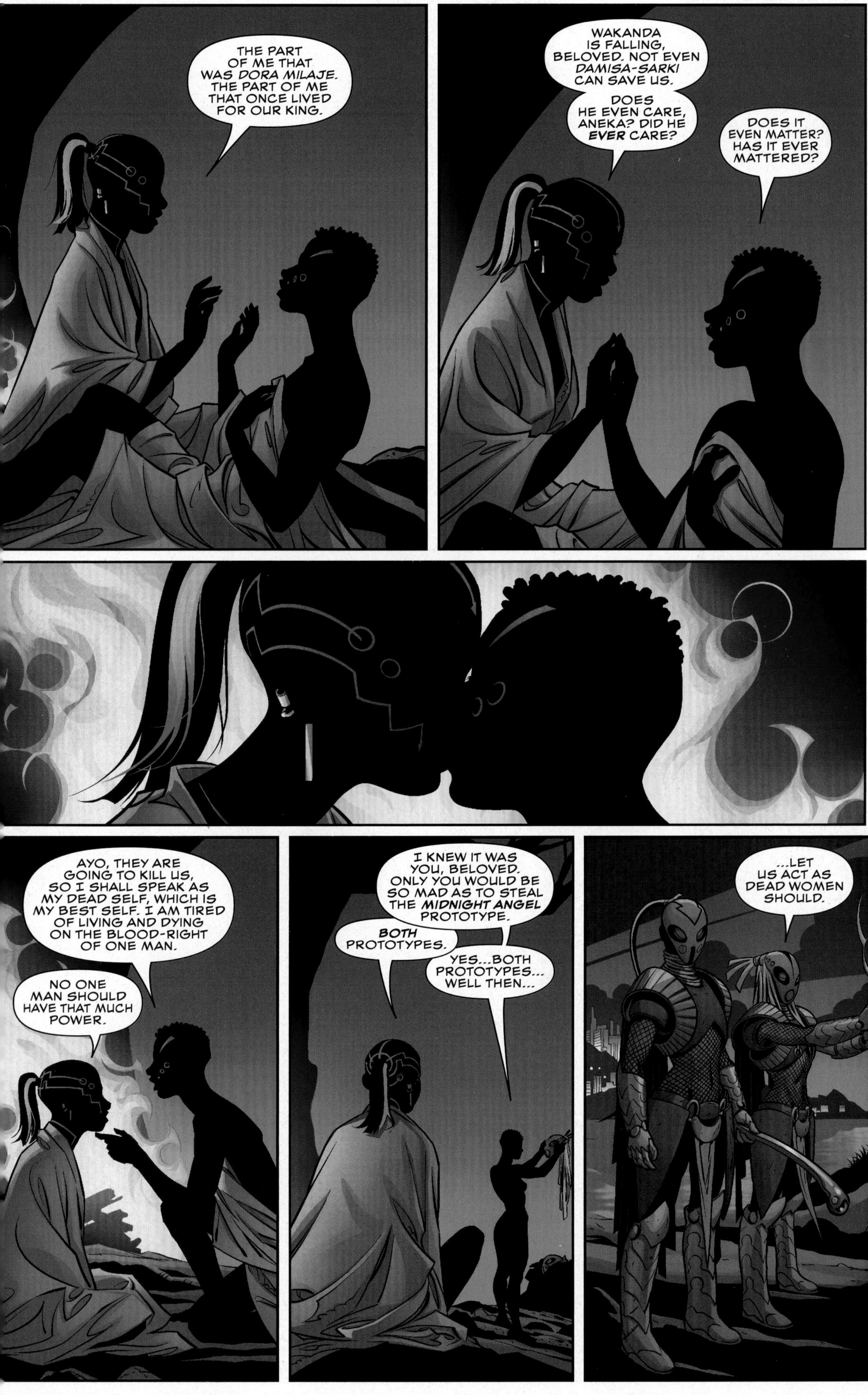
THE PART OF ME THAT WAS DORA MILAJE. THE PART OF ME THAT ONCE LIVED FOR OUR KING.
WAKANDA IS FALLING, BELOVED. NOT EVEN DAMISA-SARKI CAN SAVE US.
DOES HE EVEN CARE, ANEKA? DID HE EVER CARE?
DOES IT EVEN MATTER? HAS IT EVER MATTERED?
AYO, THEY ARE GOING TO KILL US, SO I SHALL SPEAK AS MY DEAD SELF, WHICH IS MY BEST SELF. I AM TIRED OF LIVING AND DYING ON THE BLOOD-RIGHT OF ONE MAN.
NO ONE MAN SHOULD HAVE THAT MUCH POWER.
I KNEW IT WAS YOU, BELOVED. ONLY YOU WOULD BE SO MAD AS TO STEAL THE MIDNIGHT ANGEL PROTOTYPE.
BOTH PROTOTYPES.
YES...BOTH PROTOTYPES... WELL THEN...
...LET US ACT AS DEAD WOMEN SHOULD.

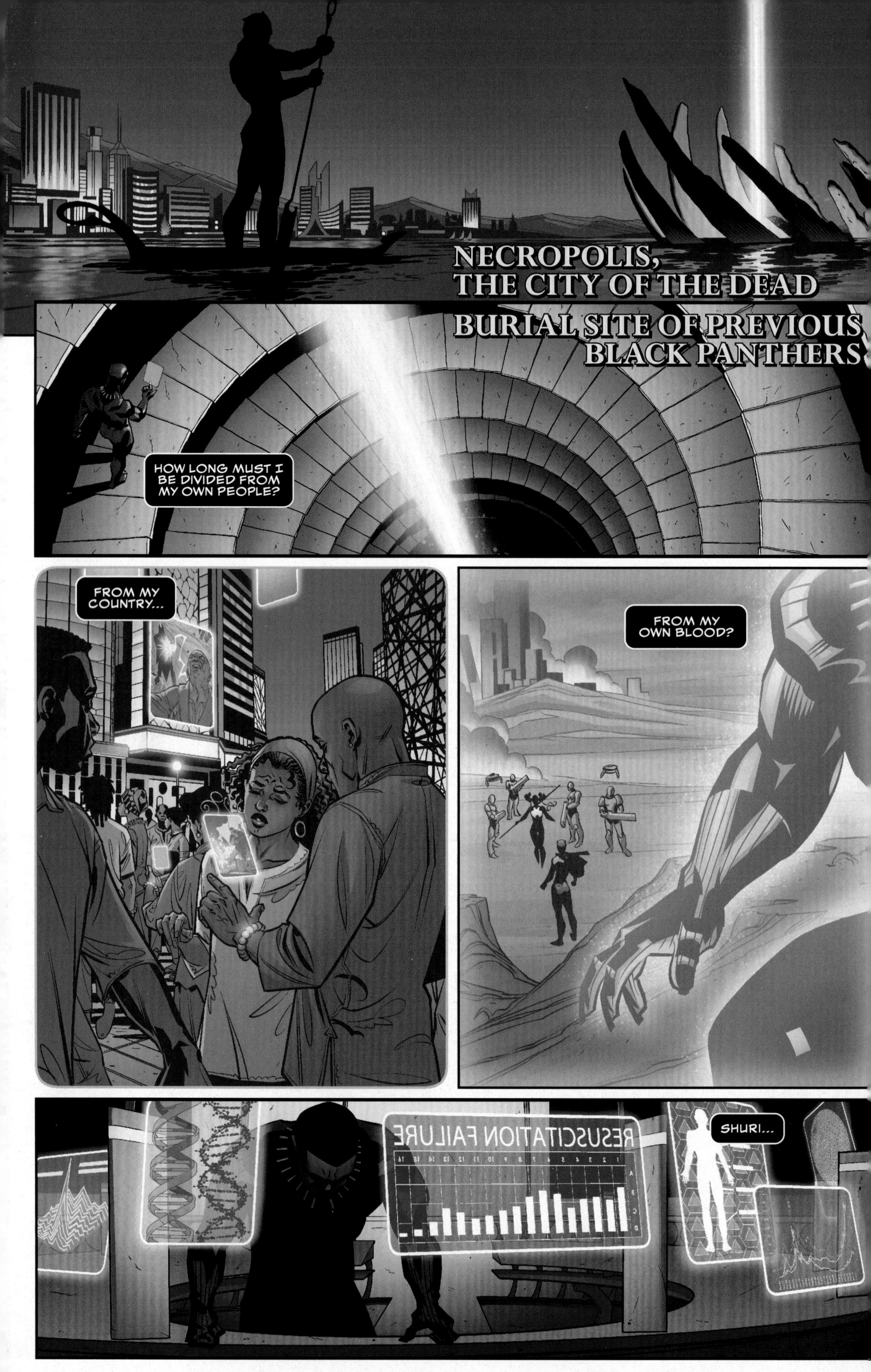
NECROPOLIS, THE CITY OF THE DEAD
BURIAL SITE OF PREVIOUS BLACK PANTHERS
HOW LONG MUST I BE DIVIDED FROM MY OWN PEOPLE?
FROM MY COUNTRY...
FROM MY OWN BLOOD?
RESUSCITATION FAILURE
SHURI...

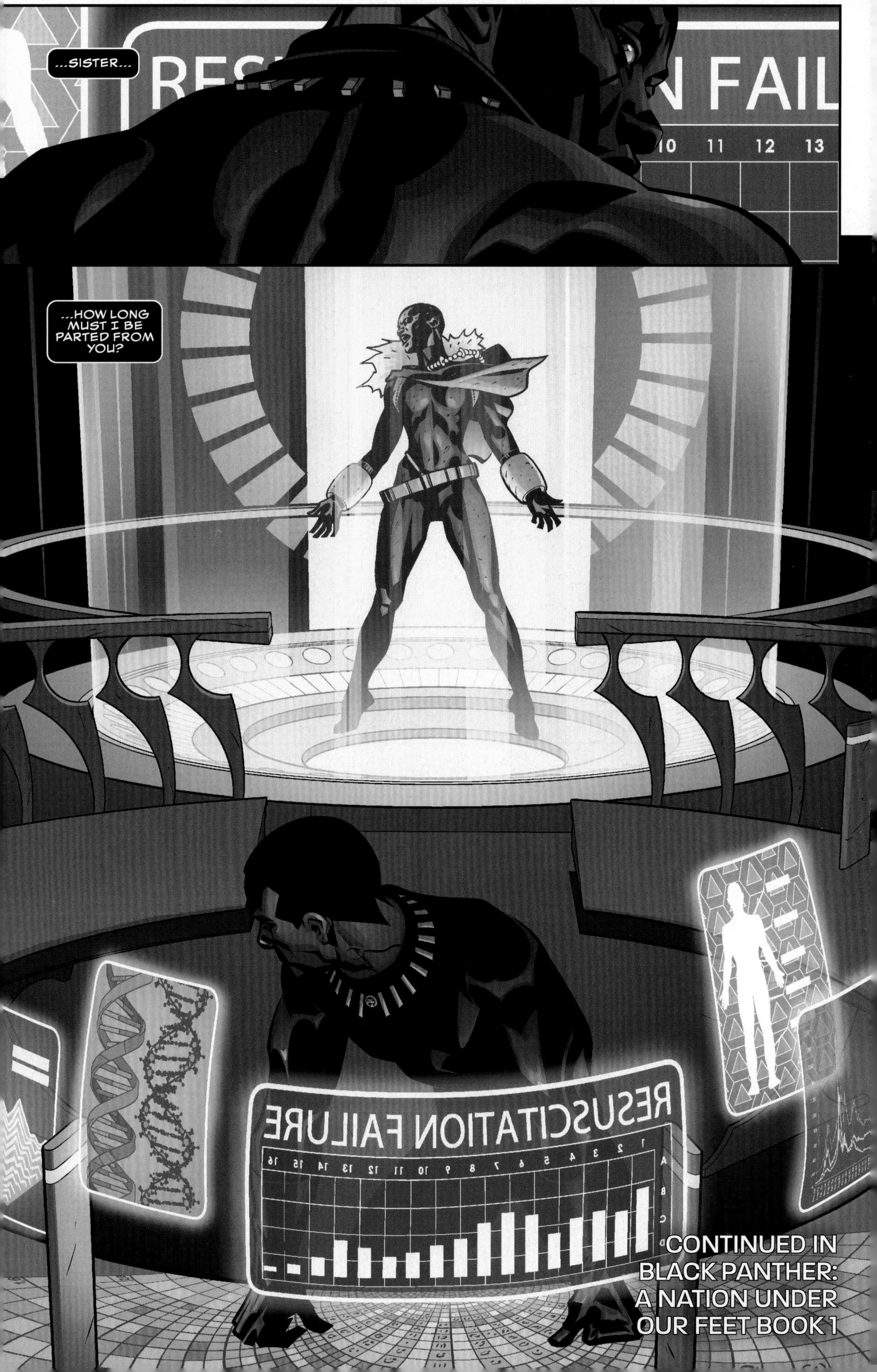
...SISTER...
...HOW LONG MUST I BE PARTED FROM YOU?
RESUSCITATION FAILURE
CONTINUED IN BLACK PANTHER: A NATION UNDER OUR FEET BOOK 1

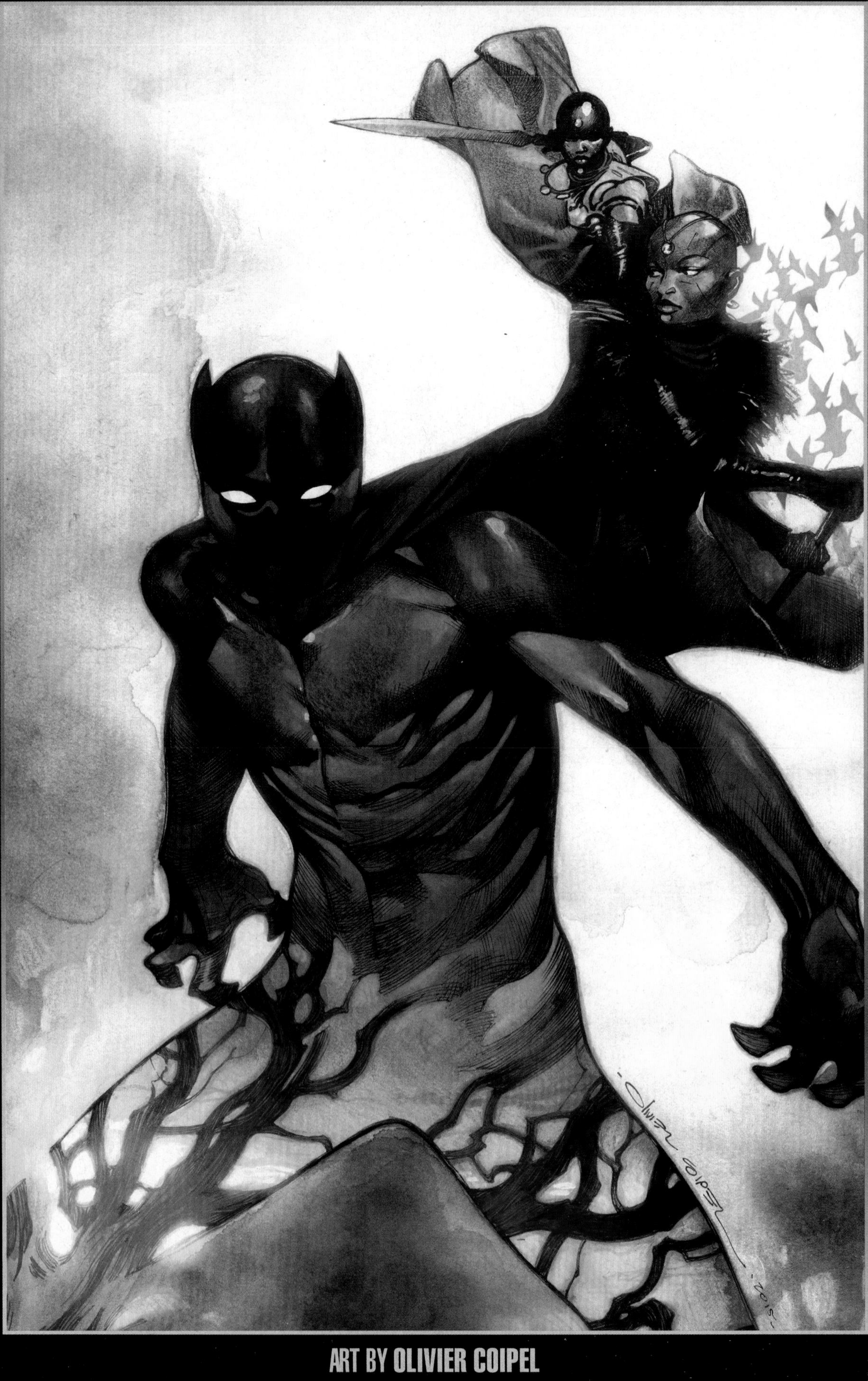

ART BY OLIVIER COIPEL